WE'RE GOING TO MAKE YOU A

STAR *by Sally Quinn*

SIMON AND SCHUSTER · NEW YORK

Designed by Irving Perkins
Manufactured in the United States of America

1   2   3   4   5   6   7   8   9   10

Library of Congress Cataloging in Publication Data

Quinn, Sally.
   We're going to make you a star.
   1.   Quinn, Sally.   I.   Title.
PN4874.Q5A35   070'.92'4   75-11932
ISBN   0-671-22084-5

My thanks first of all to all my friends who changed their whole lives around to get up at 7 A.M. to watch me on TV.

To Hughes Rudd, who really supported me through the whole horrible episode, even though he jeopardized his own career by doing so.

To my editor, Alice Mayhew, whose energy and insight and humor kept the tone of the book on an even keel.

To Warren Hoge, who encouraged me through the worst time at the beginning and whose patience and understanding were limitless. He also kept a scrapbook of the reviews I wasn't reading, without which I probably couldn't have written this book.

To my parents, who always told me how wonderful I was, and who allowed me to see only their pride, never their disappointment.

And finally to Ben Bradlee who kept me believing in myself.

For Hughes

PART
ONE

THE COUNTDOWN: Dick Salant, president of CBS News, was beaming. Hughes Rudd was chuckling to himself and Sally Quinn was fending off questions about her sudden rise in TV news. The setting was a luncheon at "21" in New York and the guests included members of the press, who were given an opportunity to meet and chat with the CBS correspondents who will go on the air next Monday. Salant was saying he'd love to switch the time of the *CBS Morning News* show from 7 A.M. to 8 A.M. but he'd run into opposition from the fans of *Captain Kangaroo*. "I know because I raised all my children on *Captain Kangaroo*." If the new team is a success, Salant said naturally he'd take credit for the show, but if the show bombs he said he's going to find someone to point the finger at. Who dreamed up Rudd and Quinn? he was asked. "That was Lee Townsend." Townsend, the executive producer, however, modestly disclaimed credit. "It was a group effort," he told *Eye*.

Eye, *Women's Wear Daily*, Tuesday, July 21, 1973

The previous Tuesday Hughes and I had arrived in Los Angeles at the Beverly Wilshire Hotel on the last leg of our promo tour, and the first thing Wednesday morning I had called Warren Beatty. He lives in a penthouse apartment in the hotel.

"Where are you?" he asked.

"In my room downstairs," I said.

"I've been trying to reach you ever since I heard you got the job at CBS. Why don't you come upstairs this afternoon after your interviews. I want to talk to you. CBS is doing a terrible thing to you."

"What do you mean?"

"They're doing the same thing to you they did to Gardner McKay."

"Who's Gardner McKay?"

"Exactly."

By six o'clock in the afternoon I had finished my last interview in the bar. I was exhausted, frustrated, punchy and so bored with myself that my jaw was twitching. I chewed swizzle sticks while reporters drank and asked the same questions. Did I think being a blonde bombshell helped get stories and jobs? They heard the confirmation before I could answer that I didn't actually think I was a blonde bombshell. Actually, I thought I was a serious journalist who happened to have blond hair. "She thinks it helps," they scribbled.

Still, I was somewhat elated by the sudden whirlwind I had been caught up in . . . the flashy job offer; the flattery of having been chosen, with no experience, over all the others, for a much-sought-after position; the idea of making a lot more money; instant recognition as a "personality. . . ."

And it had been amusing, after four years of interviewing other people and asking their opinions, to have people asking me what I thought about things.

"It seems strange to be on the other side of the pad and pencil," I would tell them, "and a little scary." What I didn't say was that it was fun.

It had become less and less so as the week of the promo tour wore on, and as I read the results. I came away from interviews thinking I had been wonderfully clever, witty, cogent, frank, honest, sensible, intelligent, warm, friendly— Ms. Terrific. Then I'd pick up a paper and read some of the things I had said and want to die. It was like looking in one of those distorting circus mirrors and seeing oneself suddenly fat or thin or wiggly or green. I scarcely recognized myself.

During an interview with *Women's Wear Daily* I had raced to the telephone to answer a call from the doorman and had identified myself as "Mrs. Hoge." I was living at the time with Warren Hoge, metropolitan editor of the *New York Post*. I hadn't thought about how it sounded until I picked up *WWD* and saw myself stammering an explanation: "I didn't do it for any moral reasons, believe me, it's just that he wouldn't know who I was if I said Sally Quinn."

In Cleveland I was interviewed by a man I remember only as wearing very white shoes. He wrote, "This mere wisp of a girl with the blond halo and the blue-green eyes said she was scared, all right, and it was all the big strong man reporter could do to resist throwing his arms around her and saying, 'There, there, little girl. . . .' "

"Who do you consider the sexiest member of the Senate Watergate Committee?" the reporter asked.

"I don't think in those terms," Miss Quinn replied.

"Senator Baker," Rudd volunteered. "No question about it."

"How are you going to dress on the program?" the reporter persisted.

"Very low key," replied Miss Quinn. "Very much like this —a pants suit. I have fat legs."

In Chicago I read in an interview that "Most of the country has never seen Quinn and Rudd on television together. Yet the mention of their names in the same breath already strikes boredom in the heart of millions."

And: "Miss Quinn dwelt most heavily on what she called the 'will-women-like Sally' question; that is, will housewives gladly suffer those blonde good looks? 'I find that women are actually much more sympathetic to me and men are more hostile,' she said. 'The whole idea of my not getting along with women is ridiculous. It's actually rather boring.'"

In *Harper's Bazaar* I was quoted as saying, "It's a big jump from day person to night person. And now I'll have to get along without martinis." I've never drunk a martini in my life.

I gave what I thought was a political interview to a syndicated writer, and found this on my desk a week or so later.

The brainy blonde, who makes her TV debut this week as co-anchor woman on *The CBS Morning News*, talked in one of the CBS executive offices on Manhattan's West Side.

"I can't tell you how good my spaghetti is, but half the time I'll cook spaghetti and everybody will groan and say, 'Oh, no, not Sally's spaghetti again.' I just go and pile my plate higher and ignore them."

The journalist said, "Smiling Sally's a sunny, happy girl with a delicious sense of the ridiculous. She looked stunning in a beige silk safari suit."

The National Observer: "She makes men think of sex. Sally is sexy, Hughes is solid. When Sally smiles, men tend not to care much what she says or writes."

A reporter from the New York *Daily News* asked me what famous people I knew well in Washington, who I had done stories about, and how they had responded. I read, "She drops names like Sen. Barry Goldwater (a family friend), and speaks of how 'Big Ruby,' George Wallace's mother-in-law, called her up last week to congratulate her on a story Sally had written about her in *The Washington Post*."

Also in the *Daily News* that week: "The confrontation [between Sally and Barbara Walters] has taken on such horrid sexist overtones that one almost expects Miss Quinn to sally forth tomorrow with, 'Say, big boy, if ya wanna know what went on last night at the House Armed Services Committee, just whistle.'

"A panting reporter later asked, 'Would you look at her twice on the street?' Me cooly, 'Once and a half.'"

Also: "I want to state for the record that at no time during our interview did Sally lay a hand on me, but then the press agent left the door open."

Surprisingly, even to me, the whole thing wasn't about a desire to have a go at being a television reporter, or an anchorwoman, or even to learn a new trade. Nor was it any inclination to be famous, to be a star. There may have been a sense of wanting to better myself, a sort of puritan work ethic of not wishing to turn down a "good" opportunity. But what has made me question the validity of my own motivations, values and goals is what I finally concluded to be the real—and, I feel, frivolous—reason for accepting the CBS offer. Curiosity.

It was as if I had accepted an assignment from *Esquire* Magazine to be the first woman astronaut and then only as countdown approached realized that I would actually have to go up in space.

Warren Beatty is surprisingly nice. Most of the movie stars I have met have been in an interview situation. I was covering the Democratic Primary in California in 1972 for *The Washington Post* and had been assigned to interview Beatty when he was campaigning for George McGovern. I had read an enormous amount about Warren. I had gotten through Smith College on movie magazines, and I knew everything there was to know about Warren Beatty. I had never liked what I read, and I was predisposed not to like him. I expected him to be a shallow, boring, insensitive, not-very-bright playboy. I was wrong. He is bright, sensitive and serious and has a clearer understanding of his environment than most people I know in any situation. For this reason, and because now I had suddenly been catapulted over to his territory, a territory I knew nothing about, I would trust his judgment about CBS.

He greeted me in a terrycloth robe over a bathing suit, apologizing that he had been out on the terrace of his tiny apartment, reading scripts in the sun. He offered me a chair inside, flopped down on the pile of pillows on a studio couch in his very unglamorous, unmovie-starish living room, and gave me a Dubonnet on the rocks. He doesn't drink.

"So who's Gardner McKay?" I asked.

"Remember years ago when *Life* Magazine had a beautiful black-haired guy on the cover and did a story on how he was the new star of a TV series called *Adventures in Paradise?*"

"Vaguely," I said.

"Well, he was built up as the biggest thing since Cary Grant, Clark Gable and Tyrone Power. He hadn't had much acting experience, but he was handsome and that's what they cared about. Nobody could have lived up to that reputation. He was the victim of overpromotion. And so are you. I think you're terrific. If you recall, I once told you that there were only two people in my career who had ever interviewed me who I thought should be interviewed themselves. You and Gloria Steinem. But you've never had any experience, and if you're going on the air in two weeks there's no way you're going to be able to live up to the publicity. Nobody could. You've been made out to be a smug, tough, competitive little cock-teaser, and people aren't going to like you for it. There is no way you're not going to be attacked. Sometimes I just don't understand how people who run these giant corporations can be so stupid. I wish I could have gotten to you before all this happened.

"But I can tell you one thing," he said. "There are an awful lot of people you admire and respect who are going to be repelled by you on sight after all this terrible publicity."

There was a knock at the door. It was Paul Simon of Simon and Garfunkel.

"Paul, I want you to meet a friend of mine," said Warren. "I'm sure you must have read about her." Then with a grin he made a sweepingly dramatic gesture toward me. "This is Sally Quinn."

Simon had read about me.

"*Yecccchhh,*" he said.

"You see what I mean?" said Warren with a sympathetic shrug.

The first week in February of 1973 Barbara Walters, the cohostess of the *Today* Show, had come down to Washington to do a week of tapings for *Not for Women Only*, a daily half-hour program she tapes for after the *Today* Show. She was doing a series on women journalists in Washington, and she had asked me to be on it. The segment was divided into two days of society reporters and three days of political reporters. Barbara had included me in the latter group, and I had appreciated that, because she knew I had been trying to get out of the strictly "society" category that so many women reporters in Washington find themselves in, no matter what they write about. I was surprisingly unnervous, and I seemed to find plenty to talk about. I had felt confident and at ease. It was my town and a subject I knew well. That was not my first experience in television.

I had worked with Gordon Manning, the news director of CBS News, one summer when Dick Salant had hired me for the Presidential conventions. I had been working for Robert Kennedy's Presidential campaign, but after Kennedy's tragic death, a friend who worked for him persuaded Salant to put

me on his convention staff in Chicago. Most of what we did
was type memos, and mostly it was a lark, and because of our
strategic location we spent a good part of our time hanging
out with the correspondents and the higher-ups. When Bill
Paley and Frank Stanton came down to Salant's trailer–office
at the convention hall, we were the ones who arranged for
their picnic lunches, bought the paper plates and napkins, set
the table, and saw to it that Mr. Paley had the kind of pas-
trami and kosher dills he liked.

Since that obviously did not consume a great deal of my
time, I was loaned out to Gordon Manning as his assistant
in Central Control, from which *everything* happened. I was
liaison with the anchor booth. Gordon would yell, "Tell
Walter the Kennedy people are about to hold a demonstra-
tion in their corner of the convention hall," and I would do
just that. Much of the time, however, I was bored or pre-
occupied, and several times I fell asleep in Central Control.
Gordon was good-natured and never really seemed to mind.
We would laugh about it later with Salant and Bill Leonard,
who was Gordon's counterpart, vice president in charge of
special projects, encompassing *Sixty Minutes'* hour magazine
format, the special on the moon shot and other big deals.
Manning and Leonard were always together, were extremely
funny, and were called Rosencrantz and Guildenstern, I assumed affectionately, by their coworkers. That was the
extent of my television "experience" until then.

About a week after the show, Barbara had told me that
CBS had asked to see tapes of the *Not for Women Only*
segments I'd been on. "They're very interested in you," she
said. "They thought you were terrific."

I was flattered. Then I forgot about it.

Sometime later that month Barbara gave a party in New
York. After dinner I had gone back to her bedroom to make

a phone call. Her alarm clock was beside the phone on her bedside table, set for 4 A.M. Later that night I remarked to a friend, "If they paid me a million dollars, I would never accept Barbara Walters' job. That is simply no way to live."

A few months later, in May, I heard that CBS was looking for a woman to co-anchor the *Morning News,* and that a big talent search was on for *the* woman who could take on Barbara Walters, and that they were going to pay her $75,000 a year. "I'm glad I'm a newspaper reporter and not a television reporter," I thought. "At least I won't be tempted with an offer for a terrible job like that."

June 6 was my fourth anniversary as a reporter for the Style section of *The Washington Post.*

When Gordon called from New York and asked me to have dinner with him in Washington on June 6, I accepted but it never occurred to me that he wanted to talk about The Job. Bill Small, the CBS Washington bureau chief, had offered me a job as Washington correspondent several times during the past few years, and I had never shown any interest, but that's what I assumed it was all about. Aside from the *Not for Women Only* appearance with Barbara Walters, my three or four ventures into television had included a five-minute interview on a local program and two half-hour group interviews on Martin Agronsky's public television show. That sort of thing was fun, but it seemed superficial compared to the digging and observing one does as a print reporter and the exquisitely painful challenge of sitting down to writing.

The standard operating procedure when one has been offered a job is to spread it around the office. That way "management" hears about it before you tell them and has time to figure out how much of a raise they are willing to pay to keep you at the paper. It happened that while I was out in the newsroom spreading the word, Benjamin Bradlee, editor of the *Post*, walked past and overheard that I was having dinner that night with Gordon Manning, his old friend from *Newsweek*. He asked where, and I told him the Cantina d'Italia.

I remember walking from the office to the Cantina to meet Gordon. I had on a beautiful new Sonia Rykiel pants suit, I had a great tan, I had lost weight, and I had just finished what I thought was a very good piece for the paper the next day. I felt golden. And figuring Gordon was about to offer me the Washington job, which I was going to turn down, made me feel particularly confident.

Only he didn't offer me the job as Washington correspondent.

Gordon Manning is a short, round-faced, balding man who looks very much like a chipmunk. He has the mannerisms of a chipmunk too. Everything he does seems speeded up somehow, his gestures and the way he talks, and he has the shortest attention span of anyone I've ever known. He spurts things out, fires jokes, quips wisecracks and ideas like bullets, and is onto something else before you've barely absorbed his last remark. He has a wide mischievous grin, almost pixieish, and he is very, very funny. Because he's so facile, it's hard to know how smart or how talented he really is.

He was in a good mood. We laughed a lot about the old days at the convention. He told me I'd come a long way, and he joked affectionately about his wife Edna, apparently a marvelous woman, whom I had never met, and how she'd splattered yellow paint all over his shoes when he told her he was having dinner with me. We gossiped about mutual acquaintances.

Gordon was paged. "I'll bet it's Bradlee," he said. He was on the phone just a short time. When he came back he was rubbing his hands together gleefully. "Who was it?" I asked. "Ben Bradlee." "What did he say?" "He said, 'Fuck you' "

"Well, I guess I'd better tell you why I'm here," Gordon finally said as I was finishing my veal francese. "I've told Bill Small time and time again to get you to come to work for us and he's never been able to persuade you, so I decided I would have to come down to Washington and persuade you myself."

"Gordon," I said, "I know what you're going to say and before you go any further I want to tell you that I have the perfect job at the *Post*, I am deliriously happy there, and I have no intention whatsoever of leaving."

"We're going to revamp the *CBS Morning News*," Gordon continued, ignoring what I had said, "and we're looking for a woman. A woman who can knock Barbara Walters off the air. We think you're the one who can do it."

Suddenly I felt very sick. Not for the last time.

I did some minor tossing and turning that night but rather quickly, amazingly quickly in fact, I dismissed the whole notion as ridiculous and fell into a deep and peaceful sleep. Gordon had told me not to answer, that I was to put the idea out of my mind and he would call me the next day. I did. The next afternoon I was sitting at my desk when Ben Bradlee and Gordon walked back to the Style section. We joked a bit. Gordon was acting very smug, as though they were both on a fishing expedition and he had produced a highly superior bait.

Bradlee looked a bit uncomfortable.

I sent him a note that afternoon telling him I had absolutely no intention of leaving the *Post* for CBS no matter what kind of a job or how much money they were offering. Later I also told that to Gordon on the phone. I meant it.

But Gordon asked me when I was going to be in New York. I told him I would that weekend.

"Well, then," he said, "why don't you stay over on Monday and have lunch with me and Hughes Rudd."

My heart sank a little. It was Hughes, Gordon had told me the night before, whom they were thinking of putting on as co-anchor. I had never met him, but I'd watched him on television and he had always been one of my favorites, a highly individual personality, iconoclastic and funny. I had always wondered why he stayed on television announcing, instead of writing, which he does extremely well. I also wondered why they had kept him on television. He had never quite developed a happy homogenized television image.

"Well, lunch can't hurt," I thought.

We met at Le Poulailler, a popular French restaurant near Lincoln Center in the West Sixties. I arrived first and checked my suitcase. I was going back to Washington right after lunch.

A few minutes later, Gordon arrived with Hughes and Sandy Socolow, assistant news director. We fell into a lively, amusing conversation. One of the first things I said was, "This may seem like a silly question, but I know Barbara Walters has to get up at four in the morning. Would we have to get up at that hour?" "It's not silly," said Sandy, looking a little uneasy. "Actually, one thirty. You'll be writing the whole show." "No way," I thought and relaxed.

Hughes looked as though he had just stepped out of a World War II cockpit and, as I was to learn, Hughes usually viewed things with an attitude that suggested he had. He had been a pilot in Europe during the War and his trench coat had the bullet holes to prove it.

Hughes was born in Waco, Texas, where he learned to love chili, and moved to Kansas City when he was in his teens. He left the University of Missouri before graduating to join the Army and served as an artillery spotter pilot. Hughes has never gotten over his military experience. He refers to it often, he likes people who have been in the military, and he admires toughness.

He looks a little like Edward R. Murrow and talks like him, too. He has a deep, gruff voice that sounds best when he is barking out some obscenity and sounds strange when he is being gentle. Hughes's face is a basset face, sagging slightly when he is sad or angry. Even when he laughs his short, loud, one-syllable "Ha!" his eyes droop.

He is a rebel, a troublemaker, and he likes to be ornery out of pure delight.

When Hughes got out of the Army he began a rather checkered career in writing and journalism, beginning at the *Kansas City Star* and then the *Minneapolis Tribune.* After a scholarship at Stanford, he became the editor of the Rock Springs *Daily Rocket and Sunday Miner* in Wyoming. There was another fellowship at a writer's colony in Taos, New Mexico, and then he got a job writing industrial movies in Kansas City. It was about that time, in the late fifties, that Hughes called his old buddy Walter Cronkite and asked him if there was any possibility of a job at CBS. Cronkite said sure, c'mon to New York, and Hughes landed a job on the night desk in New York.

It was there that he began really writing seriously, for the *Paris Review* and magazines like *Harper's.* From those essays and short stories, Hughes put together a book called *My Escape from the CIA and Other Stories,* a brilliant and hilarious collection.

Hughes went on to Moscow, then to Bonn, as foreign correspondent for CBS, and sent back memorable, zany pieces different from those of the other reporters. For all the fifteen or so years that Hughes has been at CBS, he has not allowed himself to become pasteurized one bit, and he's the only one in the entire network who'd just as soon disagree with Bill Paley as look at him. Hughes is special. And Hughes "don't take no shit from nobody."

I liked him at once, and before long we were laughing and

talking as though we were old war buddies. In fact, we did talk about the Army a lot. I'm an Army brat, and that pleased him. Hughes was looking me over carefully. Gordon had told me that Hughes had the final approval for his co-anchor. I couldn't tell what he was thinking, but at one point I asked for one of the Parliaments that he was chain-smoking and a little piece of paper fell out of the box. "Oh, Hughes," I joked, "already writing me little notes. Let's see what it says," and I opened it up. It was an ad. But I read aloud, "For God's sake don't take the job at CBS."

"No, no, it doesn't say that at all," said Hughes with genuine alarm, and I saw Gordon and Sandy look at each other significantly. Hughes approved of me. After that, Gordon asked me to stay for dinner with him and Hughes to meet Lee Townsend, who was to be the producer.

"But I've got my suitcase here."

"Take it home," said Gordon, "and meet us at six thirty."

Gordon chose the Coffee House, a little-known club on the West Side near the Algonquin Hotel and *The New Yorker*. It's a rather faded-looking little club of two rooms, with older women as bartenders and waitresses, and has enormous cachet as a writer's club. It had been founded in 1914 by the editor of *Vanity Fair*, Frank Crowninshield, who just happened to be Benjamin Crowninshield Bradlee's uncle. Gordon was shrewd. I had expected to be taken to someplace obvious and extravagant like the Four Seasons. But here we were in this quiet little, slightly shabby club, and I began to think that maybe people in television were sensitive after all.

Since we had just finished lunch three hours before, we weren't particularly hungry, but when you're negotiating big deals in television, I have since discovered, you do it over meals even if you have to eat twelve times in a day.

Lee Townsend is a short, skinny little man with a rather bad complexion, granny glasses and a high voice. If Gordon is a chipmunk, Lee is an animated Mickey Mouse. Before he came to CBS, where he was national assignment editor, he had been the last city editor of the *World Journal Tribune* and had a very good reputation as an editor. He was exceedingly nice, but rather reticent that evening, and didn't seem particularly sure of himself. I imagined it was because Gordon and Hughes and I dominated the conversation.

We really didn't talk about CBS very much; it was more a meeting to meet Lee and to let Hughes see me one more time. What we did talk about in the most general terms was the informal news show that they wanted.

The *Today* Show had been on the air for twenty-one years, I was reminded. The *Morning News*, in different forms, for ten. Jack Paar, Walter Cronkite and Mike Wallace had all done stints on it.

None of them had ever been able to make a dent in the *Today* Show ratings and, Gordon was explaining, they would have just let it ride except that Bill Paley, who is head of the network, has insomnia and therefore always watches the *Morning News* and takes a special interest in it. And Bill Paley does not like to lose. He may have the best hard news show on the air at 7 A.M., but he doesn't have the ratings. And ratings are *everything....*

Nielsen ratings, which we read about in *TV Guide* all the time, are determined by little boxes called Nielsen Audimeters, which are attached to 1,200 TV sets across the country. They belong to families of varied economic and social backgrounds. The audimeters record impulses on 16 millimeter film to show which channels are being watched. At the end of each week the film is sent to Nielsen headquarters in Chicago, where it is data-processed.

Each household represents 2.3 viewers during prime time (7:00–11:00 P.M.) and anything over 17 per cent of the viewing audience is considered a passable score by the networks.

So the make-or-break effect of the Nielsen ratings is determined by 1,200 families out of 60 million TV households in America. What if they all go on vacation or out to dinner the same night?

William S. Paley is the dynamic "king" of the Columbia Broadcasting System. In 1927 Paley bought a tiny radio station staffed by only a few people and turned it into the largest (30,000 employees) and most powerful network in the world.

Those who know Paley will tell you he is a giant, an extraordinary mind, and has a sense of curiosity and imagination, a decisive manner, and energy to carry through that is rare even among the most active men. Although most people who work for him are scared to death of Bill Paley, there is no one who doesn't admire him.

To add to his glamour, after he divorced his first wife in 1947 he married Barbara Cushing Mortimer, a New York and Boston socialite who wrote for *Vogue* Magazine. Mrs. Paley, better known as "Babe," *is* style, fashion and beauty, and she has dominated the pages of *Vogue, Harper's Bazaar* and *Women's Wear Daily* for years, named so often as one of the ten best-dressed women of the year that she was finally elevated to the Best-Dressed Hall of Fame. The Paleys are one of New York's glittering couples. His way of living adds to the myth of the distant ruler, and socially Paley intimidates those who work for him.

Several years before, the Paleys had taken a trip to China and Gordon Manning had accompanied them. There are varying reports around CBS on how they all got along. The way Gordon tells it, the trip was very successful. But others say that it was something less than that. In any case, it was on that trip that the subject of revamping the *Morning News* came up.

The *Morning News* is a sore subject at CBS, so it was courageous of Gordon to broach it. But it had been on his mind because the two correspondents who were doing it then had made it clear to him that they were interested in moving along. John Hart and Nelson Benton were both bright, competent and successful correspondents who enjoyed their jobs as anchormen on the *Morning News* but found the hours, the low ratings and the lack of response depressing. Hart, from New York, and Benton, from Washington, had a strictly hard-news format with occasional film pieces and interviews. It was a good, fast-paced, traditional news broadcast, irreproachable. It had zero ratings. Both were anxious to live normal hours again and get back to the streets and do some reporting.

The hard-news format was obviously not the answer to the *Morning News* problem. Or at least not what they had meant by hard news. Hard news is a straight telling, like Cronkite's *CBS Evening News,* except that the *Morning News* is an hour long, and the *Evening News* a half hour. The *Morning News,* it has to be said, is less "hard" than the *Evening News.* The top stories in the morning, as newsmen like to point out, are mostly foreign news, fires and other natural catastrophes. For this reason, an informal format seems to be easier to swallow at that hour of the morning.

When Gordon had brought up the subject in China with Bill Paley, he already had a vague idea of something more informal and he had Hughes Rudd in mind. Bill Paley liked Hughes and Gordon knew it. The Paleys had visited Hughes and Ann Rudd when Hughes was the CBS Moscow correspondent, and they had all had a marvelous time. Hughes had taken them around to some of the more rowdy restaurants, and the Paleys got a better taste of what Russia was like than the usual VIP tour. Paley, who has a rather offbeat sense of humor, had always liked Hughes's irreverence. He agreed that perhaps Hughes could be put to better use than just as a general-assignment correspondent.

I admire Bill Paley for his recognition of Hughes.

CBS had no intention of hiring a woman anchor when they decided to change the show. Gordon had been off on a trip to Vietnam and when he arrived in Fuji or some other remote island, he was paged with an urgent telephone call. It was Salant. He had just come from a CBS women's meeting, one that most companies are now well accustomed to, where the women demand better pay and working conditions, equality, etc., and at this meeting they had demanded a woman anchor.

Salant, backed to the wall by the women, had apparently promised them that the next anchor hired would be a woman. That is what he informed Gordon on the phone. So there was Gordon in the South Pacific, with the task of finding an anchorwoman. Gordon thought of me. There was not and is not now a female anchorperson on a major network. Barbara Walters is not an anchorperson because she does not read the news. Lew Wood reads the news. In fact, it was not until Frank McGee's death that Barbara, after eleven years on the *Today* Show, was elevated to the status of co-hostess.

The irony of *CBS Morning News* trying to hire a woman is that Barbara Walters' first job after she graduated from Sarah Lawrence was as a writer for the old CBS *Good Morning* Show, when Walter Cronkite, as anchorman, was unsuccessfully trying to compete with *Today*. After that she worked in public relations with Bill Safire, who later became President Nixon's speechwriter at the White House, and in 1961 Barbara went to work for the *Today* Show. After three years as a writer and reporter she began to do air interviews and slowly made a niche for herself as a permanent member of the *Today* Show team along with Hugh Downs and Joe Garagiola.

Barbara likes to tell a story about Don Hewitt, perhaps the most successful and professional producer in the business, currently the producer of *Sixty Minutes*, the Sunday evening "magazine" show. When she went to him for a job years back, he told her about all her liabilities and advised her to forget television. She didn't have what it takes.

In fact, regardless of her immense success, Barbara still has many detractors, both viewers and critics, who mention her lisp, her harsh delivery, her brittle manner and her interruptions of interviewees as faults on television. Because I never get up early and had never seen her on television before we met, I had no preconceived idea of what she would be like.

It wasn't until I went to New York that I ever saw her on TV, and by then I knew her well. I do feel that she comes across harder and less sympathetic on television than she does in person.

I find her a warm, generous, loyal, dignified, humorous woman with a vulnerability that makes her immediately likable. Barbara is a woman's woman. She would be my first choice of someone to call if I were having romantic problems, someone to have a long gossipy lunch with, someone to go to for advice if I were in trouble. She has enough insecurity to make her very human and approachable, and she's not afraid to admit it. And she has more curiosity than anyone I know, is always interested in others and their problems, is always concerned. When you talk to Barbara you know she's listening, not looking over your head to see who's more interesting. I know it may sound trite, but she's a very private person in a very public environment. She is easily hurt by criticism, and is extraordinarily ambitious, and works longer hours and harder than any one I know, man or woman, and she is totally professional. As Barbara and I have often discussed, she, like any other woman, looks forward to a successful relationship with a man, and her separation from her husband, Lee Guber, was very difficult for her. She anguishes over not being able to spend as much time as she would like with her adopted daughter, Jacqueline, and often will give up social engagements in order to stay home with her. Barbara is a normal woman in an abnormal situation.

Anyhow, if I was being offered the job of knocking Barbara Walters off the air, it couldn't have been because of my extensive television experience. It must have been my background and my reputation as an irreverent Washington reporter.

As an Army brat, I had been in Washington on and off all my life. First as a first-grader, then as a fifth-grader, then again when my father came back the summer before my senior year in high school. In between, I went to twenty-two schools, including five high schools. We traveled from Washington state to Florida, to Washington, D.C., to Colorado, to Texas, and we lived in Japan, Greece, and Germany twice.

In those days, before my father made general, we went everywhere third class, stayed in crummy motels, and always ordered the cheapest thing on the menu. Bologna, peanut butter and jelly, and American cheese were the cheapest. I can't eat any of them today.

But my father was a dedicated soldier, West Point, the brilliant G-2 of the Seventh Army during World War II. He interrogated Goering in Germany; was director of the OSS, formally in charge of the transition period, before it became the CIA; and he was a front-line hero in Korea as the commander of the 17th Infantry regiment, 7th Division, where he earned the nickname "Buffalo Bill."

We uprooted ourselves from year to year, hauling around from one Army post to another, from castles to Quonset huts. And my sister and brother and I learned to be adaptable, to fit in, to become one of the gang quickly. If our new schoolmates spoke with Southern accents, we did too before a month was out. If they wore streamlined saddle shoes with rolled-down pink angora socks to match their pink angora sweaters, so did we. If poodle skirts and crinolines were in, we got them right away, and then scrapped them when the next move required kilts, loafers and button-down shirts.

It became a game, trying to psych out what people wanted of you and giving it to them. There was no time for iconoclasm. That would have to come later, and it would come on strong because it had been repressed for so long.

It seems calculating. And it was. But it was survival. If you knew you would only be in a place for perhaps no more than six months, you had to make friends fast and you had to be sure not to make the wrong friends. What I learned from all this was a rather scientific sense of observation, an awareness of people's social habits, an acquired skill, a natural instinct (and subsequent disgust) for the most sophisticated and subtle social climbing.

This was invaluable experience for a would-be reporter and writer. Noticing the little things was important in being able to fit in. It was cultural adjustment, and once I had checked it out I was okay. If you're a reporter, that's the first thing you have to do—move right into the situation, size it up, make friends with the people you need to talk to, and move right out. There's no time to waste.

Social climbing and power climbing—the two are often synonymous—are what make Washington run. To understand a society it is essential to understand how people climb. If there are more than two people together, if there are three, one of them is climbing.

My life was different from most brats' because my father, who was eleven years older than my mother, rose in rank very quickly. He was a brigadier general by the time I was ten, so most of my Army life was as a general's daughter. Being a general's daughter is like being a princess. Army posts are closed communities, and whoever "rules" the post is the final authority.

There are limousines and orderlies and aides and airplanes and boats and private trains. A wish becomes a command. People's rank and position are on their shoulders, so there is never any confusion as to who anyone is or where they stand. For this reason, observing Army life is seeing raw power in action. It is fascinating, and it can be ugly and frightening. The best vantage points are military social events—dinners for commanders' conferences, "hail and farewell" receptions at the officers' clubs, officers' wives' meetings (the women are said to wear their husbands' rank on their shoulders), military reviews, events honoring foreign dignitaries, and most important, visits from civilian secretaries of the Defense Department. The ass-kissing is blatant, calculated and expected. As the general's daughter, I was expected always to be a junior hostess or, when my mother was away, surrogate hostess. I learned to stand in receiving lines, smile, be polite and gracious, make conversation.

But one thing most people don't understand is that to be in the service is to be poor. In the old days, when West Point still had some cachet, it was fashionable for the young lieutenants to marry rich Vassar, Wellesley and Smith girls. This way they could lead the genteel life of an officer and a gentleman, dressing for dinner every night, and have money on the side to entertain the commanding officer properly. For some reason, my father, class of '33 and a poor boy from Crisfield, Maryland, passed up his chance to marry a rich Wellesley girl and married my mother, the daughter of a surgeon from Savannah, Georgia. He now kids her that he thought she was rich—and in fact her family lived in an enormous house in the best section of town, but my grandfather had lost most of his money during the Depression.

So we were always broke. We gave dinner dances for kings and princes in our occasional palatial houses, wearing evening dresses we had bought at government employees' merchandise stores. We ate meat loaf and tuna casserole prepared by a cook and served by an orderly in a dining room that seated twenty-four.

Because money was scarce, we all worked summers at a very young age. My first job was as a camp counselor at the Fort Lewis Youth Camp in Tacoma, Washington. I was sixteen and I didn't even know how to tie a knot, and I made about $125 for the entire summer. Having been put in charge of the drama group for lack of any skills, I presented Dylan Thomas' *Under Milkwood*, which was considered risqué for eleven-year-olds and outraged the parents. Since my father was commanding general of Fort Lewis, I wasn't fired. The following summer we moved back to Washington, D.C., and I got a job working for Barry Goldwater on Capitol Hill. I did dull clerical work and sneaked out to the Bobby Kennedy–Hoffa hearings.

My father was Assistant G-2 of the Army, and a major part of his job was dealing with military attachés. That meant an invitation almost every night to an embassy national-day reception or dinner party. As anyone who has lived in official Washington for more than a month can tell you, embassy national-day receptions are the lowest form of social life. The ambassadors hate them because they have to give them. The social secretaries hate them because they are a lot of work. The American officials hate them because they have to go to them. The guests hate them because they are so unexclusive. And everybody hates them because they are truly boring.

I loved them.

My mother took advantage of that and would often send me in her place with my father, who also hated them. You can bring anyone. In fact, you don't even have to be invited. There are a lot of people in Washington who have lists of national days and just go to an embassy on its national day, walk in, head for the bar and the buffet and eat free meals half their lives. This practice is not looked down upon. And there are those who feel that since most of the national-day receptions, which often cost thousands of dollars, are in a roundabout way paid for by United States aid, they deserve, as taxpayers, to eat there free.

But I loved them because everybody in Washington goes to these horrible events at one time or another, and so I used them as a sort of training ground to meet and talk to and observe the famous and powerful people who make the town move. Soon I was getting invitations myself, and because I spoke some foreign languages (at various points in my life I have spoken some, and forgotten, Japanese, Greek, French, Spanish and German), I became a relatively familiar face on the circuit. I was apprenticing Washington.

I spent my last year in my fifth high school at Mt. Vernon Seminary and then was accepted by Smith. That summer I barely passed the Civil Service typing test and got a job in the protocol office at the Pentagon, where I spent my time arranging dinner parties and luncheons for Washington dignitaries. I once wrote a thank-you note to Queen Elizabeth for the Secretary of Defense. I liked the job a lot, and I earned enough for spending money through my freshman year. I had a scholarship for the year so the tuition was paid for.

I was apprehensive about the clubbiness at Smith. I knew I was about to hit the big leagues, that there was a network of girls who were all from certain families and had gone to certain exclusive boarding schools in the East and who summered in the same places.

When my parents drove me up to Northampton, Massachusetts, to let me off, I didn't know a soul and I was scared to death. I walked into Talbot House, the house I had been assigned to, known as the "preppy" house, and watched everyone flinging themselves into each other's arms, screaming with delight about their summers and their trips to Europe and their tennis lessons and beaux. I don't think I've ever felt so alone or left out. But I made some friends and decided to become a political science major.

I made my debut that Christmas at the Holly Ball in Arlington, Virginia, a third-rate organization that would present almost anyone who could dredge up some kind of social credential and enough money. While all my friends came down from Smith to the elegant Washington Debutante Assembly, which is now defunct, I was out in Arlington at the Army–Navy Country Club, where my parents belonged, dancing with corny boys I didn't know, who carried bottles of liquor in brown paper bags.

My parents didn't make me do it. In fact, they really couldn't afford it, but we all felt I should have some semblance of respectability and security and identity, and somehow in our minds, after having moved around forever, "coming out" was supposed miraculously to do the trick.

That Christmas I got mononucleosis and was in bed for over a month once I got back to school. I did poorly on my midterms and was put on the registrar's list for the rest of my college career, and I lost my scholarship that year.

I had to take out a government loan, which I just finished paying off several years ago, to get through college. And I decided to become a theater arts major.

When school was out and all my friends had packed off for their summer resorts, I headed back to Washington for a dreaded summer of nine-to-five clerical work as assistant technical librarian at the Institute for Defense Analysis. There were, however, a number of interesting men who worked there who knew their way around Washington, and I befriended several of them and their wives and met a lot of State Department and administration people, had an interesting time, and got paid well.

I worked there for three summers, and I thought if I ever saw another book by Herman Kahn I'd kill myself. But I learned a great deal about Washington. I knew that I would always want to spend time there. I had become addicted to politics.

It was intoxicating to be around real power—to have senators pay attention to you, sit across from famous administration types at little Georgetown restaurants, be invited by ambassadors to visit their countries.

And I became a *Washington Post* freak. I loved the editorials, Herblock was my idol, and the news there seemed more interesting and colorful than it did in other papers. But what intrigued me most were the "women's pages." They weren't like any other "women's pages." There wasn't a day you couldn't find some delicious little tidbit or piece of gossip from a political reception or embassy party or the White House the night before. Sometimes there is real news in the women's pages, because the gossip columnists and society reporters are political reporters as well. They have to be, in Washington. I thought it was the most interesting way to find out what was going on that I had ever read.

My senior year at college I faced the terrible prospect of deciding what to do with my life. I had starred as Lily Sabina in Thornton Wilder's *Skin of Our Teeth,* and I had done well enough that I had put on my vocational office form—under desired occupation—"movie star." This enraged the vocational office, and I had to be bailed out by Miss Fitch, my class dean, who had nursed me through four years of registrar's lists, narcoleptic fits, botany classes and psychiatric excuses to get out of Sociology II exams. I was a hopeless student.

But when I played Sabina there had been an MGM talent scout by the name of Dudley Wilkinson in the audience. Legend had it that he had discovered Paula Prentiss at Northwestern several years earlier. I still have his card in my wallet.

After the play, Dudley had come backstage and had told

me I was divine. "We're going to make you a star," he said. He was the first one.

Dudley's plan was that I would be the answer to a nationwide search for a girlfriend for TV's Doctor Kildare. I had always thought that Richard Chamberlain, who played Kildare, was sort of a loser, but now I saw him in a new light. I raced out and bought all the movie magazines I could find and read them avidly, clipping out pictures of Richard Chamberlain.

The whole campus was thrilled with this new development, and everyone waited impatiently for me to get word from Hollywood about just which plane they wanted me to take. Dudley had said he wanted me to go out to "the Coast" for a screen test. A screen test!

Unfortunately, I had already been chosen to be a resident actress at the Monomoy theater in Chatham, Massachusetts, on Cape Cod. It was a small summer stock theater, and the positions there were very much sought after. So my big problem was how to stall Dudley. I explained how important it was to me to be on the "legitimate" stage. He agreed. Sort of.

So I went to Monomoy, having graduated at the exact bottom of my class, far more of a distinction than being second from the bottom. I expected to hear from Dudley sometime in August. My stay at the summer stock theater was something less than a raging success. At one point I thought I had lined up the role of Anne, Helen Keller's nurse, in *The Miracle Worker*, but it was given to another actress and I ended up with a blackened face playing Viney, the maid, in a two-line walk-on. I left before the summer was over, with one consolation: My picture was on the cover of the local Cape Cod magazine.

My father paid an Army photographer to make some professional movie-star-looking pictures for me to put in my portfolio, but I looked like what I was, just graduated from Smith, having starred in the senior play.

I got in touch with Dudley, and he said he'd meet me in New York. We met, and he broke the bad news. They had decided that Dr. Kildare would not go steady after all, and that his girl friends would be played by a series of well-known starlets, the first being Yvette Mimieux. I knew I had had it. But Dudley wasn't about to give up on his talent. He had a friend coming East to make the movie *Flipper*, about a father, son, girl friend and dolphin. Maybe there was a part for me as the father's girl friend. Dudley called one morning and asked me to rush down to the office—one of the big wheels had flown out from Hollywood to cast the girl friend. I dolled up in my best Sunday outfit and raced over there, only to find a greasy, fast-talking hustler of questionable sensitivity.

He described the part, told me they were to begin shooting in "the islands" relatively soon, and asked what I could do. I told him I hoped I could act. He told me there would be other requirements for the job. He raised his eyebrow and leered, or so it seemed to me at the time.

I told him I'd have to talk it over with my father.

He told me they'd call. They never called.

I had to go back to Washington that fall to do my Junior League provisional course. My mother had always regretted not joining the Junior League because she said it helped when you were moving around to have a ready-made group of friends wherever you went. Everyone thought that I might marry within the Army even though I insisted I wouldn't; but, having just blown my theatrical career, I figured the Junior League was a nice pastime in preparation for being a socially acceptable wife and mother.

While I was doing my Junior League course I worked as a salesgirl at the Shop for Pappagallo, a chic little boutique in Georgetown, where Jackie Kennedy shopped and which hired only post-debutantes. We were paid a minimal wage, which we bartered away for very expensive clothes at a discount. I was living at home and passing the time away until someone asked for my hand.

John F. Kennedy's death changed my life, as it did the lives of most of my friends. Somehow everything that had seemed important before became trivial and stupid. The Tuesday after Kennedy was killed, I went into the shop and announced my resignation. I wanted to do something important, to help, but I didn't know what or how.

I had a friend who was a junior instructor at Princeton and was about to go to Mexico on a research project, so I asked if I could go with him. Then I quit the Junior League. I was running out of money in Mexico just about the time my father was ordered to Germany to be the Commanding General of the Seventh Army. He was, by that time, a lieutenant general (three stars). I decided to see what Europe had to offer.

It was midwinter when we arrived at the airport to be greeted by an honor guard, limousines, sedans and endless generals. I had taken my shoes off on the plane and my feet were swollen, so I limped down the ramp while the honor guard screamed and yelled and did fantastic things with their bayonets, and the band played something that resembled "Hail to the Chief." Our entire stay in Germany would be like that, I was to discover. We were taken to our home in Stuttgart, an enormous mansion with thousands of orderlies, cooks, drivers, maids, limousines, sedans, aides, private trains, airplanes, helicopters. Nobody lives like a general or an admiral stationed outside of Washington except the President of the United States. Washington is considered a hardship post because there are too many generals.

There was about a month of inspection during which my father traveled around Germany on his private train, which he renamed the Mobile Command Post so that Congress wouldn't get the impression that it was anything frivolous. (The wife of the former ambassador to Germany had blown it by taking the "girls'" bridge game out on the train every day to tool around Germany at the cost of about $50 a mile. The government took the ambassador's train away. But the generals still had theirs, and I went along as my father inspected his command.)

Then I had to get a job. I had exactly no money. A slot was found for me to work in G-1 (logistics). My job consisted of doing nothing, as far as I can remember. I was salting my money away, being bored to distraction by my job, and meeting a few lieutenants and German barons, princes and counts, whom I saw occasionally. Most of my social activities were devoted to playing co-hostess at the dinners and receptions my parents gave for a Secretary of the Army or Chancellor Kiesinger, our next-door neighbor, or *bürgermeisters* of the various towns we visited.

I kept the job for about four months, until I thought I would be physically ill if I had to go in one more day. My father was furious. Things got so tense around the castle that I took off for Spain with a German lieutenant I had been seeing and stayed there for several months. In Spain my German got very good. By the time I got back, however, I was again out of money.

My father knew the head of Mercedes-Benz, which is headquartered in Stuttgart, and I got a job translating German to English and occasionally a little Spanish and French. This was also a boring job. But at the same time I became reinvolved with theater at the *Amerika Haus* in downtown Stuttgart. Everyone was trying to fix me up with lieutenants so that I could become a nice Army wife.

My mother and I did not want me to become a nice Army wife. So I became ruthless about turning down invitations for dates with young career officers. Every ambitious young officer hopes to marry a general's daughter. Unlike the days when my father was young and officers married for money, these young men were after power. It works. Marrying a general's daughter is almost a guarantee of a successful career, unless you blow it on the battlefield.

At any rate, I was being proposed to at a rapid rate by a number of climbing young men who would just as soon have married a cow. I finally boycotted them all, except for the reserve types who were in for two years, and consequently acquired the nickname of "The Cobra," which was to stick long after. Kris Kristofferson, who is an Air Force brat and who was my first love in Fort Lewis, Washington, was stationed in Germany at that time. Years later, when I went to interview him, he told me hilarious stories about what a bitch I was supposed to be.

The second summer, I took a leave from Mercedes-Benz and went to Madrid with a friend from Smith to study at the university. We went to classes occasionally, met a lot of Spaniards whom we didn't like, and took on several jobs. I got a job modeling gloves, which I did for a few weeks. Later I translated and edited for an Israeli writer who spoke no English. That, you might say, was my first venture into the world of journalism. The summer ended and I went back to the translation department of Daimler-Benz. The rest of that year we waited for my father to get his orders. We had heard he was slated to become Chief of Staff. But instead there was a crisis which resulted in his retirement.

Barry Goldwater, a family friend, was running for President. At a Washington party, he mentioned casually that he might visit my parents after the convention. He hadn't contacted my father but had been invited to come whenever he wanted. Lyndon Johnson went into a rage. Goldwater had refused his invitation for a military briefing, knowing full well that Johnson would try to make him out a fool. So the White House leaked a story to the *Herald Tribune* that Goldwater didn't have to go to the briefing because he was already getting military secrets from Lt. Gen. William W. Quinn, former director of the Defense Intelligence Agency.

It was also leaked that my father and Goldwater planned a trip to Berchtesgaden to pay homage to Adolf Hitler.

Other papers followed suit. But the most damaging was a story by Daniel Schorr of CBS in Bonn. Schorr reported that Goldwater planned to go to Germany right after the convention as a guest of General Quinn, and that he had accepted an invitation to speak at a lakeside seminar in Bavaria. That meant, Schorr pointed out, that the first speech he gave after the convention would be in Germany. He would be staying with his old friend, General Quinn, at the General's private cottage in Berchtesgaden. Which was, by the way, Schorr informed his viewers, Hitler's favorite retreat.

Schorr also passed on the news that Franz Joseph Strauss, the leader of the Conservative party in Germany, had told him that he was happy that Goldwater was coming to Germany because they had a lot to talk about.

In the same report, Schorr quoted a right-wing German newspaper which had carried an interview with Goldwater and had then gone on to editorialize that there was a great deal in common between the German and American right wings.

Military men are not allowed to be political, and Schorr's broadcast made it look as though my father was siding politically with Goldwater. Shortly after the convention in San Francisco, Johnson put out word that my father would never get his fourth star. Any hopes he had of being Chief of Staff were dashed. It was a cause célèbre among the military. General Eisenhower called from Gettysburg, and General Lyman Lemnitzer from Paris.

My father decided that, rather than be "put out to pasture," as it is politely known in the military, he would quit. So in February of 1965 the Chief of Staff sent General Abrams, the late Chief of Staff, over to Germany in his plane to pick us all up and bring us back to Washington, where my father would turn in his uniform at the Pentagon. It was a wrenching experience as we stood at a full military review to watch a brilliant military career go down the drain because of vindictive politics. And it was a lesson in politics which I was never to forget.

Back in Washington, staying temporarily at the bachelor officers' quarters at Fort Myer, the post where we had lived before going to Germany, we were a grim threesome. My brother was at the University of Arizona by then, and my sister had gotten married the summer before. So we were alone in a dreary town, with no quarters, no orderlies, limousines, aides—no nothing.

But my father got a job as a vice president with Martin-Marietta and bought a house in Chevy Chase, Maryland. I had to find a job. I called Ellen McCloy, my college roommate, and she told me to come to New York and we would find jobs and get an apartment together. I went to New York and found several jobs, but none of them sustained me either financially or spiritually. I wasn't very serious about a career because I had met a young Harvard graduate in Germany who was doing his time in the Army, and we had decided to get married. I was planning to go to Europe to spend the summer with him, then return, find another job, and wait for him to come back the following year for the wedding.

But during this time the job I liked the best was as freelance public relations agent for Murray Zarat's Pet Festival and Animal Husbandry Exposition at Coney Island. I had to take the subway out to Coney Island every day, although Murray began to feel sorry for me and would slip me five dollars most days for taxi fare. He would also slip me my salary, which varied from week to week depending on how good a job I did. The Pet Festival, claimed Murray, had the world's largest collection of animals. If you pressed him, he looked at you, shrugged his shoulders, and said, "Two million ants?" There were, of course, other animals, but it was the ant colony that made up the bulk.

My job was to publicize the Pet Festival. Part of the time I worked out of the bridal suite of the Americana Hotel, writing press releases for Murray. He smuggled me in as a hotel employee. I liked the accommodations; it was convenient, and the bridal suite was nice and roomy.

My first publicity stunt was the landing of Noah's Ark at Coney Island. Murray went bananas over the idea. We would rent an ark, then get two of each kind of animal that Murray had and put them on the ark. Then we would sail it around for a while and land it on the beach in front of the Pet Festival. Several other animals would be at the landing to greet the ark. We would alert the press.

We got the ark. Somehow Murray and his staff got the two-by-twos on board and it took off. After several near-sinkings, the ark was ready to beach. I was on the beach, ecstatic at the number of reporters and television crews that had shown up. I had done my homework. There was, though, one small consideration that had not occurred to me. The law. Suddenly I looked up, as the ark was about to land, and saw what seemed to be hundreds of police cars, red lights whirling, pulling up and racing out to the beach as though it were the Normandy landing. They ran up to Murray and asked if he was the owner of the ark. He said he was. "You have to have a permit to land an ark on the beach here," said a very mean-looking policeman. "Noah didn't need a permit," Murray screamed back, in what I thought was his finest moment. "We're taking you off to book you, buddy," said another policeman, and they started to drag him away.

There was a scream and Murray turned and ran toward the water, where the animals were disembarking. Unfortunately, nobody had thought about what to do with them once they were on the beach. The animals, plus the horses and zebras and the elephants that had come down to meet them, were running up and down the beach. Murray was running about like a crazy man trying to gather them up, and the two policemen joined in. Then there was another scream and Murray, hysterical by this time, dashed over to where the second cry had come from, took one look, and threw his arms up to the heavens in supplication.

One of the goats had just given birth to twins. Now there was a complete change in tone and Murray played it like a violin. He named the twins after the arresting officers, Al Olson and Bob Mahoney, and went peacefully off with them as the cameras whirred. We got four minutes on the seven o'clock news.

That was my most successful venture. The others didn't turn out to be quite the coups I had hoped for. The parachute jump, which I had transformed into the world's largest bird-feeding station, did not attract a single bird, and the otter's sliding board was a total bomb. But nothing was as bad as the Miss Superchick contest. I had placed an ad at the bottom of the front page of *The Times*. There was to be a contest to choose a woman to sit on duck eggs and hatch them. This would take place at the Pet Festival, and people could come and watch. The woman would wear some form of costume and sit on a throne which would have a seat like an inner tube with the eggs inside. The incubation period would be eighteen to twenty-one days. She would get a hundred dollars a day plus a thousand-dollar bonus if the eggs hatched. I had persuaded Louis Nye to go out there with me and act as the judge, and I had questionnaires printed that asked, "How much egg laying experience have you had?" And the contestants were to be judged on their answers to the questionnaire and to Louis Nye's interview.

I was shocked to arrive at the Pet Festival the morning of the contest and find nearly 500 women and an enormous number of reporters. I had set up a counter with Danish pastries and coffee for the press.

There was every kind of contestant, from prostitutes to respectable mothers trying to put their children through college. I felt sick. What had started as a gimmick—an attention-getting joke—had turned into a grotesque and demeaning spectacle aimed at taking advantage of desperate women while stripping them of their dignity. Nobody much seemed to see it that way. It makes me realize now how far we've come in the last few years. I tried to get Murray to cancel the whole thing, but he was thrilled with it. Louis Nye's interviews of the contestants, after they had filled out their forms, were going splendidly, and they were being filmed and recorded by several TV and radio crews.

The finals were to be held at the Americana Hotel, but I became so revolted that I went off and never came back. As it turned out, the contest never took place. The big New York newspaper strike came along just then, and there was no more publicity to be had. I later heard the Pet Festival had gone out of business.

I decided to go to Europe to visit my fiancé that summer, and when I came back I became a Kelly Girl.

That way I would move around to a lot of interesting and exciting new jobs each day. I found, to my disappointment, that although I did move around each day, it was to type file cards and do other work nobody else wanted to do. I also found I was being relieved from each job for incompetence, which is why I didn't last as a Kelly Girl too long.

Ellen McCloy and I had not found an apartment, which was just as well, since I didn't have any money. So after Christmas when my fiancé came over from Europe to see me, I decided to go to Washington and stay with my parents until he came back in May and we could prepare for a June wedding.

That meant I had to find a job.

A friend of mine had just come to Washington to work for Charlie Guggenheim, the filmmaker, and he hired me to be his assistant production manager. I was terribly excited because I was finally going to be in films. What I wasn't aware of was that the production manager has to deal with all the business arrangements of the company. There was nothing artistic about typing up orders. So that didn't last too long. But I did leave on good terms, having met a lot of interesting people through the company. In fact, one friend I had met led me into my next job, which was the most fun of all.

I became the social secretary for Cherif Guellal, the Algerian ambassador, a thirty-five-year-old bachelor who gave the best parties in Washington. He was handsome, bright, sophisticated and nice. At the time I began working for him, Cherif was involved with a former Miss America, Yolande Fox. Together, they were the most sensational couple in Washington, and an invitation to Cherif's was the most recherché invitation one could have.

My job was to plan and organize his parties, making sure the guest lists were fascinating, diverse, controversial and gay. Doing this job, I learned about Washington and the people who lived here. And I was often a guest as well as a social secretary.

Shortly after I went to work for Cherif, the Arab-Israeli war broke out in June 1967, and Algeria severed relations with the United States. Cherif was recalled, as were all the Arab ambassadors, and Embassy Row virtually died. It had been the Arabs, during the Johnson Administration, who had kept things going in town, and without them, Washington folded up socially.

It was during this time that I met Warren Hoge, who was then the Washington correspondent for the *New York Post*. Warren had gone to work as a reporter for the *Washington Star* immediately after graduating from Yale and had taken the job at the *Post* a few months earlier.

Reporters had been anathema to me, after my father's experience in Germany, and I was not only suspicious of them but felt that they were socially inferior. Once, at a dinner at the German ambassador's in Bonn, I was seated next to the *New York Times* correspondent and felt terribly insulted.

But Warren was totally dedicated to the newspaper business and so full of enthusiasm that I became interested in it myself. He introduced me to a whole new world in Washington and a completely different group of people, who were later to become my closest friends. Through Warren, I got an interview with Philip Geyelin, the editor of the editorial page of *The Washington Post*. He hired me as a secretary after a hilarious hour-long interview, but called to say he had had an attack of guilt and that I was fired before I started for being overqualified.

Next, in the beginning of September, I got a job as a GS-7 working in the Smithsonian Institution. I reported directly to a man I couldn't stand, who hated the way I made phone calls and coffee, called me a goddamn idiot twice a day, and talked in very esoteric sentences, which made me feel dumb until I realized nobody else knew what he was saying either. Finally, in February, I went to work for Eugene McCarthy's campaign. I got two hundred a week in the fundraising area working for a wonderful zany man named Tom Page. Page liked the McCarthy campaign because it was so crazy and atypical. So did I. At first.

But one day in April a couple who thought they were running the campaign, Jeannie and Curt Gans, moved all the office furniture out of the campaign manager's office during his lunch hour and locked the door. That was the day the McCarthy campaign began to disintegrate internally. Tom Page called up his old friend Frank Mankiewicz and asked for a job with Bobby Kennedy's campaign. He said he wouldn't go, though, without his trusty companion, Sally Quinn.

Tom and I packed up and went out to San Francisco to be, respectively, the media coordinator and assistant media coordinator for the Northern California campaign.

My job was to line up celebrities from the East Coast to come out to California and campaign for Kennedy. I would get a George Plimpton or a David Susskind, make sure they had tickets, hotel reservations and someone to pick them up at the airport, and book them for as many TV and newspaper interviews as I could. I also arranged several publicity stunts reminiscent of the old Murray Zarat days, including a celebrity tennis match with four prominent personalities and tennis pros. The problem was that I had booked it at a high school without asking permission, and the school canceled the match after more than a thousand pro-Kennedy tennis freaks had arrived to see it. I was later told that we had probably lost more than a thousand votes. I was also told to keep a low profile.

On June 5, 1968, Robert Kennedy was shot in the Ambassador Hotel in Los Angeles, minutes after I left the San Francisco armory where the Northern California campaign victory party was going on. I didn't hear the news until the next morning. Later that day, many of us in San Francisco were put aboard a campaign plane and flown back to Washington, a dazed, disbelieving, silent group.

For a week I did nothing but stare at the ceiling, until I heard about an emergency committee on gun control that was being set up to fight the free sale of handguns. I worked for them for the rest of the month, then went to New York for a weekend to visit Ellen McCloy, who was working as special assistant to Richard Salant in CBS News. Salant took Ellen and me to lunch at the Ground Floor, Bill Paley's creation at the bottom of CBS headquarters. We had a marvelous lunch, and Ellen and I convinced him that I would be indispensable as an extra assistant at the Democratic and Republican conventions. He agreed and I was hired.

At that point I had never met a single television personality, and I was terribly impressed with the proximity I would have to all the "stars." Salant was kind and generous and, I

must say, he certainly let us have our own way, and the summer was a great adventure. We got to be friends and I liked
and trusted him. By the end of the summer we were all exhausted and emotionally overwrought. So when Salant asked
me to come to New York and work for him there, I refused. I
really loved Washington and politics and felt that my career,
whatever it might be, lay there. Besides, I really had no interest in television. And at that point, Warren and I were very
much involved.

That fall I had a difficult time finding a job, mainly because
I had resolved that I would not again do anything I hated. I
rented a tiny apartment in the only slum in Georgetown for
$100 a month. It had a Pullman kitchen and a sofa bed in a
room so tiny that the bed took up all the space, and I had to
step over it to get to the other side of the room.

Finally, desperate after about a month of job-hunting, I
went to Cherif Guellal, who had returned from Algeria and
had taken on a job as a writer-historian at the Institute for
Policy Studies, an organization headed by Marcus Raskin and
Richard Barnet. Cherif's project was a book on the revolu-
tionary Frantz Fanon, and he hired me as a research-secre-
tary. But I was bored and terrible at it. I hate research. I
wasn't getting paid much, sat alone in a tiny office, never got
out, and eventually caught pneumonia.

But it was my engagement to Warren during that period,
and our subsequent breakup two months later, which really
drove me to a near breakdown, and I knew I had to get away.

I decided to quit my job and move to California. I went in
mid-February and stayed with my sister and her husband,
Donna and Bill Robbins. After a few terrible, sad and unpro-
ductive months I decided to return to Washington. Warren
and I got back together, but I still had to find a job. So I borrowed some money from my parents and planned an enormous party for Barry Goldwater, Jr., who had just been
elected to Congress. I invited every celebrity I knew in town,
and reporters and photographers, bought a designer dress,

used my parents' house, and had a lavish party which was splashed all over the society pages the next day.

It was my way of announcing I was back in town. What I hoped was that someone would see it and offer me a job.

It worked.

The next day I picked up the phone and a voice said, "Sally, you don't know me but I'm Ben Bradlee and I would like to talk to you about a job at *The Washington Post*. Would you be interested?"

I said yes casually and we arranged an appointment for ten the next morning. I carefully chose my nicest dress and pondered all the way down to the *Post* how to explain that I would only accept a secretarial job if there were "opportunity for advancement."

We had a marvelous interview. He explained that most of the women in Style, a feature section that had been created six months earlier from the old women's section, had turned down covering parties and society. They insisted it is sexist for women to be stereotyped as party reporters while the men were the major political reporters.

I didn't care. I was too broke to be discriminating. When Bradlee asked if I would be interested in being a party reporter, I said yes. He told me I would start the next day and that the *Post* had a six-months' trial period. I figured I wouldn't last more than six months, but at least it would keep me for a while.

Philip Geyelin wandered by as Bradlee was asking me if I would leave him some things I had written. I told him I had never written anything. He stared at me for a minute. And Geyelin said, "Well, nobody's perfect," and Bradlee added, "You're hired."

Later the story got shortened to eliminate Geyelin, and "Nobody's perfect" was put into Bradlee's mouth. That's the way it's told now because it's shorter, less confusing, funnier and more commercial.

The next day I was taken to a party by Dorothy McCardle,

then a sixty-five-year-old veteran reporter of nearly fifty years, who instructed me on how to cover a party. "The first thing you must always do," she said to me solemnly as we stood in the doorway of the Greek embassy, "is go immediately to the bar and get a drink." We did that as she explained that you never have more than one, you just have that first one to relax you and make you look sociable.

I watched Dorothy move around the room, laughing and chatting and having what looked to me like a good time, occasionally jotting down something in her notebook. I wandered around wondering what on earth anyone could write about the party.

Afterward Dorothy sat down at her typewriter and banged out a story. To my surprise, it was not only clever and amusing but filled with interesting gossip.

The next night I was dropped off at a party alone by Mary Russell, another reporter. I felt as if I were soloing in an airplane for the first time with no previous instruction. She told me she would pick me up in two hours. It was an art opening, and I knew nothing about art. I went in to the party, saw a few friends, spent the entire time gossiping. (The only notes I took were just to make people think I knew what I was doing.) I had no idea what to ask anybody and there didn't seem to be any news, or anybody famous, for that matter. Mary picked me up two hours later and we drove back to the office. I was told I had an hour and a half to write the story. I didn't know how to write, and I didn't have any story. The phone rang and it was Warren. "How was the party?" he asked. So I told him, and he laughed most of the way through my description. "Don't laugh," I said. "I'm on deadline"—I had just learned that expression—"and I don't have anything to write." "Well, write what you just told me," he said. "That's a pretty good story." So I did, and it turned out to be a pretty good story.

A week later I suggested covering a flashy victory party in

New York given by Carter and Amanda Burden, the then beautiful young rich social little couple. He had just been elected city councilman, and their celebration was supposed to attract every celebrity in the city. The party was held in a rather rough area of New York and had about half ghetto people and half richies from Fifth Avenue. The contrast was delicious, and it may have been the beginning of radical chic. My editors were pleased and the story ran on Sunday as the lead piece in the Style section. During the following months I went to parties and receptions and balls nearly every night, and I loved it. Somehow it seemed that all my past pursuits had prepared me for this kind of work. I know my way around, know most people in town, understand enough politics and am fascinated by the people who make political news.

And being a society reporter in Washington is different from being a society reporter in any other city in the world. Because Washington is, for one thing, the news capital of the world. And for another, it is a company town. Most of the interesting people in Washington either work for the government or write about it.

One day Maxine Cheshire, our VIP columnist, said, "Your résumé may look terrible to everybody else, but for a reporter it's a dream. You've done a little of everything and met everybody. It will be a great asset to you."

This is what makes covering parties interesting. All parties are working events: the people have simply changed uniforms. Society reporters in Washington are political reporters as well, and they have to be as well informed as the national-desk reporter. Party reporters have broken major news stories. Policies have been altered and reputations have been ruined by an offhand remark at a party.

At one of the first parties I ever covered, a senator told me what the vote count on the ABM was going to be. I put it at the end of a story on page 5 of the Style section. Two days later, the managing editor, Gene Patterson, came flying back to Style to say he had heard we had the story, and his national reporters had been working on it for weeks. The next day the vote count on the ABM was in a box on the front page with the lead *"The Washington Post* has learned."

I have always carried a notebook with me to make sure people know that I'm working, even though most people in this town have long since learned they ought not to say anything at a party unless they want it in the streets the next day. My close friends have made me wear an "off duty" sign at their parties so their guests could relax.

Since those in power in Washington understand perfectly how much good or damage a write-up in the social section of the paper can do, they take social reporters seriously. Also, they look to them for an indication of where they are on the power scale.

Aside from getting the required drink, the first thing you do is to find the most important powerful person in a room and stick close. That way you know you'll see everybody. You'll get the best quotes, and you won't miss any from the star.

Because Washingtonians understand this, they look to the society reporter as a bellwether. When I walk into a room, people often wait to see whom I choose before committing themselves. Sometimes you find one powerful person and hang around him until someone more powerful comes in.

My writing was not terribly professional at first, to say the least, but it was original. At least I had never learned any bad habits. I also had never learned to write the traditional who-what-why-when-and-where leads. I was as likely to start a story with an irreverent quote and not even get to who said it and where until the third or fourth paragraph. This is one of the reasons my articles drew attention and people began to notice my byline and style.

The fall in Washington is the charity ball season. I covered what really happened, and it was sometimes not very flattering to the chairmen and the guests. But it was so clear that most of those involved in the balls were using them for social advancement rather than for any altruistic purposes. And I felt a duty to expose them. They had been getting away with sycophantic, fawning reports of their goings-on for too long, and I didn't feel like perpetuating it.

There was the expected uproar over my coverage of the charity balls. There were letters to the editors, and groups of vigilantes came to the paper in protest. I was reporting what happened.

"What do you think you are, a national reporter?" one irate charity ball chairman asked me. I became more and more cynical as people denied quotes that I had published. Occasionally when someone denied what I had written, I would get angry and confront them. Usually the reply was a startled, "But, my dear, that's part of the game, that's the way it's done." And I soon realized that in Washington and in politics, that is the way it's done.

My big chance came that fall when Barbara Howar had a party for Gloria Steinem and invited me to cover it. Among the guests was a short, heavyset, shy little man named Henry Kissinger. He was standing off alone in the corner, not talking to anyone. So I wandered over to talk to him and asked him why he was all by himself. "What's the matter?" I asked. "Don't you like parties? Aren't you a swinger?"

"Well," he said, grinning, "I'm really a secret swinger."

That was it for Henry. By the end of that week he was "The Secret Swinger" in *Time* and *Newsweek* and *Life* and newspapers around the world. Ever since, he's joked about how I made him what he is today. That was the first time that he had shown his true sense of humor in public. When asked about women reporters in Washington, he remarked, "Maxine Cheshire makes you want to commit murder. Sally Quinn makes you want to commit suicide."

That piece, written about four months after I had started at the *Post*, marked the moment when I began to be seen as a personality rather than just another reporter.

I went to White House dinners and the coverage was not often flattering. I had learned that most people weren't interested in reading puff pieces. Even if they were outraged by the truth, they continued to read. There were some cancelations of the *Post* because of my articles. But a check by the subscription department found that those who canceled papers for political reasons would resubscribe the next day. People want to know what goes on. When Julie and Tricia gave a dinner dance for Princess Anne, the Princess disgraced herself by behaving rudely to members of Congress and reporters. I wrote about it and was categorized, along with some other women reporters, as one of the "Washington Witches" by the British papers.

I interviewed the wife of the British ambassador, Lady Cromer. She ventured her opinion on the war in Vietnam. She was in favor of it.

She added that, "Saving face means more to Asians than life. Life means nothing, but nothing to them."

Her husband was nearly recalled by Parliament, and her career as a Washington hostess was severely curtailed.

I started covering Embassy Row as though it were a meaningless, dying institution. In fact, it is, since we have hotlines and traveling secretaries of state and foreign ministers. The 1967 Arab-Israeli war had pretty much heralded the demise of embassy influence, since the Arabs were the only ones who had kept Embassy Row alive. Mostly because they have belly dancers.

Still, there are too many people in Washington who depend on their favorite ambassadors for dinner, too many charities who depend on the embassies for their ballrooms and free booze, and too many old-time society columnists who depend on the embassy parties for their stories. So they continue. And my stories created more outrage, and I ended up being unofficially banned from the British, the Belgian, the German and the French embassies in Washington.

I loved every minute of it. Once I got over the shock of being publicly denounced and snubbed and of receiving hate mail, the reaction and controversy I was causing was fun. I liked to watch people at parties debating whether to avoid me or suck up to me.

For many who had always counted on some social reporters for free publicity, it was a whole new world. I imagined the agonized decisions whether to invite me to their parties and take a chance on being reported if they made fools of themselves, or doing without the publicity altogether.

In the old days, all that glorious publicity was there for the taking. But now it wasn't so easy. Quinn might just print what they really said and did, how they really behaved. Instead of Mrs. So-and-So looked divine in her pink chiffon, framed beautifully by her magnificent self-portrait, the glittering candelabra and the beauteous bouquets of anemones, she might just pick up the paper and read that she had, in fact, had a little too much to drink, tripped on her hem and fallen to the floor, knocking over a waiter and crushing her color-coordinated hors d'oeuvres into the matching carpet. (True story.)

It raised the stakes of the Washington hustle and made it more dangerous. That's what Washington is—a hustle, both political and social. The politicians and the administration types hustle the press. The press in turn hustles them. Almost everybody's scratching somebody's back some of the time. Washington is like an Oriental bazaar where people trade information and favors as if they were rugs and camels.

In the old days, society reporting was part of the hustle. An ambassador, senator or administration official invited you to a big buffet dinner and you wrote a nice story. The next time he invited you to a small seated dinner with top-ranking guests. You wrote another nice story. The next time, who knows, you might be the only reporter and be seated next to Henry Kissinger. Or your host might call you with a hot item or invite you on a trip around the world. Enterprising reporters could buy excitement, glamour, romance, fame, social acceptance and money with a nice story. What they hadn't realized was that you didn't have to write a nice story to get it all. What used to be acceptable in Washington is not any more. Some still do it, but they are now the pariahs of the legitimate Washington press corps. "On the Take" is out.

At that first party I went to with Dorothy McCardle, Jimmy Symington, former chief of protocol, the son of a senator and now a congressman himself, told me, "If you want to survive in this business, always write nice things about people."

But I learned quickly enough that not only had things changed, but that anyhow I could not resist the temptation of writing about it if I heard an ambassador's wife scream at the servants because the flambé wasn't in flames, or saw a senator get drunk and make racist remarks, or watched a famous hostess throw a drink at her guest, a White House official. If someone called Alice Longworth and said they were having Kissinger to dinner, then called Kissinger and said they were having Mrs. Longworth, and I found out about it—and I usually did—I would print it. If someone asked a Jewish senator and his wife to leave a restricted private club, I reported it. If Administration officials made anti-Administration toasts at a party, ditto. And if a disgraced official was called and told a party had been canceled, only to find out the party really took place, I printed it. And I did survive.

However, party reporting itself did not fare as well. It became obvious that it was dangerous to invite reporters, no longer harmless, and one's guests began to resent it when they arrived to find a society reporter and photographer on hand. Word got out about which hosts and hostesses allowed their parties to be covered, and soon no one who was anyone would go to them, and so reporters didn't want to cover them. I began going to private dinners as a guest, not as a reporter, if I felt I might pick up things I could use as a background, which is what most non-social reporters in this town did anyway. Once, a well-known hostess remarked that to have a society reporter covering your party was the kiss of death, but to have Sally Quinn there *not reporting* was a sign of social success.

I had been at the *Post* about two years when I asked to cover the 2,500th anniversary of Iran. The Shah of Iran and his wife, Queen Farah Diba, planned an immense celebration in the middle of the desert at Persepolis, near Shiraz. I went for three weeks to the celebration, which was the biggest extravaganza in 2,500 years. Every major paper and television network in the world was covering the event. In fact, there were so many press people that they had to take over the entire University of Shiraz and put us in the dormitory. We lived in tiny concrete cells with a single narrow bunk and communal bathrooms. Down the hall in my dormitory was Barbara Walters. We had known each other before, when I covered a party that her husband, Lee Guber, gave at his theater near Washington, Shady Grove. Barbara and I had liked each other right away and she had later sent me one of her famous handwritten thank-you notes for the story I wrote.

There we were in the middle of the desert, in the most primitive, inelegant surroundings, all struggling for stories with the least possible help from the Iranian government. There was a two-hour bus ride from the dormitory to the tent city at Persepolis where the royals were staying and where all the festivities were held. Those long, dusty rides, with no bathroom facilities and nothing to eat or drink but curdled yogurt and pistachio nuts, plus the terrible heat during the day in the desert, were sheer hell. Then at night, for the newspaper people, there was always the writing of stories and the attempt to file them via Iranian Teletype machines. It was so awful that Horst Faas, the Pulitzer Prize-winning photographer, who has covered wars and natural catastrophes, told me, standing on the ruins of Persepolis in the broiling sun, that this was the most grueling assignment of his life.

During all this, Barbara Walters, who had one major broadcast at the end of the last week, lost her researcher to the flu and had to do everything herself. So we worked out a deal whereby I would give her the copy I filed every night in exchange for any tidbits she picked up during the day.

I got the only private newspaper interview with the Queen. She told me how disgusted she was by the whole celebration and how she deplored the use of all the tacky French things brought over from Paris. She explained that the planning had been taken over by some of the older officials who were still ashamed of Iran. The interview was picked up by the news magazines, and for the first time, they gave me credit for my story by name.

Charlotte Curtis of *The New York Times* was also there, and she and I found that we were helping each other out a great deal as well. We even saved each other's lives one night in the desert, coming back from the Shah's banquet for the kings and queens, when we got caught in a dust storm and were nearly blown away.

It was during those three weeks that Charlotte and Barbara and I became good friends. It was like being in combat together.

The next major stories I did were a series of three interviews with the Wallace family during the Democratic Primaries. Having followed them around for nearly a week on various campaign planes, I finally managed to corner George Wallace, his wife, Cornelia, and her mother, Big Ruby. They were all marvelously candid and funny, especially Big Ruby, who gained national prominence by making the remark during our interview about her son-in-law, "Shoooooooooot, honey, he ain't even titty high."

After the Wallaces came the Democratic and Republican conventions in Miami, where I began writing about the media covering the media. Then I went on to do personal interviews with football player Billy Kilmer, critic Rex Reed, writer Oriana Fallaci, Birch and Marvella Bayh, film director Bernardo Bertolucci, Clare Boothe Luce. I wrote a very favorable story about Barbara Walters and was criticized for writing a puff piece. I was beginning to realize how much animosity there is toward successful women.

I covered the Mardi Gras, did a sociological study of the makeup of New Orleans, and wrote up Norman Mailer's fiftieth birthday party in New York. And I covered the sentencing of Clifford and Edith Irving. I did a series of profiles of the administration people involved in the Watergate scandal, including H. R. Haldeman, and shortly before I left the *Post* I did a profile of the famous fan dancer Sally Rand.

I had what I considered to be the perfect job. It was glamorous, exciting, I made a good salary, there was a new story every day, I traveled constantly, I met every famous person there was, and I had made enough of a reputation to have caught the public eye.

To my mind there was nothing anyone could ever offer that would make me consider giving up *The Washington Post*.

Most people never believed that. For one thing, there has been such a mythology built up around the supposed glamour of television life that it is hard for the average person to imagine turning down anything on TV. Gore Vidal once told me, "There are two things one always does, my dear, when one has the chance, sex and television."

Secondly, the word had gone out that there were at least

sixty names on an imaginary list of candidates for the *Morning News* slot. Sixty quivering females all dying for the job and willing to scratch and claw their way to the anchor booth. It seemed hard for me to believe that. However, I knew there were several who had been considered, even though Gordon always later insisted that there had *really* been no others. Gloria Steinem and Bess Myerson had been mentioned, but no one thought that they would give up their jobs for something like the *Morning News*. Connie Chung, of the Washington bureau, had done a week-or-so tryout on the *Morning News*, and Leslie Stahl had decided against the tryout. Several other women were taken for perfunctory lunches, and interviewed for potential.

Margaret "Meg" Osmer, a producer for *Sixty Minutes* who had acquired a certain celebrity as a sometime companion of Henry Kissinger's, was also an initial possibility. Meg had done very little on camera before, so they brought her down to the Washington studio to try out as co-anchor from there with John Hart in New York.

Meg had not wanted to, but had finally allowed herself to be persuaded to do it for three days. She asked if she would be expected to write anything and was told no. The first morning, she appeared in the studio to find that she was expected to write the entire Washington portion. When she got on the air with John Hart she received no camera cues, her TelePrompTer was blank, and her earpiece (Telex) kept falling out. After the show was over she asked to see a playback to see her mistakes and was told she couldn't view it.

The next day they presented her with an interview of two foreign women on the subject of women's liberation, for which she was unprepared. And finally she was told at the end of her tryout that I had already been offered the job.

I never saw Meg on camera, but she is a beautiful and bright woman who should have been able to perform perfectly well under decent circumstances. Instead, she apparently came across as nervous and unsure.

Naturally it didn't work out. They thought she didn't have "it" and she left CBS. She is now doing very well as correspondent-producer for ABC.

So, as Gordon says, there was never any question in his mind from the beginning that he would hire anybody else but me.

The *Today* Show is on from seven till nine, the *Morning News* from seven until eight. Gordon said they would continue with a hard-news format but with two interesting, lively and "controversial" (he stressed that word) personalities, both writers and journalists. We would begin with hard news—and nobody was ever to forget, Gordon kept repeating, that *The CBS Morning News* was the hardest and best news show on the air; that wasn't going to change. Then we could combine it with some light conversation, ad libs, interviews and lively film pieces and wipe out the *Today* Show for that hour. After that, we'd most likely expand and take them on for the full two hours. It was very simple.

And, I thought, this is the largest, richest and most powerful network in the world. They must know what they're doing.

By the time we had finished our steak and carrots and potatoes shortly before nine at the Coffee House I had agreed to stay over the next day and write a pilot.

The next afternoon around two I arrived at the CBS News building at 524 West 57th. It is an old, fly-infested converted milk barn, painted completely gray on the inside, and looks and smells depressingly like the inside of an Army hospital. I should have known that was a bad omen. I have a very keen nose and I have never been happy in a place where I didn't like the smell.

I was taken back to the *Morning News* section, a little

corridor of offices right off the newsroom and next to the *Evening News* section, henceforth to be known as "the Cronkites." There is a little square room with glaring light bulbs, four desks pushed together and four typewriters, which is called the Bullpen. Hughes and I were shown the script from the John Hart broadcast that morning and then given a pile of wire stories and that day's *New York Times*. Jim Ganser, one of the producers, was supervising and he took a sheet and outlined the major stories of the day, giving half to me and half to Hughes. I couldn't believe it was that easy. I was assigned to write about Vietnam at peace but where people were still getting killed. From several wire stories and *The Times* I put together a few paragraphs, half news, half editorial, with a conclusion that left no doubt about how I felt. I wrote the rest of my stories the same way, then with time to spare, I dashed off a minute-and-a-half essay on what social life was like in Watergate Washington. Hostesses were having a terrible time trying to find dinner guests from the Nixon administration who weren't "criminals" and I quoted an unidentified woman as saying she didn't care, she was going to invite so-and-so anyway because, after all, he was only a white-collar criminal. It was a true story. Everybody seemed amazed that I had written my part so quickly, and Hughes was pleased and said I reminded him of his wife, Ann, who was spending the summer in their house in France. "She's meaner than a junkyard dog," he said admiringly. "And so are you," he said, smiling. Lee Townsend was pleased too, and Gordon told me how impressed everyone was with me.

I agreed to stay over and film the pilot the next day.

That night I had dinner with Hughes and Roger Mudd, CBS news correspondent and anchorman, who was in New York for the summer substituting for Cronkite. We ate at a tiny French bistro near CBS called the Cafe Brittany and drank a lot of wine, and Hughes began to feel compelled to warn me about the television business.

"I've been in it for fourteen years," he said, "and it's a terrible business." Everybody says Hughes is a little bit crazy. Hughes says so,.too. "You have to be crazy to stay in this business," he said. Roger who is also a very funny and very nice man, took Hughes's cue and told me all the television horror stories he could think of. Each wavered between encouraging me to come to CBS and being protective.

I liked Hughes even more that night. He is a marvelous raconteur, one of the best I've heard, and with his Midwestern background and accent, combined with his Francophilia, he can be the best old company in the world. We got along, as he would say, "just dandy."

The next morning I went to the "studio"; I was informed by one of the producers that this was the news business, not Hollywood, and that we called it the "office." It seemed like a studio to me and I never could call it the office, which I think annoyed some people. We went upstairs to one of the huge studios (that's okay; it's also used for the soaps) and they put us on high stools in front of a lectern.

We had typed our scripts out on special typewriters that produce enormous letters. The page slides under a large magnifying glass attached to the camera, and as one looks into the camera the copy is visible. The TelePrompTer is a fairly recent invention.

The pilot was only about a half hour because we had no commercials or interviews. We had written some lead-ins to film pieces and had allowed space for two ad libs. After a film piece about Willy Brandt in Israel, Hughes and I chatted about our experiences living in Germany. After a film piece about Kissinger, I talked about his reputation with the ladies.

When we had finished, we did it a second time, and then everyone came rushing over to say how fantastic it was, and how incredible it was that I could read the prompter like an old pro. They did say that it would have looked a little better without the dark glasses, but that they were sort of sexy so it wasn't a big thing. It was a big thing. I didn't have my regular glasses with me and I couldn't see the camera, much less the script, without them.

I told Gordon I had to get back to Washington that afternoon, and he said he would call me by the end of the week. I thought about the whole experience going down on the Metroliner and decided that it had been fun but I definitely did not want to go into television. It was too easy.

Gordon called Friday to say that everybody loved the pilot. He didn't say who everybody was. I was to learn that "everybody," just like "they," is never defined. That way nobody is to blame for anything. More people had to see it and Gordon would call me the next week.

By that time I had mouthed off all over the place about the pilot and the $75,000 that I had originally heard CBS was going to pay. Everybody who heard about it was calling or coming by my desk to get the details, and most were enthusiastic. They all thought I would be terrific on television, a real natural, and what an opportunity, all that money and fame; one of the gang makes good, etc. It was sounding better and better.

Monday I heard nothing. Tuesday Gordon called to say that Salant loved the pilot. I thought that was odd, because Salant had watched the taping from the control room with Gordon and had said then that he loved it. Apparently this was Salant's official approval. Then Gordon laid it on me.

"We want to go to Blackrock with it. But we don't want to unless we have pretty much assurance from you that you'll take the job if it's approved."

"Who's Blackrock?" I asked.

"Blackrock," said Gordon, "is the CBS network headquarters across town on Fifty-second Street. It's where Paley and Arthur Taylor, President of CBS, and Jack Schneider, President of CBS Broadcast Group, and Bob Wood, President of CBS Television Network, are. It's called 'Blackrock,' as in *Bad Day at. . . .*"

I did not want the job but I didn't want to be turned down either.

I took a deep breath and lied. "Yes," I said, "I'll take the job if Blackrock approves the pilot."

Wednesday I spent all day going from person to person in the newsroom soliciting opinions, and calling up everybody I had ever known. Ben Bradlee told me he thought it would be a mistake. He didn't think I would be satisfied by television and he said I was just beginning to develop as a writer. Phil Geyelin, editor of the editorial page, agreed. David Halberstam, former *New York Times* reporter, Pulitzer Prize winner and author of *The Best and the Brightest,* said he thought I should try it. Bob Woodward and Carl Bernstein, *The Washington Post* Pulitzer Prize Watergate reporters, authors of *All the President's Men,* said I should do it. "You'll hate it," said Carl. "But you've got to do it," said Bob.

But it was Warren who finally helped me decide. "I think you are a writer," he said. "I don't think you'll be satisfied with television. But I think you will never be able to forgive yourself if you don't try it. It's such an extraordinary opportunity. And if it doesn't work out or if you don't like it, you can always go back to writing."

And there was always another thing in the back of my mind. It never occurred to me that I would be anything but terrific.

Thursday afternoon, late, the phone rang. It was Gordon. "Victory is ours," he said. I put my head down on my desk and sobbed.

I told Ben Bradlee. It was the only time in my life I have ever wept in a professional situation. Bradlee consoled me by saying that if the CBS thing didn't work out I could come back to the *Post*. That made me feel a little better, but not much. The second thing I did was get an agent. Hughes had told me I had to have one and suggested his agency, N. S. Bienstock, Inc., which handled, either as agent or accountant, almost everyone else at CBS as well—including Gordon. The minute Gordon hung up, my phone began ringing with agents calling to sign me. International Famous sounded too show-biz. And after all, this was the news operation.

I called up Hughes's agent, Richard Leibner, at Bienstock. I felt he at least would know everyone and understand the setup, and God knows I didn't know anything. I didn't even know what an agent does except take 5 per cent of your salary. I'm still not sure I do. Leibner is a fast talker with a heavy New York accent, almost a parody of what an agent should be like. He is a hustler. That was a good sign.

"Richard," I said, "before I say anything, I want you to know that I don't want this job. I'm taking it because I promised Gordon I would. So if the contract is not exactly the way I want it they can forget the whole thing."

"Sweetheart," said Richard, "before I say anything, I want you to know something. If you're twice as good as they say you are, if you can make the switch from the newspaper medium to the television medium, if they use all the potential they have to make this a great show, if they spend the amount of money they'll have to spend to make it any good, if you have a good vehicle and they get the best producer and staff in the business . . . your chances are one in ten you'll last out the year."

"Richard," I said, "I don't want this job."

"I'll call you tonight after I have my preliminary talks with Don Hamilton in accounting. Then we can start talking salary and benefits." In fact, Hamilton is Director of Business Affairs at CBS.

That night Leibner called in the middle of dinner.

"All right," he said, "I've talked to Hamilton. They're talking in terms of $40,000."

What had happened to the $75,000? Why had I agonized over this decision? Fabulous experience or no fabulous experience, that was a joke.

"Forget it."

"Well, wait a minute," Richard said. "We're just starting negotiations. We can get them up a little, I think."

I told Richard I had heard they were going to pay $75,000.

"Forget it."

"Well, what do you think they'll pay?"

"They'll never go higher than $50,000, and if they pay that much I'll be surprised."

"All right, Richard. I'll never go lower than $60,000. And if they can't do that then they'll have to find another woman. Remember this, Richard, and make sure they understand: *I do not want this job.*"

I felt saved. They wouldn't go up.

Richard said he'd call Hamilton.

He called back. He explained with great drama that he and Hamilton had been sword-to-sword all day, that they were both exhausted, and that he had done all he could. He had finally dragged out a promise of $50,000.

"Forget it."

"Listen," said Richard. "They just don't believe that you don't want this job. Neither do I. Do you realize there are millions of women in this country who would take it for nothing?"

I was beginning to enjoy this.

"Fine. Go hire one of them. Oh, and by the way, Richard, I want a limousine and a clothes allowance."

"You're out of your mind," said Richard. "Nobody gets a limousine."

"Barbara Walters does."

"And nobody has a clothes allowance."

"There aren't any other anchorwomen."

We talked about the contract. They wanted a five-year contract. I wanted to sign a one-year contract. We compromised on a three-year contract with the stipulation that if they removed me from the anchor job I could quit. I wasn't crazy about the three years, but apparently I couldn't budge them. There were all kinds of other details, such as that I had to get approval before I wrote anything or appeared anywhere, and that if I quit I couldn't appear on any other network for three years. In other words, they owned me.

Richard said with exasperation that he would go back into the ring with Hamilton and let me know.

He called back. "They've agreed to $56,000, to go up each year until you reach $60,000 by the third year. And I won't go back for more. I know when I've pushed them to the limit. You get a limousine and you get a $3,000 clothes allowance. Oh, and by the way, this whole contract is subject to change if they decide to put you on the *Evening News* as an anchor."

"The *Evening News!* Walter Cronkite's job? Oh, God help me," I thought. It was getting more unreal by the minute.

"Well, do you agree to the contract?" asked Richard.

I waited a long moment. I was in it that far, I might as well take the plunge. "Yes."

Later Gordon told me that Richard had called him. "Gordon, you've got lightning in a bottle."

When Gordon and I first discussed the job I told him I had grave reservations about his choice. I reminded him that I was controversial, opinionated, flip, open and had no intention of changing. Was he sure this was what he wanted on television? Did they really want me to say what came to my mind during the ad libs, and would they not try to turn me into a bland, opinionless, dull-but-safe marshmallow? And I wondered aloud whether, if we were supposed to be journalists, we could maintain any kind of objectivity and still express controversial opinions—or any opinions, for that matter.

"Paley wants controversy," Gordon had said. "And so does Salant. You can get away with much, much more at that hour than you ever could on the *Evening News*."

I had doubts and so did a lot of people I talked to, but I figured CBS knew what it wanted.

I also pointed out to Gordon that I had a rather unconventional life style. I had been living on weekends with Warren, I explained, and if I moved to New York I would move in with him. I would also be talking about him openly and freely in interviews. I saw nothing wrong with it, and I had no intention of hiding the fact.

I think Gordon gulped a little at that one, but he gamely said that was just fine, I could say anything I wanted to. After all, CBS was not hiring me because or in spite of my personal life.

On Friday morning, June 22nd, the first piece about me appeared in *The Washington Post*. The head ran "SHOWDOWN AT SUNRISE," and it carried pictures of me and Barbara opposite each other. I wasn't too crazy about that. It created an atmosphere of rivalry I would have preferred to avoid. But my editors laughingly pointed out that I was now a public personality and had no say in the matter. They also pointed out that it was clearly the right angle for the story. They were right.

TV critic John Carmody had written, "Although a number

of her candid interviews had attracted CBS's attention, it was, ironically enough, her appearance on Miss Walters' *Not for Women Only* TV program that whetted the network's interest." He quoted Salant as saying that the format of the revamped show would "have no relationship to the *Today* Show" and would "retain the integrity of the basic news show." But also as predicting that "*Today* is ripe to be taken."

Stuart Shulberg, the producer of the *Today* Show, was quoted: "We welcome fresh competition. *Today* has led the morning field for so long that we could run the risk of growing too fat, smug and sassy. This will speed up the pace, sharpen our competitive spirit, and provide the kind of honest competition we need and relish. May the best program win."

Barbara Walters was quoted: "The only thing I can say as a woman in broadcasting is that I welcome any new member to the fold. . . . I have respect and friendship for Sally. I know her very well. And I applaud both her and CBS for a very smart choice."

And Sally Quinn said: "Barbara is a great friend of mine and one of the most professional people I've ever known. As far as competing with each other, we covered the Shah's celebration in the desert of Iran together last year and stayed in the same dormitory. That's like being in combat together, and I imagine this will be a somewhat similar situation."

And we were off.

Over the years, Clay Felker, the editor of *New York* Magazine, had offered me a job as a writer several times. In March 1973 he had invited me to be the guest editor for a special issue he was going to put out, called "Couples." He had promised to pay me $5,000 and we had signed a contract, but before I got involved a trial issue bombed and the whole deal sort of died. When Felker heard that I was going with CBS he called with his final offer to work for *New York*. He offered "to make me a star." I had heard this before. This time he was not only going to make me a star but he was going to pay me as much as his other big star, Richard Reeves. Clay told me he paid Reeves $48,000 and said that with TV appearances and other sidelines, Reeves probably pulled in about $75,000. I could do the same, if only I would come to *New York Magazine,* where I belonged. I refused. "For the last time, Sally," he said. "You were born to be a star. You should have let me make you one." He hung up.

Several hours later he called back. "Well," he said. "I want to do a cover story on you."

I said I'd check with CBS and see how they felt about it. Gordon was impressed. We decided that Clay was figuring the story as mutually beneficial. It was not the wisest decision we ever made, but I told him yes.

The following week, on Monday, June 25, I went to New York because I was to be at the "office" the next morning at 7 A.M. to watch the "broadcast." I learned that I was never to say "show." This was a *news* broadcast. I went to CBS and Hughes, Lee Townsend and I watched the John Hart broadcast, and then we spent the rest of the morning discussing the show, reading our mail and dealing with the publicity people. We had two of them assigned to us. One was from the Blackrock publicity department and acted as a liaison. The other was with CBS News. They both spent their time setting up endless interviews, and Hughes and I never had any idea what was going on. One thing I demanded, which Hughes did not, was that no publicity person sit in on an interview with me. That did not go over well. As a reporter, I had always been turned off by having a flack sit in on an interview and had always found it to the subject's disadvantage to have another person jumping in to say, "What she means is . . ." There was some rumbling, but I announced I would not do any interviews under those conditions. I won. For the moment.

After a while I didn't care any more.

We had lunch that day with Gordon and Salant and some of the big advertising executives from Blackrock in the CBS News executive dining room. They were all scared of Gordon and Salant and, I think, a little in awe of my flip relaxed attitude toward them and it.

The subject at lunch was what we would call the show. Hughes and I liked *Bulldog*, which is an old newspaper expression for the first edition. They didn't buy that. It was pointed out that it would lend itself to rude jokes. Thank God. We suggested *First Edition*. They didn't like that. Nobody had any good suggestions. Salant liked *The CBS Morning News*. I remarked that I didn't think that was very catchy. If we were going to have a new show we should have a new name. Finally everybody decided (Salant decided) that if the Cronkites were called *The CBS Evening News* then . . .

I was to meet Aaron Latham from *New York* Magazine that afternoon at the photographer's studio for the cover picture. He was a friend and had been a colleague at the *Post*. Shortly before he left he had done a very good investigative series on an adoption center in Washington called Junior Village. He had written a book on F. Scott Fitzgerald, become an editor at *Esquire*, and had recently gone to *New York* as an editor. This was one of his first pieces for it. I was rather looking forward to the interview.

I walked into the studio. In the middle of a vast room, there was a double bed with mussed sheets and a man's pajama top. The idea, Aaron explained to me, was that I should get in the pajama top and be crawling out of bed for the photo. The caption was to read, "Won't it be nice to wake up with Sally Quinn?"

I said he must be kidding. He wasn't. He seemed embarrassed and was scared he was about to lose his story. I felt sick. I called Townsend. I told him of course I had no intention of posing like that and wanted to know whether I should pull out of the story. He said to go ahead with the story but, obviously, to refuse to pose for the bedroom scene.

Aaron called Sheldon Zalaznick, the managing editor of *New York,* to tell him I wouldn't do it. Zalaznick suggested I sit on a pile of trunks and have the caption read "New Girl in Town." I called Townsend. He agreed. I agreed. I should have walked out, but this shot seemed so harmless by comparison. The caption Felker finally used read "Good Morning, I'm Sally Quinn. CBS brought me here to make trouble for Barbara Walters," as though I had said it.

I was uneasy during the next few days, more cautious about what I would say to Aaron than I had ever imagined I could be. What I couldn't realize was that it probably wouldn't have made any difference. I think they already knew what they were going to write and would have written it, in fact were writing it, without my help.

(I was only to find out I had been double-crossed when I saw the magazine on the stands. So maybe they didn't deliberately distort the truth. But I can't believe it. I can't believe that a serious and experienced journalist like Aaron could have managed to get so much wrong—and in such a neat pattern. Maybe.)

The next morning Hughes and I were taken to Blackrock by Gordon for the first time. We were to meet Bob Wood. We didn't know it then, but he was the biggest cheese we were to meet. We never saw Schneider or Taylor. Paley was out of the question. I used to imagine that he didn't exist, that he was a name conjured up to frighten people. However, I would see his pictures, with his wife, Babe, in *Women's Wear Daily.* We went up elevators—into one office where we picked up a vice president in charge of something, who looked terribly nervous, then to another and bigger office to pick up another higher-up, equally nervous. Then our little caravan trooped into Bob Wood's office, very plush with two enormous windows to the floor, looking down God knows how many floors to the street below.

"Aren't you afraid you'll fall out of those windows?" I asked in horror, nearly reeling.

"No, but sometimes I'm afraid I won't," he joked. I wondered if he meant it.

Bob Wood is a bachelor and attractive in a crew-cut business-executive way, though his sense of humor misses and he seems rather square. There was some joshing about how we would have to get together and how much prettier I was than Hughes. That became a standard line and got harder and harder to laugh at. So did everything.

There was some half-serious talk about the show, but it was really just a "getting-to-know-you meeting." We talked about CBS's *Captain Kangaroo,* the eight-to-nine show. The ratings were very high. There was no way it was going off the air to give us another hour unless we destroyed *Today.* We talked about the affiliates. "What are affiliates?" I asked. Gordon just looked at me and I wished we were back chatting about how Bob Wood was going to take me out. Affiliates, it turns out, are local TV stations around the country which are affiliated with the CBS network. In the most recent survey, some segments of the two-hour *Today* Show on NBC were being shown on 209 of the network's 219 affiliates. Of CBS's 200 affiliates, only 110 carried its full hour of morning news. The plan was to sign up as many of our affiliates as possible. We were not, as had been previously allowed, to permit them to use portions of the hour-long morning news. It was all or nothing.

The conversation turned to politics. Wood asked what political stories I had done recently. I told him I had done a profile of Haldeman and made a nasty remark about H. R. Haldeman's being Nixon's stooge. Gordon gave me a dirty look. Bob Wood is from California and is a close friend of the Haldeman family. "One thing you've got to learn," Hughes told me later, "is never to confuse CBS News with the CBS network." I had the feeling the meeting hadn't gone too well.

As we were walking out, one of the nervous vice presidents remarked that he had heard that *New York* Magazine was doing a cover on me, and that they were all terribly excited. They understood that Felker and Latham were friends of mine. "So it will be a sweetheart piece, eh?" He winked and gave me a smile.

That afternoon Hughes and I were interviewed separately by *Women's Wear Daily*. He was scared he would make a faux pas, just what *WWD* loved, so he asked a flack to go along. My interview went fairly smoothly except when I identified myself to the doorman as Mrs. Hoge.

Hughes called. "Well, sheeeeee-it," he said. That was his favorite expression, and it soon became mine. Before long we both found it appropriate for almost any occasion. "I've really done it this time," he said. "The reporter asked how I was going to like getting up in the middle of the night. And I told him it wouldn't bother me because at my age I was used to getting up a lot in the middle of the night anyway. And then I really blew it," he said. "I just couldn't help adding, 'but that's okay because we're going to piss all over the *Today* Show.'"

I screamed with laughter and relief. At least Hughes was as outspoken as I was.

Aside from my explanation of why I had identified myself as Mrs. Hoge, I was pleased enough by my piece. I was quoted accurately worrying about becoming a celebrity: "Being a celebrity takes you a little farther away from being a journalist—that's the danger. I feel impotent without a pad and pencil." And worrying about having to look pretty, and about making an ass out of myself with the ad libs; about not having any experience, and about the feud people were trying to create between Barbara and me. "That's very sexist," I said. "Why haven't they pitted Hughes Rudd against Frank McGee?"

Hughes was saved. He didn't get quoted as pissing all over the *Today* Show. But his piece ended with a poignant remark. "I've been a field hand for fourteen years and I thought I'd be doing stories for the rest of my life about people who keep collecting giant balls of twine," he said. "But two weeks ago I discovered everyone in this business takes stomach pills, and that's when I started taking them too."

I thought he was joking. He was serious.

That afternoon Aaron Latham flew down to Washington with me and spent the next two days talking to me and asking around about me. I told him nothing that could possibly be damaging to me.

The following Monday, July 2, I was back in New York for several hours of taping. We had to be at CBS News at 6:30 or 7:00 A.M. We were going to discuss what to use for a studio. It was decided that the John Hart studio upstairs, which was also used for the soaps, was too large and impersonal. Also, we decided, we would rather have a newsroom effect so that we could get up from our typewriters and read the news as if we were real journalists. There wasn't enough room in the newsroom itself, but there was a tiny room next to it called the "Flash" studio. If there is a sudden urgent newsbreak, you go in there and "flash" it. The Flash studio would be ours. One wall would be torn out and filled in with glass so that a camera stationed outside in the newsroom could photograph Hughes and me through the window, giving the impression that we were actually in the newsroom. There would be three cameras in the Flash, and two small platforms, one with a triangular desk with Hughes on one

side of the narrow part and me on the other. The other platform, several feet away, would have chairs and a coffee table
and would be the interview area. It meant, of course, that
there would be no room for dancing bears, but we weren't
thinking of that at the time. According to Salant, it would
cost a quarter of a million dollars just to convert the Flash.
But that was okay. Nothing was too good for the New
Morning News.

I went upstairs to the makeup room where everybody—
including the soap-opera stars—was made up, and a nice
lady came in and told me I was gorgeous and made me up
to look gorgeous. For the next three hours Hughes and I sat
on desks in front of the newsroom or on high stools, and we
talked. Lee Townsend told us simply to joke around and talk
about anything, just as if we weren't on camera. They would
take out the best parts and use them for promos (promotion). That meant that in prime CBS time, segments of
thirty seconds or a minute of Hughes and me chatting infor-
mally would be run as commercials. The audience would see
what kind of ambiance they could expect on the show.

My office was a tiny little room set up with a mirror and
bright lights so that the makeup could be done there. I did
my own hair and it never occurred to me to ask for a hairdresser, although I remembered that Barbara Walters had
told me she had one. There was no precedent for a woman
anchor, so nobody thought about those things.

I asked for a sofa so I could lie down before I went on the
air. I never imagined how much I would be using it.

We had still not met the staff, but it was to be the same
as John Hart's except for Lee Townsend, who would be the
producer. It didn't concern me that he had never produced
anything in his life. I thought it was kind of funny. There was
Lee with no experience, Hughes who had never been an
anchorman, and I who had scarcely been on television. They
must know what they are doing, I thought.

We had not yet discussed the format, except in the most general terms. No matter. Somewhere there were thousands of brilliant minds, cloistered, spending twenty-four hours a day dreaming us up a fabulous format and five spectacular shows for the kickoff week, with special taped interviews for me to do with elusive stars nobody else could get to—maybe Greta Garbo and Howard Hughes. Bureaus all over the world had been alerted to produce the best film pieces they could find, and there would be a couple of investigative pieces that CBS had long been working on and that they were planning to break that first week. All this was going on, and they would tell me about it and begin to prepare me as soon as it was all together.

It didn't even worry me that they planned to go on the air July 23. After some thought they moved it up to July 30. That gave us four weeks. Plenty of time, I thought. They moved it to August 6. That was the absolute final date. Great, I thought. More time to get ready. That was the week Bill Paley was planning to leave for vacation, so he wouldn't be around for the debut in case anything went wrong. It didn't matter. He heard about it.

So that Monday, July 23, after Hughes and I did the chit-chat for the promos—and everybody thought they were great, so natural and unaffected—we did a few in-house promos, for the affiliates, which were outlined but which we ad-libbed. Hughes would explain who we were and what we planned to do in general terms, and then we joked around a bit and added something like, "See you August 6, hope you'll be watching." These were strictly in-house, meant only for the local station managers, who were supposed to like us and take the show. But they were not previews and were not meant to be reviewed. Unfortunately, some were shown to TV critics around the country, and Hughes and I were shocked when we read a few snotty little reviews about what we had believed to be a private exchange. We should have been forewarned. People were lying in wait.

After all the promos were finished, Hughes and Lee and I had lunch and I brought up the subject of clothes, hairstyles and glasses. I had just bought a pair of rimless glasses that I thought would be unobtrusive, but I had to wear them so I could see the prompter. I have tried contacts and can't wear them. Lee said that was fine. He said he didn't care what I looked like. This was a news show. Not Hollywood.

We were swamped with requests for interviews, both in person and on the telephone. There were sometimes nine or ten a day. One was from the beauty editor of *Ladies' Home Journal*. She had called me several times to do a beauty layout, and she talked in the inside, tough, pseudo-intimate jargon that New York fashion people use.

"Listen, doll," she said over the phone. "Come on by Tuesday morning. We'll talk. Byyyy-eeeeee." Click.

I was a little hesitant about that one. It didn't seem terribly hard-news-oriented somehow. But the CBS publicity department thought it would be good. So Tuesday morning I went. She offered me a chair in her green-and-white, very decorated office, and introduced what became clear were the details of a "make-over." "Hon," she said. "You've got a lot of potential. Good cheekbones, a nice long nose and the best streaking job I've seen outside of New York." (My hair is blond and gets blonder in the summer sun. In the winter I help it along with a forty-nine-cent bottle of Clairoxide and a piece of cotton. When I got the TV job I decided I should have it streaked professionally. In Washington. From then on out my roots showed.)

"But, you'll have to have it streaked again. I'll have my man, Leslie Blanchard, do it. He's the best in the business.

You've got to remember, sweetie, you're in the big time now. Oh, and, puss, your eyebrows are a disaster. They have got to go."

I was intimidated. I agreed to everything, and then ran out to tell the PR people at CBS to make up some excuse. I didn't want my eyebrows removed by the *Ladies' Home Journal.* Later they told me that when I refused to have my eyebrows pulled out and my hair dyed, the editor remarked, "But she doesn't understand. If she doesn't go along with us, we'll simply have to kill the piece!"

Tuesday afternoon Hughes and I were to attend a meeting at Blackrock with the CBS flacks. We were conducted to a large conference room where there were twenty or so people sitting around. Each had a pad and pencil. Nobody wrote anything down. They were supposed to get an idea of what Hughes and I were like. So we performed the act we were slowly developing and at which we became quite good. Until we went on the air.

Hughes would say how I was meaner than a junkyard dog, and I would talk about how he was a good ole boy, and he would discourse on how there wasn't a decent place to get chili in all of New York, and I would reminisce about how I was an Army brat, and then we would chat about how we were never going to be able to get up at that hour in the middle of the night, and then Hughes would reply that at his age. . . .

Afterward they talked us into going downstairs to have our pictures taken. I had dirty hair and no makeup and a busy blouse, and Hughes hadn't shaved properly and had soup stains on his tie. We protested, but they said these would not be the official photos. They were going to line up Richard Avedon for those. Nothing was too good for the new *CBS Morning News* team. The photographer posed us leaning forward with our heads together like the old Steve Lawrence–Eydie Gormé, Marge and Gower Champion pictures.

At one point, when the photographer came over and pushed our cheeks together, Hughes screamed, "Get me off this horse immediately."

We collapsed in laughter, much to the photographer's consternation, and I asked Hughes what he was talking about.

"Oh, Christ," he said, breaking up again, "haven't you ever heard the story about the time the famous cowboy was the Grand Marshal of the Rose Bowl Parade?"

"No."

"Well, one time when this cowboy was the Grand Marshal of the old Rose Bowl Parade, he was supposed to lead the whole thing. And he showed up at the pen where all the horses and floats were waiting, completely drunk. His costume was a gold lamé cowboy suit that he had to be sewed into. But once they got him sewed into the suit and on the horse, he kept falling off, he was so tight. Finally they had to strap him on the horse as the parade started. They left the pen and began making their way through the cheering crowds. About three or four blocks out, the cowboy, cursing and swearing, reined in his horse and the manager of the parade rushed to his side, thinking he was about to fall off again.

" 'Get me off this horse immediately,' he shrieked in a loud voice. 'I've just shit in my pants.'

"I always say that when I'm in an uncomfortable situation." It became our byword.

The photography session finally ended. We were both unhappy with the contrived, posed pictures. But what the hell, we thought, they're not the official pictures.

They were the official pictures.

I was still working for *The Washington Post*. I had to go back to Washington to clear out of my office, pack my furniture, get rid of my apartment and sell my car. CBS said they really didn't need me for the next couple of weeks and they would let me know when they did. They had set up a promo tour for the week of July 23rd.

PART
TWO

WAS IN Washington the following Monday when the issue of *New York* Magazine appeared on the stands. I had heard rumors that it was not going to be a sweetheart piece.

I don't want to cry foul because a piece was written about me which I didn't like. And, God knows, I have been accused often enough of doing hatchet jobs and misquoting to find that response distasteful. But I have never misquoted anyone knowingly, and I have never made up anything to make a story better. I have always insisted that I don't do jobs on people, they do them on themselves. And if you are a good interviewer you don't have to fictionalize. There had been no way I was going to give Aaron the ammunition to get me. If he was going to do a job on me, he was going to have to do it all by himself.

I don't want to blow the piece out of proportion. But it did have a tremendous effect. It painted me as a tough, mean, bitchy woman, who had no women friends, who had slept her way to the top to get the interviews and jobs, who had used her father's position to wield power, who considered herself a sex symbol and played it to the hilt, and who would scratch and claw anyone anytime to get what and

87

where she wanted. It was a caricature of a sort of 1930's Hollywood ball-breaker. It was written in a snide way, a sort of pornographic primer of "Look, look, see Sally run, see Sally sleep her way to the top."

I couldn't believe it.

I had known this would be a cover story, so I had been careful about what I said both on and off the record. Because Aaron and I knew each other and had so many mutual friends and were planning to spend some time together during the interview, it was important to me to establish ahead of time what was "on" and what was "off" the record.

In any normal situation, just to say "This is off the record" would be enough. But I had gone even further with Latham, making him promise before we even began that when I said something was off the record, that was it. After that bedroom scene at the photographer's studio, I was edgy. He had agreed.

There were very few off-the-record remarks, mainly because I was being particularly careful; but as Latham reported them, they all sounded lascivious. One conversation, which I had specifically made Aaron agree was off the record, was with Judith Martin, another Style reporter on the *Post* and a mutual friend. Judy and I have a kidding relationship that from time to time lends itself to racy humor. Aaron took part in that exchange and, leaving out his own obscene observations and several risqué remarks of Judy's, he condensed the conversation into the following:

Sally said, "My agent told me to say that I make in excess of $45,000."

Judith Martin, a Style writer, said, "Unfortunately that was after you had already told us you were making $75,000."

Sally said, "*Playgirl* wants to interview me."

Ms. Martin said, "Sally has a lot of redeeming social value."

Sally said, "I have little tits."

This in-depth, on-the-scene reporting followed me to the newsroom, where I made a date for a farewell dinner with Bob Woodward and Carl Bernstein, also former friends and colleagues of Latham's.

Woodward says, "Remember telling us about the live-sex show you went to in New York? You said you had to pretend you had never seen one before."

Sally said, "I'm a good actor."

(What we had actually talked about was how a colleague, Karl Meyer, had been assigned to cover a live-sex show by the *Post* and had asked a group, which had included Aaron, to go with him. We did, found it disgusting, and left minutes after it had begun.)

Bernstein said, "She once went through my closet to see where I bought my clothes."

(Bernstein had described how his former wife had asked me one night at a dinner party to go through his wardrobe with her and give her advice on where to buy his clothes.)

Executive Editor Ben Bradlee walked out of his glass office onto the newsroom floor. Ms. Quinn went to talk to him. When Bradlee had learned that Gordon Manning of CBS was coming to woo Sally Quinn from him, he had managed to find out where they were having dinner. He had called the restaurant, Cantina d'Italia, and asked them to page Manning. Bradlee said to tell Manning that his office was calling. When Manning came to the telephone, Bradlee said, "Screw you."

The only thing Aaron changed was that Bradlee had said "Fuck you." Aaron knew it, but he was too intimidated by Bradlee to print it.

That incident made me realize that a man's reputation, both personal and professional, is valued a good deal more than a woman's. Somehow, in Aaron's mind and in Clay Felker's, it was okay to misquote me, to distort conversations, to attribute sexual looseness, a moral laxity, a vulgarity of speech and manner to me. I was only a woman. People, the thinking obviously goes, wouldn't take it as seriously. But to quote Ben Bradlee as saying "Fuck you," or Carl Bernstein and Bob Woodward using colorful language, well, it just wouldn't happen. They were, after all, men, serious, respected journalists who had important and valued reputations. The Latham example would not be the last.

Latham also made up a feud between Barbara Walters and me. His piece led with a quote from Clare Boothe Luce's play, *The Women.*

SYLVIA: You know I go to Michael's for my hair. You ought to go, pet. I despise whoever does yours. Well, there's the most wonderful new manicurist there. (*Shows her scarlet nails.*) Isn't that divine? Jungle red.

NANCY: Looks as if you'd been tearing at somebody's throat.

He misquoted me as saying that Barbara and I "used" to be friends. When I told him we were in fact quite good friends and mentioned that I had gotten a kind letter from her that day, he asked if he could see it.

I said no, that it was my private business.

After I left work that night, the letter disappeared from my desk and coincidentally reappeared in *New York* Magazine in a context which made it sound insincere. It said:

"Dear Sally—CBS could not have made a better choice. I mean this in all sincerity and look forward to seeing you very often now that you'll be in New York. I won't be able to catch you on camera, but I hope we'll get together off camera. For God's sake, let's avoid all those people in and out of the media who may try to create a feud between us. We like each other too much. Much luck and affection, Barbara."

Naturally Barbara was offended when she saw the letter in print, assuming that I had betrayed her confidence by giving it to Aaron. It took several friends to explain that it had been stolen. But Latham nearly managed to create the feud he had wrongly accused us of having.

Latham also intimated that I had slept with most of the men I interviewed and noted that I rarely interviewed women. In fact, more than half of the people I have interviewed are women. And I consider those my most successful interviews. He invented a line from a piece I had written about Bernardo Bertolucci, the director of *Last Tango in Paris,* in which he has me following Bertolucci into his hotel bedroom. Not only did I not go into his bedroom, but Latham did not mention, as I had in my piece, that the PR man was there.

I had told him that, as a general's daughter, I hadn't gone out with lieutenants because they might have wanted to further their careers through me that way. I had told him I must have had fifty proposals and none of them for love. He quoted me as saying, "She says she had 50 proposals while she was in Germany. . . . She once said: 'I thought I could get any penis I wanted.'"

But the remark that stunned me and my friends was: "One evening at a Washington dinner party, Sally Quinn was the center of attention as she verbally measured many of the town's most prominent politicians. Her conversation was a Gallup Poll of penis sizes. Then she outlined her theory of how all the best men in Washington 'screwed beneath themselves.' She also said that the women in the city like to make love above themselves. It makes a nice Washington compromise."

The party in question had been at the home of Walter

Pincus, the editor of the *New Republic,* and his wife, Ann. I was not there. Someone else had discussed not a "Gallup Poll of penis sizes" but the alleged sexual problems of one politician. A week later Clay Felker was a guest at the same house, and Ann Pincus repeated the story. I was there briefly that night. I arrived shortly before Felker and left to catch the 10 P.M. shuttle back to New York. Aaron Latham was there on neither evening.

Mary Breasted of *The New York Times* interviewed me and wrote nearly four columns about the piece, listing its distortions and those in another article Latham had written about Gay Talese, the writer, a week earlier.

I think the *New York* article was most responsible for my unhappy experience at CBS. Clearly there were a hundred other reasons for it, but that article set the tone for the rest of the publicity, and the publicity created an atmosphere of open hostility and resentment toward me. Instead of sympathy for being caught in a corporate disaster and for my own lack of experience, I got destroyed, almost always in a personal way, by the majority of the critics and reporters, who continued to write about me long afterward.

Salant was upset. He called me to say that they understood that I had been victimized, and sent out a memo in response:

Because it is of utmost importance to what CBS News and I stand for, let me emphasize this as strongly as I can as a guide to future CBS and CND publicity concerning the *Morning News*: Sally Quinn was chosen by us as co-anchor person for the *Morning News* because, and only because, it was our conviction that she is a first-rate professional journalist and a first-rate broadcaster. We will not—repeat, not—in any way encourage, and to the contrary we will *discourage,* any publicity, or any attempts at an "image," which emphasizes or even adverts to anything other than Sally's journalistic competence. The kind of publicity which has recently appeared is demeaning to Sally, to CBS News and to journalism. Happily, we had nothing to do with it.

CBS News does not hire people because they are sex bombs, male or female, or because they are blonde or brunette or bald. We hire them for their journalistic competence. That is precisely why Sally was hired, and we will exploit, publicize and promote that and nothing else.

I heard that Paley went bananas when he read the article. The following Wednesday I appeared on *The Dick Cavett Show*. I had met Cavett when I interviewed him about two years before for the *Post*. He had been nice and friendly and, I thought, clever and funny. But it had been a disaster. I had gotten nothing out of him. He is the most difficult person to interview I've ever known, except for Warren Beatty.

For some reason I wasn't nervous about going on his show. I arrived early, and Cavett asked me to come up to his dressing room to chat while he got ready to go on. He had seen the *New York* piece and thought it was a hatchet job. I agreed to talk about it on the air if we didn't mention the name of the magazine or the author.

Just before we went on, Cavett said, "Feel my hands." They were ice cold and damp and shaking terribly. "Thanks a lot," I said. Until then I hadn't been scared, but after that I was in a state of terror. By the time we went on, I had managed to calm down a little, and my friends told me the only sign of nervousness was a slight giggle. But generally the appearance was thought to be reasonably successful and I was pleased. But not surprised. I still thought I was going to be good on the *Morning News*. After the show Cavett took me and Warren to the theater to see *Uncle Vanya*. Warren and I had to fight our way through the mobs of autograph seekers outside the studio, but Cavett, more experienced, made a dash for the car and they never even saw him. I got caught in the middle of the crowd and everybody was yelling, "Who is she, who is she?" "I don't know," someone said, "but she must be famous, get her autograph."

And so I signed my first autograph, and felt foolish. Not at all flattered, as I had thought I would. It seemed ridiculous, the whole exercise, but worse, I didn't feel like a journalist any more. I felt tainted.

"Sally Quinn, it's Sally Quinn," said the person to whom I handed the autograph.

"Who's Sally Quinn?" yelled someone else.

I dove for the car. We went to the theater, then backstage to meet George C. Scott, then to an Italian restaurant, then back to Cavett's house to watch a show he had taped a few days earlier.

I enjoyed the feeling of hanging out with someone like Cavett without a notebook in my hand. That, I thought, would be a plus about television. Once you were away from the camera you could have easy friendships. In the end, if you're a newspaper reporter, you're never not working. It's a small distinction, but important. While I was on television I could have given a big party for Henry Kissinger and that would have been okay. For a reporter it would somehow be a conflict of interests.

Two days later I got a letter from Latham, which he has refused me permission to reprint, but which was self-described as "gushing." He'd seen me on the Cavett show and had thought I was "terrific" and looked better on TV than in real life.

What the letter was really about was the fact that he'd had conflicting reports about whether I'd been upset by the article, which he'd not meant to be "malicious" but to "add to" and "confirm" the legend he thought I'd worked so hard to establish. Had he "miscalculated," he wondered aloud; perhaps he'd "misunderstood" me—? In a dazzling piece of logic, Latham concluded that the person he'd described would have loved the article. Trouble was, who was that person? Perhaps it was not me, he pushed on. Then, in a lovely irony, he concluded his letter by saying that he would love to see me "in person" so I could tell him what I thought. Amen.

I spent the following week in New York giving interviews. I was beginning to get an uneasy feeling that maybe all those people who were putting together the fabulous show were on vacation. Each morning, before the interviews with *Women's Wear, Harper's Bazaar, Time* Magazine, *Newsweek* or the *Daily News* would begin, Hughes and Lee and I would "toss around ideas."

Lee suggested I go down to Alabama and interview the Wallaces. The idea depressed me. I had interviewed them for the *Post* nearly two years before, so it would be going over old ground. Besides, there was no way they would say the same things to me on television they had said in private. And thirdly, where the hell were all those great interviews they were supposed to be lining up for me with all that CBS clout? In retrospect, I find it absurd that I didn't press my questions. But at that point I was so busy blabbing away mindlessly in interviews about what a terrific show we were going to have that it only vaguely occurred to me that it wasn't being set up. And maybe, because I was already so locked in, I was afraid to ask.

Hughes was concentrating on film pieces in our idea sessions, and he was coming up with what sounded to me like pretty good ideas. They were new and offbeat and they appealed to me. But I didn't know anything about film and wasn't particularly interested. I'd leave that up to him. He was not all that crazy about doing interviews and that, I assumed, was why they had hired me. It was the one thing I knew how to do, and I was only a little worried about doing it in another medium. I was anxious to get on with it.

I had voiced some apprehension about interviewing on television to Lee Townsend.

"Oh, don't worry about that," he said lightly, "that's the easiest part."

I didn't think the Wallaces were such a good idea, but "they" did. I was instructed to set up a day the following week when I could fly down and interview the Governor and his wife. Lee Townsend suggested that we should try to get Pat Nixon to come on the first day. I thought that sounded like a great idea. Now we were getting somewhere. I figured that if he suggested it, it was a pretty strong possibility. What didn't occur to me then was that Pat Nixon would as soon have given an interview to *Rolling Stone* as CBS. Furthermore, I soon learned that I had had more clout as a reporter for *The Washington Post* than as an anchorperson on the *Morning News*. People didn't care about the show.

Another idea was to get Norman Mailer and Norman Rosten. They both had books on Marilyn Monroe coming out that month. August 6, the day we were to go on the air, was the eleventh anniversary of Monroe's death. That sounded jazzy, and Mailer is always entertaining, if not a little dangerous, to take on live. Earlier that year I had covered his fiftieth birthday party for the *Post* and afterward he had referred to me in *The New York Times Book Review* as "Poison Quinn," which of course gave me a modest cachet. I didn't know whether Mailer was annoyed with me or not, though we had maintained a sparse and arch correspondence since.

He was to have a press conference that afternoon at the Algonquin Hotel. I waited around through the conference and, as I tried to approach him, his female secretary pushed me away, telling me that Mailer refused to speak to me because he was so furious. I tried crawling behind a curtain and inching my way toward him, but the same secretary, dressed from head to toe in a leather motorcycle outfit, threatened to crush me personally if I didn't leave Mailer alone.

So much for Norman Mailer.

The next idea was to use a piece of a Mike Wallace film on Everett Alvarez, the POW who had spent eight years in North Vietnam. We went back to the *Sixty Minutes* section to view it; it was quite good. It was eight years that month since Alvarez had been captured. My only objection was to the idea of using something by Mike Wallace on *our* first day on the air. It would be obvious that we hadn't been able to come up with anything of our own. In fact we hadn't. I had some ideas, but I couldn't seem to understand what they wanted, and I still believed they would choose what they thought was the best vehicle for me—which would show off my talents, make me look good.

The Alvarez film was scrapped. I didn't know that, though, until the day we went on the air.

There must have been other ideas tossed around and rejected, but as far as I knew that was about the extent of it.

The tone of the interviews that I was giving had changed considerably. I had myself changed in reaction to the *New York* Magazine piece. Most of the New York press were familiar with the magazine's sensationalism; even at that it really wasn't as bad as it could have been.

Still, one disapproving reporter from *Time* refused to believe that I had been misrepresented. "Suppose someone quoted you as saying, 'I thought I could get any penis I wanted'?" I asked her. "But that would be impossible," she gasped. "I would never say that." "Exactly," I said.

Sometimes someone would tell me right off that he or she didn't believe a word of it and then ask, "Why do you hate women?"

I found that there was more notice taken of an open admission that I was living with a man I was not married to than I had expected. Many articles remarked, "She admits unashamedly that . . ." or "She says without embarrassment that . . ."

Some wanted me to be that person in the magazine and would turn the questions around to sex no matter what I tried to talk about. It wasn't that I objected to talking about sex. I objected to talking about it exclusively. And nearly everyone seemed to approach me with a certain amount of hostility. There were interviews and pieces about me, favorable and unfavorable, in which I scarcely recognized myself. I rarely had the impression that anyone was trying to find out what I was really like.

In the middle of the last week in July there was a sales meeting, and Hughes and I and Gordon went over to Black-rock to talk to the salesmen. We were to give them a big pep talk about how great the show was, and they were going to get all fired up and go out and sell it to the affiliates. We were led into another conference room, where we were seated at the head of the table and, again, there was a group of twenty to thirty advertising men. (If there were any advertising women there, I didn't see them; the room was quite dark for some reason, and they kept addressing each other as "gentlemen.") It was a very Madison-Avenue crowd, wide ties, wide lapels, wide cuffs, wide trousers, loud colors and sculptured waists and haircuts—and as such, further distinguished from the news crowd, with their sloppy corduroy jackets, funky ties and chinos.

There was a large box in the middle of the table that produced a lot of static. We were "hooked up" to several of the advertising divisions of some of the larger affiliates, such as Chicago. When Hughes and I did our number, they were to get all fired up, too, and then go out and sell like crazy.

The "hook-up" didn't work. All we could hear was static and people from several different cities screaming, "We can't hear, talk a little louder." Another thing was that the men didn't want to hear our number. They wanted to find out if I really was the little piece of ass *New York* Magazine had said I was.

"Hughes," I whispered, "get me off this horse immediately."

If there was a point the advertising men wanted to discuss, it was getting ads for the *Morning News*. And the first thing, they forcefully allowed, was that of course we all understood that their hands were tied. I mean, how could they possibly get advertisers to lay on all that dough if Hughes and I weren't going to advertise the products ourselves. If we were, as we said we were, truly serious about competing with the *Today* Show, then we were going to have to do Alpo Dog Food ads and stocking ads and whatever, or else we just weren't going to get the ads.

Salant, Manning, Hughes and myself were violently opposed. The program was to be a news broadcast, not an entertainment program. Besides, CBS had a policy against anyone in news doing advertising of any kind. I agreed one hundred per cent. But we all turned terribly pious on the advertising people, who were, in fairness, trying to do their jobs. I felt more like a piece of meat that day than I had before. It was the day I learned that anyone on the air, correspondent or anchorperson or whatever, is called "the talent." We were drifting further and further from journalism.

I have the impression the meeting didn't go too well, though Gordon said it had. And anyway, what did I know from advertising? Later I found out that the advertising people were telling the affiliates that "the Piece" was great publicity. One of them was quoted to me as saying, "That little girl sure has a lot of spunk."

One afternoon that week Hughes came back to the publicity department of CBS News around four. I was running on to the zillionth interviewer of the day. (I had been telling her my political philosophies for about two hours, not realizing that she was going to do a piece about my spaghetti recipe for her cooking column.) He told me that "the women" were having their meeting that afternoon at five, the same kind of meeting in which they had threatened Salant about getting a woman anchor. Hughes had heard a rumor that they were up in arms about me. Because, as an outsider, I had been chosen over women already at CBS who could have done the job. Also they were angry that CBS had chosen a "blonde bombshell." I have to laugh just to write that expression. Everyone had read the piece, and two portions had particularly annoyed them.

Latham had not been interested in my attitude toward the women's movement. I had tried to talk to him about it, but he kept changing the subject. Finally I had persuaded him to come to the *Post* cafeteria, and for one hour I explained to him how I felt about the movement. The state of women in professional situations is important to me, and I think women have a very bad deal most of the time. I had been active in *The Washington Post*'s women's group and had been among those who had represented them in a meeting with management. So I spent an hour telling Latham how valuable and worthwhile I thought the movement was, how much I liked Gloria Steinem, and I then mentioned two concerns. I thought that there was too much infighting and that that detracted from the movement's effectiveness, especially where it was most needed, outside the New York/Washington axis. I also said, with what I hoped was some humor, that the movement might reach more women in the country who were ready to be enlightened but were frightened by the grim ideological approaches taken by so many.

Latham had quoted only my criticisms and had ended that segment with the blind quote, "She treats women like Kleenex."

There were apparently also bad feelings about an opening

speech I had made in Washington earlier that year. I had been on a panel of newspaperwomen at a *More* (a journalism review) convention. The topic, as I had understood it, was the special difficulties of women journalists. I had been annoyed by the behavior of a small group of women at the convention, most of them from the National Organization for Women, which was convening in another part of the Mayflower Hotel but taking part in those *More* panels that were of interest to them. During these sessions they would hiss and boo and stand up, interrupting at the mention of anything they interpreted as sexist (the use of the word "newsmen" instead of "newsperson"). I thought they were making fools of themselves, getting themselves laughed at by both men and women, and doing a disservice to the cause of women.

When my turn came to speak, I had decided to talk about a problem that I knew every woman in the room had faced as a journalist, which was how the men one has to deal with, especially on an interview basis, often treat a woman condescendingly or patronizingly or, at worst, as a sex object.

It seems hard to believe that even revered, respected and proven women journalists like Mary McGrory, the columnist for the *Washington Star*, or Meg Greenfield, the assistant editor of the *Washington Post* Editorial page, will occasionally be patted on the head or cajoled in a patronizing *you-don't-really-mean-all-those-awful-things-you-write* sort of way. The fact is that most men don't respect women journalists as much as they do men. Every time you go out you have to prove that you're good. You have to produce a better story than a man would so that the next time the man won't condescend to you or patronize you. And other men who read you will know you're good.

The problem is especially acute if you can be viewed as a sex symbol. So I had said in my talk that at a certain point one must sometimes decide whether one is a journalist first or a woman first. I was a journalist first. And I said—here it comes—that if a senator put his hand on my fanny and was about to tell me how he would vote on impeaching the President of the United States, I would face a crisis of conscience. I wasn't sure whether or not I would remove his hand before he had a chance to tell me. Obviously I had made it up around the biggest political story of the year.

There was a considerable brouhaha. The most noise, I noted, came from some of the women I knew to have exploited their sex the most. I was also amused to note that Bob Woodward, on another panel, had talked about how he and Carl Bernstein had taken out the secretaries of the principals they were investigating and had visited their wives during the daytime at home. This was received with applause and admiration by everyone. In an aside I had added that several male reporters from large Eastern newspapers who were doing stories on massage parlors had handed in expense accounts for "massages." That was greeted with hilarity and respect for their initiative by everyone, including the "feminists."

So this afternoon Hughes persuaded me to go to the women's meeting at CBS. He thought they wouldn't attack me if I was there and that it would look as if I were supportive of them—which I was. So I went. I sat alone as everyone gazed at me—there were more than a hundred there—and made up my mind to speak once Salant had finished his rosy presentation of all the wonderful things CBS was doing for the women's causes.

I think now that getting together the courage to stand up, introduce myself, and try to clear my reputation was the hardest thing I ever had to do. Even harder than going on the air with no preparation, though God knows that runs a close second. My palms were sweaty—in fact I was perspiring all over; my heart was beating so fast I could hear it in my ears; my mouth was so dry I could hear my tongue scratch against my lips and I was shaking from head to foot. There was a lull, and I forced myself to stand up and be recognized. "I'm Sally Quinn," I said, unconvincingly.

Salant, seeing my misery, broke in. He said that before I said anything he wanted to point out that I wasn't anything like the way that magazine piece had pictured me, and that I had gotten a very bum rap. I tried to talk. It was all I could do not to weep. For one thing, I was exhausted, and the tension of all those interviews had gotten to me. My voice was unsteady as I explained how I felt about them and how I supported what they were doing. In what sounded to me like a half sob, I told them I was scared and that I needed their support too. When I was finished I got out as quickly as I could. Sylvia Chase, a correspondent, told me she thought I had done all right, and another woman wrote a note. I don't know what the others thought. The whole experience made me think that perhaps some of us are not as passionate about wanting our sisters to get ahead as we want to believe we are, or as much as we are about getting ahead ourselves.

It made me feel sad. Mostly, at that moment, sad for myself, because right then I really felt rather pitiful. And there's this extra element for women that men don't have to contend with in terms of competition. There isn't enough room right now for all of us because the men, who run things, will only let a few tokens in. And the ones who get in fill the available places. Everybody can talk about the fact that the more successful women there are, the better the chances for all women. But we know that that is a while off. So women sometimes fight each other for survival. And men love it. It's putting the female Amazons in the arena and letting them fight to the death. There's something sensual and exciting about it for men. There's something about seeing women fight each other for something they all want that turns men on. Like lady wrestlers. Men can laugh and smirk and jeer at them and feel superior. It's known in their circles as a cat-fight. Aaron Latham, not sensing a fight, had made one up. It was essential to the sexual titillation of his story.

Basically I am sympathetic and protective toward women. Those are my gut instincts. Those are the ones that tell me that if I protect other women they'll look out for me too. The ones that tell me women are probably smarter and more capable and more understanding than men to deal with.

But what I found that day is that most women aren't there yet. They are still in a position of self-protection, survival, a position inflicted upon them by men who run the show.

There was another minor crisis that day. Did I want the sign on my door to read "Ms. Quinn" or "Miss Quinn"? I received several notes from women arguing both ways. I decided on "Sally Quinn." It was a decision that brought me praise, and which I now believe to be the only wise decision I made until I decided to quit CBS.

I had spent that first July weekend in Washington with the movers, and Sunday night I flew to Cleveland to meet Hughes for the promo tour. We were accompanied by Bernie Roswig, a CBS publicity man from Blackrock who was acting PR liaison between the news division and the network. He is fairly short and wears platform shoes, is a spiffy dresser, and has a slight skin problem. The trip had to be the worst three days of Bernie's life, though he claimed it was very successful.

It's all a blur—one awful interview after the other, and the worse it got, the more Hughes and I took it out on poor Bernie. I still don't know why he came with us, because we were met each place by limousines and whisked to hotels by local PR people, so there was no real reason for Bernie to be along unless it was to sop up our hostility so that it wouldn't spill all over the interviewers. He kept us in line. I suppose if Bernie hadn't been around we wouldn't have shown up for half the appointments.

In Cleveland we had a breakfast interview at our hotel, the Hollenden House, the city's best, though it looked a bit seedy to me. We went to the Cleveland *Plain Dealer* to be interviewed by its TV critic. That was the guy who wore white shoes. The photo department wanted to take our pictures—Hughes at the wire machine, me posed like a pinup sitting on a fake fence in the photo lab. I refused. That was just the beginning, and that's what I mean about the *New York* piece. Outside of New York the only people who read it are the press, because they think it will keep them in touch with what's going on in the Big Apple. There seems to be a general attitude that what a kicky, hip, trendy magazine says goes, and there is a lack of self-confidence to form one's own opinions.

Walking down the street with Hughes and me, the reporter from the *Plain Dealer* turned to Hughes and said, "Well, Hughes, how does the situation in Washington look to you?" They chatted for a while and then he turned to me and asked, "Sally who do you think is the sexiest politician in Washington?"

We did a couple of TV and a few more newspaper interviews, then we went to a radio station where a man-woman team had a local show. When we walked in, the man, a youngish type with body-hugging bell-bottoms and a sculptured haircut, avoided shaking my hand. When we went on the air, the first thing he remarked was that my roots were showing. I was puzzled by his flirtatious rudeness until he began talking about the *New York* piece. Then I got his message.

The next day in Chicago the local critics were by far the most sophisticated group we had met on our trip, and Hughes and I had a pleasant low-key exchange with them. They were hip to what the *New York* piece was all about, and the subject was happily dismissed.

At lunch, in what I think was called "The Luau Room" of

some Polynesian restaurant, we had an unpleasant interview with a rather haggard woman who seemed resentful that the interview wasn't about her. She talked about herself except for a few asides: "My, my, you're certainly getting a lot of attention and money for such a little girl, aren't you, honey?" She would ask us a question, tell us what she thought, and then write her answer down. "We're getting awfully tired of ourselves," I ventured.

"And each other, I bet, hummmmm?" she said, and I watched her jot down, "tired of each other."

We were both getting tired of everything.

After a session of interviews on the West Coast, I called my mother in San Francisco.

"I saw the ads for you on television," she said. "They're all over the place."

"Oh, what did they use?" I asked. Neither Hughes nor I had any idea what, out of that four-hour rap session we taped, would be used for promos.

"I think it's the senator-with-his-hand-on-the-fanny one," Mother said.

"What!" I screamed in horror. I had never referred to that at all, so I couldn't imagine how it had gotten on the air. It turned out my mother had mistaken it for an old line I had used, "A senator will tell you more over a martini at midnight than he will over a microphone at noon." But I had only used *that* jokingly during the in-house promo session.

I went out of my mind. I told Bernie Roswig that if they didn't get that promo off the air immediately I was going to "get off this horse immediately," and he knew what I meant. They pulled it, but it had already done its harm. I found out later it had been Gordon's idea. And I was sorry to learn that. It was the antithesis of how I had thought they had wanted to project me, as a serious newswoman. It was exactly like *New York*—the blonde bombshell who uses sex to get her stories.

We headed for our last stop, Los Angeles. Again, a car to speed us to the hotel, the Beverly Wilshire. More fruit from the manager. I was exhausted and fell into bed. It was the next morning that I called Warren Beatty and he told me to come up and see him. I had a foreboding that he was going to tell me something I didn't want to hear. I was right.

The first thing I heard from the reporters at a press luncheon was that the Los Angeles publicity people had sent copies of The Article to all of them. I was bombarded with questions about sex, and how I got stories, and finally a black male reporter asked me if it was true that I had slept with a famous man I had once interviewed. I made up my mind then that I was not going to subject myself to this kind of degradation any more. Once we got back to New York I was never going to give another interview. I was hating the impotence of having no control over what was said and hating the reporters for being so gullible and single-minded. And I was beginning to hate being a celebrity. It is boring to talk about yourself all day, demeaning to put yourself at the mercy of someone else's point of view, to be tempered by their values, morals, prejudices, resentments, fears and jealousies. It was the first time that I understood what people who are written about feel, and I felt a little ashamed at how I had used to scoff at those who complained about the press.

Hughes, on the other hand, was being marvelously funny, really at his best, and people were loving him. He was trying gallantly, as he had throughout the tour, to defend me, but they didn't want to hear it.

At the end of the lunch I was interviewed by two women who were doing a series on women in television and I found them bright and sympathetic, which did put me in a better humor. We walked back to the hotel and to more interviews. Hughes and I were so punchy we didn't know what we were saying and we had begun to use each other's lines unconsciously. We were sitting in the darkened bar of the Beverly

Wilshire Hotel having our last interview. I had done my number and I had tuned out while Hughes ran on about the chili and the getting up in the middle of the night. Then I heard the reporter say, "Oh, really, why that's fascinating. Is that really what you want to do when you get out of the business?"

"Oh, yes," drawled Hughes. "I've always wanted to have a Maltese cat farm, and Texas is the only place you can raise them. You see," he continued, as the reporter wrote, "the terrain in certain parts of Texas is the same as in Malta. Why, I've already saved enough to buy three hundred head of cat and I have a friend who manufactures the little stools you milk them with, so . . ."

I excused myself with as much control as possible and went upstairs to see Warren Beatty.

Later, over dinner, Hughes and I got quite drunk and roared over the story, but we never saw it in print.

That weekend I went to a wedding and the bride's mother, whom I had never met, said, "I saw you on *The Dick Cavett Show* and I thought you were just terrible." I was devastated.

Monday, rehearsals began. Thank God. Now they were going to roll it all out for us, lay it on, let us in on all the fabulous plans for the first week of shows. And it was about time. I had begun to have doubts, but I knew that they would disappear as soon as we got to the studio and saw what they had for us.

We were to arrive at 6 A.M. to start getting the feel of getting up early. We would watch the *Morning News*, then go into a simulation of what our anchor booth was going to look like (it wasn't nearly ready) and tape a news broadcast. We were to write it from the same wires and newspapers that John Hart had used hours earlier.

Lee Townsend was jittery. Townsend, the most even-tempered man I know, was also as irritated as I had ever seen him. He had been against the promo tour (though he didn't object violently enough) because he felt we could have better used our time rehearsing. His objections had been overridden by Blackrock, which—who? I never got the pronoun straight—had insisted that it was necessary. So Townsend was nervous and angry because we had been away and virtually co-opted by the PR department, and because it was then clear to him that we didn't have a super-duper razzle-dazzle show to put on the air in a week's time. And no real studio to rehearse in.

He had reason to be more than nervous, and we did exactly what we had done for the pilot except at greater length. We wrote a little news and a few lead-ins to film pieces, and Hughes wrote an essay. I couldn't think of anything that morning, and besides, I'm not an essayist. I'm a reporter and interviewer. Hughes would do essays, which he did marvelously, and I would do what I did best.

In front of the camera, they outfitted me with an earpiece on a wire, called a Telex, which enables them to talk to you from the control room. They handed us mikes, rolled our copy onto the TelePrompTers, and away we went. It was a disaster. There were two cameras and I didn't know which one to look at. The stage manager waved his hands around, but I hadn't a clue what he was trying to tell me. I was fumbling my words and couldn't read the prompters. They were shouting in my ear through the Telex to do this and do that, and three minutes here and twenty seconds there, and ad lib here. The ad libs were always by surprise, and I would fumble around trying to think of something clever to say about a film piece we had just seen. It might have been a bloody plane crash or a dairy farm. It BOMBED, and I was shell-shocked by the time it was over. Suddenly I *knew* this was the way it was going to be. There was nothing I could do about it. It was too late to get out of it.

I was even more upset when everyone came out of the control booth and said it was just fine and all it needed was a little smoothing out and we would be just great by the end of the week. No mention of any guests for interviews, no mention of any special film pieces that would lend themselves to interesting, informative ad libs and, most frightening of all, no mention of anything I should do to improve myself. I realized fully for the first time that I didn't know anything, and I panicked.

As we were filing down the stairs to the *Morning News* section, Jim Ganser, one of the producers, caught up with me. He was to be the only one at CBS who really tried to help me.

"Try to punch your words a little more," he sort of whispered out of the side of his mouth, as though he didn't want anyone to hear.

I fell on him. "What? How? What do you mean?" I said desperately. "Tell me, for God's sake. Tell me what I'm doing wrong."

And he told me. "You're wrong to expect anyone to give any help or guidance of any kind. You're a big star now, and people figure if you're a big star you must know what you're doing. Nobody's going to stick his neck out to help you."

I went to the ladies' room and threw up. But I had to hurry. Hughes and I were the "big stars" of a large press luncheon at the "21" Club, and we were late.

That was the lunch where Salant made the remark quoted in *Women's Wear Daily* about pointing the finger at someone else if the show was a bomb.

Hughes and I sat at the head table with Manning and Salant and some of the other biggies. I could hardly talk and I don't remember a word that was said. Hughes was mildly depressed about the show, but it didn't seem to be getting him down. After lunch we were taken from table to table for ten or fifteen minutes to talk to the press and answer questions. At the first table there was an enormously fat woman with a mustache and black hair. It was Kay Gardella, TV critic of the New York *Daily News,* and she attacked straight away.

"What did you think of the *New York* Magazine piece?" she said, her tiny eyes squinting behind the folds of fat.

"I thought it was vicious and distorted," I said wearily.

"Well," she announced, "I happen to know many of your closest friends, and they all say it is just like you."

I mustered a weak smile and the wan retort that if they thought it was just like me, why on earth were they my friends? Several others at the table were so put off by her that they began to defend me, especially Mary Peacock, an editor at *Ms.,* whom I had met only casually. I think I will never be as grateful to anyone, because I was about to burst into tears. That day I seriously considered quitting. I knew, or at least thought I knew, what I was in for, only I never guessed how bad it was going to get. But I had already signed the contract. There was nothing I could do.

I don't remember much else. I remember a woman from *The New York Times* asking me if it was true that I had really been offered $45,000 by *The New York Times,* because if so everyone there was furious. That figure had been printed somewhere but was nonsense, and I tried to explain that I hadn't ever discussed money with *The Times* because each time I had been approached I had turned down the offer. I was tired of defending myself for nothing. I was tired period.

I thought I had hidden my feelings well, but a wire story about the lunch later read, "Rudd, 52, seemed more at ease and mildly amused at the goings-on. Miss Quinn, 32, appeared slightly tired and worried. . . ."

We got more bad news that week when Lee Townsend finally decided, along with the staff but against the wishes of Hughes and me, that the set's background would be blue. That wouldn't have been so bad except there is something called a blue chroma key, which means that if you have that color as a background you're not allowed to wear that color or anything with that color on the air because it will literally disappear. Wearing a blue sweater, I looked like a floating head. It's my favorite color and almost everything I own is blue or has blue in it. I would have to buy a new wardrobe, which meant that the $3,000 clothes allowance was laughable, especially when Barbara Walters turns up in $400 Jean Muirs or $600 Adolfo suits. CBS had decided upon a policy, with which I agreed, that I was not allowed to borrow clothes from designers or take a cut on clothes from designers. That meant that I had to buy summer, fall, winter and spring clothes out of that allowance—all without blue. Disaster. Not only that, but the IRS won't let you take on-air clothes off your income tax—not unless it's a costume. The rule is that the pockets have to be sewed up. They say that rule was made after Dinah Shore did a special on TV and wore ten or so outfits that cost up to $50,000 apiece.

Barbara Walters and I had been in contact by phone. She had tried to cheer me up as I became increasingly depressed. It must have been hard for her, because much of the publicity that painted me so out of proportion as an outrageous sexpot painted Barbara equally out of proportion as lifeless and boring. We were both getting a lot of mail. She, about how she shouldn't worry, nobody could knock her off the air and especially not that awful little upstart, who-did-she-think-she-was-anyway. And other mail saying, at last you're about to get beaten.

I was getting you-little-creep mail—if you think you can knock that wonderful person off the air forget it. Or, it's about time someone took that horrible woman on.

Barbara assured me one gets used to it after a while and said I shouldn't read the terrible mail, only the good. She also said she was glad it was me and not someone else. "If it weren't you they would have put another woman on the air, so at least they chose a friend of mine," and she told me to feel free to ask for her help or advice anytime. She was going to be in Israel the week after I went on, and she joshed about how she was leaving me a clear field. "Well, you don't have to go that far to help," I kidded. I gave her names of some friends of mine to look up in Israel, and she said she would have a party for me when she got back and we would invite all the press and then people could see that we were friends.

The rest of the week was more of the same. The same kinds of rehearsals, the same news, the same ad libs, the same stumbling and the same lack of advice, counsel, training and help. Some days it was better than others, but it was all depressing. Hughes didn't seem too upset, and at first I couldn't figure out why. I guess now that Hughes knew he would be good as an anchorman. He knew he had a strong, gruff, authoritative delivery, that he would read the news well, and that he was an essayist. He could write these off-beat, delightful little essays that appealed to a lot of people who disliked the Eastern establishment mentality. They also appealed to the Eastern establishment types, who found them refreshing. Hughes had been on TV long enough to learn how to be careful about ad libs. You don't say just any old thing on television, no matter what they tell you. There's controversial, and there's *controversial*. And Hughes knew where the camera was and when it was on him.

My problems were unending. There were no interviews, I said anything that came into my head (and it wasn't much at that hour in the morning), I couldn't write essays, and most important, I just ain't no news reader, no matter how you look at it. I was bored with it; it wasn't my own stuff—O.K., so I rewrote somebody's wire story—and I have what has now been pointed out to me as an upper-class Eastern-debutante Smith-College accent and sense of humor. "The great rancid masses," as Alice Roosevelt Longworth likes to say in interviews, just wouldn't go for it.

There was one bright spot that week. On Thursday Hughes and I spoke at a lunch given by the National Academy of TV Arts and Sciences at the Pub Theatrical on Broadway. A lot of people I had never seen came up and congratulated us and said how much they loved the piece in *New York* Magazine.

We were a smash. I have never been as clever and funny and neither had Hughes, and we delivered a dialogue that sounded as though it had been written for us by a great gag writer.

They loved us. For one brief and delirious moment I thought maybe they'd love us the following Monday. But deep down I knew that we would never be able to do what we had done that day on the air.

We finally got into our own studio on Friday, and we rehearsed there Friday and Saturday. Nothing went right.

Friday morning after John Hart's last show someone came into the Cronkites, where we were working, and said that the staff of the *Morning News* was having a farewell party for John and the old producer. I hadn't really seen John to talk to him. I like and respect him a great deal, but we had been so busy working the lobster shift (that's the night shift in newspapers) that we just hadn't had a chance to see each other.

"Oh, great, I'll go up and tell John goodbye," I said, jumping up from my chair.

"I wouldn't if I were you," someone said. "There's a great deal of hostility up there toward the new team. And the atmosphere upstairs is more like a wake than a party. I think you had better forget it."

That was the first I had heard of resentment or hostility on the home team front. It worried me because, except for Townsend, Hughes and me, the "team" was the same. There had been no staff changes. I had found that curious. If they had really wanted a whole new format, with more entertainment and a lighter mood, I thought that they would surely have tried to bring in some people who were more in the show-biz line. The *Morning News* staff was very good. But they were hard-news oriented, and Gordon had said the idea was to take on the *Today* Show.

That morning when I went in to get my makeup done for the rehearsals my hair was a mess. While I was upstairs, the woman who was doing my makeup said her friend Edith, the hairdresser for *Edge of Night,* was right down the hall and maybe she would roll my hair up on the hot rollers for me. She called Edith, and a round-faced woman in her late fifties, with reddish hair, big, wide innocent eyes, a very strong New York accent, and dyed-to-match pants, vest, blouse and shoes, came rushing in. Edith said she would be delighted. She had the lightest, most soothing touch, and the whole time she did my hair she told me how great I looked and how terrific I was going to be on the air and that she was honored to do my hair. Then she asked who my official hairdresser was.

"Hairdresser? I don't have a hairdresser." Both women were stunned. "You have to have a hairdresser," they chimed. "Every woman on television has one. You can't just go on with your hair like this every morning."

Edith asked me if she could be my hairdresser and said she was sure that if I asked they would let me have one. I told Lee and Sandy Socolow about it and they both went blank. Nobody had given my hair a thought. They okayed it right away, but it indicates how little thought went into the planning for the first woman network anchor. Edith was a godsend. She not only took care of my hair, she took care of my ego.

After the rehearsal on Saturday, I was about to leave. No interviews were lined up for me for the following week. The big interview for Monday was with Patrick Buchanan, the President's speech writer, and that would be out of Washington. I had no idea what film pieces were going to be used. They weren't sure.

I was so depressed and scared that I didn't really care. I wanted to go somewhere and hide. As we were leaving (Sunday was a free day) Lee Townsend gave me a big smile and said, in a way I couldn't decide was joking or not, "Let me know if you have any good ideas tomorrow for the show."

Sunday was the worst day of my life. I thought about ways to disappear where no one would hear from me for years and would think I had been kidnapped by some freak. I considered the possibility of having plastic surgery so I would never be recognized as Sally Quinn. I fantasized about going on the broadcast and saying, "Good morning, I'm Sally Quinn and we are not prepared to do this show and I don't know what I'm doing up here." I thought seriously about calling Salant and Manning and telling them. I came close to quitting.

The water pipes broke in our apartment and I had to go to a friend's place on West End Avenue to wash my hair.

When I got out of the shower, I put on a large white robe that was hanging on the door. I came out of the bathroom draped in that robe and I said to Warren, who had been babysitting me all day, "I really feel like one of those ancient Aztec virgins who has been chosen to be sacrificed on top of the temple of the Gods. All the other virgins are wildly jealous of her because she has this fabulous honor bestowed on her. What they don't know is that she doesn't want her heart cut out with a knife anytime by anyone. It hurts."

I went to bed at 5 P.M. It was bright and sunny outside, and I could hear the children playing on Riverside Drive and happy couples walking and chatting and laughing as they strolled in Riverside Park.

"I will never be happy again," I thought. "My life is over."

I never went to sleep. We had been coming in around 4 or 5 in the morning that week, but it wasn't proper preparation for coming in at 1:30. The alarm went off at 1:00 A.M. Warren was waiting to walk me to my limousine, which arrived promptly at 1:30 A.M. It was like being escorted in a golden carriage to the guillotine.

I didn't feel too hot. I figured it must be because I hadn't slept. I slipped into the gloamings of the enormous black car and we glided over to Hughes' apartment, the Apthorpe, a few blocks away on West End Avenue. He hadn't slept either. We didn't say a word. A few minutes later we arrived at the studio and went directly back to the *Morning News* area and into the Bullpen.

In front of each of us was a pile of news wire stories, the first edition of *The New York Times* and the *Daily News*. Bob Siller, the copy editor, was there and so was Dave Horowitz, one of the assistant producers. They would make up the "line-up." The line-up was a sheet on which the show was blocked out minute-by-minute. Taking all the film pieces and counting their time, they would, along with Hughes and me and Lee Townsend, decide what the top news stories were and allot a certain amount of time to each, from forty-five seconds to a minute, and then block out time for commercials (we had only network commercials for the first six weeks) and station breaks. They would leave about a minute and a half for Hughes's essay, and what was left—roughly five minutes—would be alloted for "ad libs."

While this was going on, Hughes and I read the papers and the wires to get an idea of what stories we wanted to use. When we had finished, about 3 or 3:30, Bob and Dave came back with the line-up designating which one of us would write which stories and which lead-ins to film pieces. If the film piece was ready, Hughes and I would try to take a look at it so that we could write a clearer lead-in; if not, there was generally some kind of script. Often the film piece wasn't ready. Horowitz and Siller, with our advice or without, would figure out which film piece seemed like the best topics for conversation and block in a certain amount of time for ad libs after those pieces. There was some freedom to move around, but not much. Everything we were to say we typed out on our enormous typewriters.

We had two writers who were to do the weather, sports and late-breaking news. Hughes was to read all the sports. We had tried to divide it, but I didn't understand sports and kept fumbling and breaking up in the middle of the report. Hughes hated it too, but it wasn't quite as ridiculous when he did it.

By the time Hughes and I would have read everything thoroughly, discussed camera angles with Bob Quinn, our director, who came in about 4, written all our news items, lead-ins and station and commercial breaks, had something to eat at our desks (it was called "lunch" and usually came from the CBS cafeteria, known appropriately and without affection as "the Bay of Pigs"), it would be about 6 A.M.— time for Edith and Rickey, the makeup person, to arrive and get us ready.

At around 3:30 I had started to break out in a cold sweat and I became weak and dizzy and slightly nauseated. I couldn't concentrate on what I was writing. Finally I went into Townsend's office and passed out. I tried to get up about 4 A.M. and write, but I stayed at my typewriter for about twenty minutes and then went back to Townsend's office and passed out again. I thought it was probably because I was tired and nervous, but by then my throat was so sore and I was coughing so badly that I could barely talk. I had shivers and had to be wrapped up in a blanket.

Everyone piled into Townsend's office and stared at me in horror. "Do you think you can do it?" Lee asked, terrified.

"I just don't know, Lee." I didn't.

I think at that point I was more scared not to go on than to go on.

"I'll try. I'll really try. But I can't talk. And I'm so dizzy. Is there any way I could get a vitamin B shot or something to give me quick energy?"

By then it was 5:30 in the morning and I was so sick I couldn't breathe. I kept trying to sit up and I would just fall right down. I couldn't tell whether the beads of perspiration on my head were from temperature or desperation. Finally Townsend said that they had to get me to a hospital. Somebody had a car and they carried me out to the front of the building, stuffed me in the car, and drove two blocks away to Roosevelt Hospital to the emergency room. A young doctor took me back to examine me and take my temperature. I had a temperature of 102 and he said he thought I might have pneumonia. I was coughing so badly that my body was racked. "You don't understand," I practically screamed. "I'm making my television debut in an hour."

"So I've heard," he smirked.

"Well, I can't possibly go on like this. Can't you give me a vitamin B shot or something? Anything."

He said that in my condition a vitamin B shot wouldn't do any good. The only thing he could do for me was to give me a throat spray that would stop me from coughing for a few hours. But he suggested that I get to a doctor immediately afterward for proper medication.

"Anything else I could give you now," he said, "would knock you out." Oh, how I wished . . .

He left the room and came back a few minutes later with the most enormous syringe I have ever seen, with a needle a mile long.

"Forget it," I said, backing away from him.

"Don't get hysterical," he said, laughing. "This is a throat spray. I'm not going to stick the needle in you."

He stuck the needle in my mouth and sprayed a gooey liquid, which coated the inside of my throat.

Lee grabbed me, back we went into the car, and we screeched off around the corner and back to CBS as though we were bank robbers getting away.

It was a little before 6:30. Edith and Rickey were frantic, and Hughes looked as though all his blood had drained out of him. Edith rolled my hair while Rickey sponged some makeup on me. I lay down while all this was going on. The hot rollers stayed in too long and I looked like Shirley Temple when my hair was combed out. There was nothing we could do about the frizz. At about ten minutes to seven they finished on me. I was still so weak and dizzy that I could barely move, and all I can remember is a large fuzz of Warren leaning over me asking if I was all right, Townsend in a frenzy, and Hughes pulling himself together as he walked into my dressing room. "Hughes—" I tried to smile— "get me off this horse immediately." Hughes tried to smile, too, but he wasn't very convincing. "Don't worry," he growled, "you'll make it, kid."

I tried to say thank you, but the throat spray had a numbing effect, like Novocain, and I couldn't feel whether my tongue was touching the roof of my mouth or whether I was forming my words properly.

"You look beautiful, darling, just beautiful. You'll be wonderful, I know you will," Edith was murmuring.

I looked in the mirror. I was hideous. My hair was frizzy, the granny glasses looked wrong, and the only thing I owned that wasn't blue (I hadn't had the time to shop that week) was a yellow battle jacket that made me look like a dyke.

"Well," I thought, "there's no way anybody is going to accuse me of being a sex bomb this morning."

Somebody shoved a pile of telegrams in my face and I

tried to read. They were all amiable, from close friends and family, but it was upsetting me. "Oh, God," I thought, "if only they knew how terrible I'm going to be."

They were screaming for me to get into the studio and I ran in, got behind the desk, had my mike adjusted, and somebody handed me my Telex, which I stuck in my ear.

"One minute," yelled the floor manager.

My mouth was dry. No possibility of talking. I looked at Hughes. He was looking at me as though we were copilots and I had just been shot. He tried to smile. I tried to smile back.

"Thirty seconds," said the floor manager.

I looked straight outside the glass partition to the newsroom and saw everyone staring.

"Five seconds," the floor manager said.

For a fleeting moment I thought maybe I would wake up and find out this wasn't happening.

An arm went out to me and a finger pointed. I gazed at the TelePrompTer.

"Good morning," I read. "I'm Sally Quinn."

My brother, Bill, who is the managing editor of the *Theosophist Magazine,* is also an astrologer. Several years ago he did my chart for me for Christmas, and occasionally he'll take a long look at it and give me an updating. I'm a double Cancer. When he had first done my chart he had told me that I had the most harmonious chart he had ever seen and that all my life I would have everything handed to me on a platter. That sounded pretty good.

Some time in July he sent me an urgent letter, which I found when I got back from the promo tour. He had just reviewed my chart and all signs were in opposition.

He had concluded that I was in for the worst year of my life, and especially the worst six months of my life. Every aspect, both personal and professional, would be turned upside down, and I would encounter more emotional pain than I ever had before. But, like a rock thrown into a pool of water, the ripples would continue until the following June.

He had not heard about the CBS job.

I had always sort of believed in astrology. Not enough to let it direct my life, but I find it amusing and often accurate. His letter would never have led me to change my course, but if I hadn't been so totally occupied with CBS at that point, I might have given it more thought. But the day it arrived so did my furniture from Washington and I had tossed the letter away.

Right in the middle of the first program on that morning of August 6th, just as the bouncy in-house ad jingle was winding up—"You get a lot more, right here on . . . C-B-S"— I thought about my brother's letter. I thought about the letter and I had an overwhelming feeling that I had lost all control, that no matter how smart or talented or attractive I might think I was, there was absolutely *nothing* I could do. I had had it, and there was no point in trying. Even though I had gone on the air that morning knowing it was going to be a disaster and knowing the reasons why, I had still had confidence in myself, and the conviction that if any number of people on TV whom I didn't have much respect for could make it, there was no reason I couldn't. I had the feeling that if we could just get a good show together and I got a chance to have some direction and some experience, we could make it work. Hughes, I felt, was very good, but he was being dragged down by me and the format.

But when I remembered my brother's letter I lost that self-confidence. I gave up.

There was another thing I thought of during that terrible hour. It was a quote I had given to one of the publicity people at CBS, which they had printed in the press releases. It came from being an Army brat and never living in one place longer than a year and a half.

"I remember every time I went to a new school when I was a little girl, I tried so hard to impress the teacher that I became an A student as soon as I possibly could. I learned awfully early that somebody's first impression of you is usually the lasting one."

There was no way, during the first day, or week, or even month that I would be able to make a good impression. From then on, whether or not they watched again to see if I improved, they would always say, "God, did you *see* Sally Quinn. Could you *believe* how bad she was?" Because of the publicity, that's what people wanted to believe. That's what they did believe.

Even if I had not let my brother's message get to me, I would anyhow have had the conviction that I had no chance as a "big TV star," not this time around.

From that moment it was a matter of how to get out of the job as quickly and gracefully as I could, relatively intact, physically and emotionally.

I don't remember much else about that hour. I was propped up with several pillows because I was so weak and dizzy that I couldn't sit up by myself.

I coughed a lot. I remember a swirl of sweltering bright lights, moving cameras, different noises and shouts in my ear through the Telex—"Turn to Camera 2, thirty seconds to ad-lib, five seconds till commercial, ten seconds more of interview"—hand signals, desperate and self-delirious mumblings . . . and then it was over. And when it was over I felt completely numb. Nothing.

Seven months later I screwed up my courage to read the transcripts.

SALLY: Good morning. I'm Sally Quinn.
HUGHES: And I'm Hughes Rudd. Here're some of today's top stories: There's a report that American Air Force B-52's bombed

off target in Cambodia this morning and killed some three hundred friendly soldiers and civilians.

The Skylab astronauts are having trouble with their air-conditioning. The man who made Fidel Castro what he is today—is dead.

And we'll see Marshall Efron tossing a mean green salad. Sally?

SALLY: Earl Patrick Grey finishes up his Watergate testimony today, with former Attorney General Richard Kleindienst following him.

The elegant Heywood Hale Broun will have a report on the elegance that was Saratoga, and what's happening to it. And we'll be talking with Pat Buchanan, the man who writes a lot of President Nixon's speeches.

ANNOUNCER: From CBS newsroom in New York, this is *The CBS Morning News* with Hughes Rudd and Sally Quinn.

Shouting in the ear to ad-lib for thirty seconds.

HUGHES: Well, Sally, I suppose we should begin a little bit by saying who and what we are. I suppose most people don't consider me, you know, a commonplace sight in their living room, but they have seen me occasionally, I suppose, if nothing else, saying, "And now, back to you, Walter," that sort of thing.

Sally Quinn is not a commonplace sight on CBS. She's a former *Washington Post* reporter and we're very glad to have her indeed.

SALLY: Well, wouldn't you know the first day I come on television, I start out with a sore throat and a fever. And now, back to you, Hughes.

HUGHES: Well, a fever is all right as long as it doesn't make you delirious. Actually, there've been a lot of people on television who were delirious—they're usually running for public office.

SALLY: Oh, I might be one of the next.

More shouting in the ear—this time to wind it up. I didn't have a clue how to "wind it up." Hughes, thank God, did.

Hughes: Well, I think you'd better get going with it.

We did. I read some more news, there was a film report, and then it was my turn to read an intro to the next film, a piece about child labor.

Sally: Working for a living is something grownups do, not children. That's not just custom, it's law. But you'd never know it from a visit to our fields and orchards, because on farms all across the country, it's boys and girls who do a lot of the dirty, sweaty, tedious work of picking and pruning—even, as Harold Dow discovered, in the San Joaquin Valley of California, which is the richest agricultural area on the earth.

The film piece showed children as young as ten working in the hot sun picking chili peppers, even though it was against the law, then pointed out that half the migrant families in this country earn less than $3,000 a year.

When it was nearly over, a voice screamed into my Telex that we had about a minute to ad-lib. Hughes looked at me and mouthed "You start." I think, just to be polite.

I had nothing to say.

I said, "I remember when my father and mother used to make me clean my room I complained of child labor, but—but—certainly . . .

Hughes jumped in to save me.

"You don't know how lucky you are until you see something like that," he attempted.

I couldn't be stopped.

"Have you ever tried to pick strawberries for half an hour?" I exclaimed.

"No."

"You can't do it," I continued. "It's absolutely killing work."

"I picked cotton when I was a kid in Texas, not because I

had to particularly, but because I wanted, you know, the extra money. But the figures on this sort of thing are shocking. That of 300,000 children working on farms he mentioned, over half of those are between ten and thirteen years old."

"Between ten and thirteen," I repeated.

"Yeah," said Hughes.

"Yeah, it's extraordinary," I said.

"And yet," Hughes continued, "It's been against the law, oh, for, what, thirty years or more to do this."

"Well," I added, "I mean . . ."

"The plain fact is," said Hughes, "that if they are black children or chicano—Mexican-American children—nobody pays attention. That—that's what it amounts to."

Oh, God, somebody help us, I thought, cut us off, we are sinking fast . . . but there was nothing except the director making strange hand signals at me, which I didn't understand but which I concluded did not mean to stop talking.

"And the fact is," I rasped, "if you don't have the . . . the parents trying to keep the children out of the fields—"

Please, God.

"—what are—they need the money, they've got to have it," I said.

"That's the problem there," said Hughes. "Like all over the South, where you'll see the entire family out chopping cotton, or at least you used to. Any child big enough to wield a hoe would be out there, you know."

"Well," I said, "he said on this—on—the—during the film report that the families made about $3,000 a year. You know how far that . . ."

"The whole family," put in Hughes, by this time in nearly as much sweat as I was.

There was no stopping me now.

"—that goes about a week in New York City." Giggle.

Hughes looked at me. And I knew. It was all over. A

shriek came through the Telex. "Break for commercial." He paused, drew a deep breath and said, "Yeah." He paused again. Another breath. "Well, we'll be back with Skylab and a buckburger after this."

ANNOUNCER: Now fourteen minutes after the hour.

Back again we came. Hughes read something about the astronauts going for a walk in space that day.

We were told to ad-lib for about thirty seconds.

HUGHES: You know, oddly enough, Sally, I don't think anybody is particularly excited any more about even the Russians' sending something to Mars or us having men up in space. It's amazing how quickly . . .

SALLY: It's only if something goes wrong that people get interested [I said, pleased to have something to say].

HUGHES: Yes.

SALLY: I mean, I've been wildly interested the last couple days, but that's because they may end up circling—(crosstalk) [that means Hughes is trying to stop me from saying it; he fails] right, forever.

HUGHES: [weakly] . . . people . . . down here . . .

And then Hughes introduced Marshall Efron. Marshall Efron is a fat, funny-looking man who was a big hit on *The Great American Dream Machine,* and Hughes had been enthusiastic about getting him on the show. I hadn't seen him and had taken Hughes's word for it. I couldn't believe what I saw that morning on the screen. This fat boy was making a salad using dollar bills for lettuce, then a "buckburger," placing a dollar bill between two buns and eating it.

As he was finishing I got a cue in my ear that I was to go to Camera 1.

I looked at the camera and a script rolled up. I hadn't seen it before.

SALLY: And just to put our budget-conscious viewers as well as CBS vice presidents at ease, here are the dollar bills used in the salad. They've been cleaned and dried, which proves that money can be laundered without being sent to Mexico. [Then I added, because we were told to ad-lib] But they are a little greasy, you can see the envelope, it's got a lot of grease there—

HUGHES: They're oily, I suppose—

SALLY: Mayonnaise—yeah.

HUGHES: Well, you know, originally, Sally, Marshall wanted to actually tear these dollar bills, the way you would lettuce, but we checked on it and found out that if he did he could go to jail for six months and be fined $400. Which would seem to prove that the dollar is worth more nowadays if you cut it up than it is if you go spend it.

SALLY: Well, you know, when he was making his moneyburger or whatever—buckburger—it reminded me of going to shop for a steak on Saturday and the butcher started to put some hamburger in with my steak and I said, "But I didn't order it," and he said, "Listen, lady, if you ever want to see hamburger again you'd better get it now," 'cause this is it, right?

HUGHES: A collector's item kind of thing, I guess.

SALLY: So apparently there is a boycott scheduled for Tuesday, I understand.

HUGHES: Oh, really? Well, the weather is not what you'd expect for early August.

ANNOUNCER: The time now—twenty-three minutes after the hour.

We broke for commercials, then back to the Heywood Hale Broun film on Saratoga. More weak ad libs. Then it was time for Nicholas von Hoffman, a *Washington Post* columnist.

"Spectrum," a special feature each morning, invited controversial people to speak out for two minutes on any subject they chose. The network wanted to fend off complaints of bias from the Administration, and one way to do it was to let a few dull people blab about their reactionary points of view to a minimum of views. Some of them turned out to be interesting, but mostly it was just boring, and we thought it broke up whatever little flow we had achieved. Nick was one of the good ones, and he is also one of my closest friends and had been a colleague. He was outraged by the publicity I had gotten, particularly The Piece, and he devoted his time to defending me.

Nick: Hughes Rudd doesn't need any introducing to anybody who owns a TV set. No one in broadcasting is more respected or appreciated than Mr. Rudd. But Sally Quinn may be new to you. True, there've been a lot of articles about her lately, some good and some pretty sappy. In case you've read the sappy ones, you're not getting a glamour bomb with your orange juice and coffee. Sally and I have been colleagues on *The Washington Post* for some years, and I want to tell you she's one of the best reporters around. Nobody works harder at getting a story, getting it straight, and telling it right, than Sally. Unless, of course, it's Hughes Rudd. Anyhow, in Sally you're not getting a celebrity or a personality, you're getting a first-class newswoman, none better. CBS isn't going show-biz on you. Naturally, without character, professional ability is nothing. Competence is canceled out. But in Sally and Hughes you have two people who will serve you honestly and courageously. Sally, we'll miss you at the paper, but to both of you I wish every success and big, big, audience ratings. . . . And this is Nicholas von Hoffman daring either one of you to say these opinions are only mine and not CBS's.

I was surprised and touched. But I didn't have time to think about it. They were screaming at me to go to Camera 1.

I read, "This is his opinion and not necessarily that of CBS or the station you're watching."

Later Nick was much criticized. People thought it was corny. I didn't. I thought he did what CBS should have done a long time before. The only thing that didn't ring true was why I was up there reading the news if I was this alleged terrific reporter and interviewer. Nothing I had done or was to do on that broadcast gave any evidence of it.

ANNOUNCER: The time.now—thirty minutes past the hour.

Next there was the interview with Patrick Buchanan, conducted by Barry Serafin, who had agreed to accept the position as the Washington-based *Morning News* correspondent. He had given up the job of covering the Vice President to be part of the "new" *CBS Morning News*. He was joined by Dan Rather and the interview was okay but not exceptional.

The final film piece was about the Maryland Clam Festival. As it was concluding, a voice yelled in my ear, "thirty seconds of ad lib and goodbye." I racked my brain for some clam experience. None. So I said, "You know, I've never written about clams, but one of the first stories I had as a reporter at *The Washington Post,* four years ago, was to cover the Crab Derby in Crisfield, Maryland, which is—in case you don't know—the Saratoga of Crabs."

HUGHES: No, I didn't know that.
SALLY: Well, they had—I got a copy of the *Crisfield Times* last week and it had an announcement of my new job, and as the entire bio sketch it said, "Sally Quinn once covered the Crab Derby." [laughter]
HUGHES: Well, this is terrible over there—you have a Clam Festival and the clams can't come somehow, they must be imported. That's like, a, you know, like a—what, like the French no longer have snails, and they're all—
SALLY: Or truffles.
HUGHES: Most of them are imported. No, they still have truffles, not so many, but they're mainly imported from Germany, of all places. Well.

SALLY: When you go to Maine you have to import lobsters—
HUGHES: And so this day is over. Congratulations for getting through it with the flu. And—
SALLY: Congratulations for getting through the sports all by yourself, too.
HUGHES: Oh [laughter]. And we'll see you tomorrow.
SALLY: Goodbye.

Somebody yelled in my ear to look to the right over my shoulder at the camera through the glass window in the newsroom. I thought that seem contrived but I did it—not quite being able to see exactly where the camera was— and smiled.

ANNOUNCER: From our newsroom in New York, this has been *The CBS Morning News*—with Hughes Rudd and Sally Quinn.

When I walked back into my office there were three bouquets. One was from Charlotte Curtis, then editor of *The New York Times'* Family, Food, Fashions and Furnishings, now editor of the op-ed page of *The Times* and probably the woman I admire most in journalism. One from Vic Gold, former Press secretary of former Vice President Spiro T. Agnew and now a columnist. And one from Connie Tremulis of "Flowers by Connie," Rockford, Illinois.

I still have their cards.

Everybody was talking at once and saying what a great show it had been and how did I ever get through it, and, boy, what a terrific start we had gotten off to, and how terrible the *Today* Show was outdoors in front of Rockefeller Center. I don't remember seeing Hughes. I remember Lee Townsend taking me by the hand and leading me outside to a taxi. I put my head back on the seat and stared out the window as we went whizzing up Central Park West. It was a beautiful day. I thought about all the people walking along the street and bicycling in the park and about how happy they looked. I thought how odd it was that my work day was over and it was only 8, and that that was going to be my life from now on. And how depressing it was. I did not think about the show. It had not happened. Nor did Lee mention it.

We arrived at Dr. Sidney Miller's at 86th and Park Avenue. I went into the waiting room and it seemed as if everyone was staring at me. I had the feeling they had all just seen the show and were about to start spitting. Dr. Miller came out himself and showed me back to his office. He examined me, all the while talking about how nice it was to have a big TV star in his office. When he was finished he told me I might have pneumonia but he wouldn't know until the X rays. He gave me a shot of penicillin, prescribed some antibiotics, and told me to stay in bed for at least a week but to come back the next day. I told him I couldn't stay in bed. He said I wouldn't get well quickly unless I had plenty of rest. Lee bought my pills and took me home. We agreed I should not come in until 3:30 the next morning so I could get some rest.

I got into bed and stared at the ceiling. My parents called, worried about my health, and told me I was wonderful. All morning as I tried to sleep and forget, my friends called and lied to me.

The next morning I got up at 3:30. Hughes had already gone in and had sent the limousine back for me. I had not slept, and I could hardly breathe. I was coughing badly, my throat was a mess, and I was nearly drunk on the cough medicine Dr. Miller had given me. When I got to the office nearly all my copy had been written for me. I wrote a few lead-ins to film pieces and spent the rest of the time lying down. I had no idea what my script said, what film pieces we were using, or what the top stories of the day were.

Shortly before Edith arrived I went into Townsend's office. Everyone was talking about the reviews as though I had read them. Lee said in a hesitating voice. "Well, *The New York Times* wasn't all that bad, but the *Daily News* really wiped us out."

It had not occurred to me that we would be reviewed. What was this anyway, *The Beverly Hillbillys?*

Out of the corner of my eye I saw the *Times* review, so when I left the room I got a copy and went back to my office to read it alone. It wasn't as bad as I had expected. Still, I was upset. And helpless. I had to go on that day and the next and the next, and nobody was going to do anything about it. That was clear. If that was not the best review, why in the hell weren't they all running around hysterical trying to revamp the show, coach me on how to use my voice, show me which way the camera was pointing, do something, for God's sake?

The review was written by a man named Albin Krebs, whom I had met at the luncheon at "21" and who I felt was a just and decent man. I think his review was eminently fair. Perhaps too fair. He said the show "holds promise, was brisk, well paced, often breezy and sometimes genuinely amusing. What it lacked in news value it compensated with a well selected budget of softer topical features."

The team of Rudd–Quinn is an attractive one. Rudd, a veteran of fifteen years with CBS, is a newsman whose light has been pretty much kept under a bushel basket by his network, but yesterday he proved he deserves the chance at the big time that CBS is finally giving him. On the whole, his approach to the news is wry, his delivery dry.

Miss Quinn, who has been highly publicized since CBS hired her away from *The Washington Post* for her present assignment, possesses a natural poise and can deliver a humorous line coolly, although she was obviously nervous and ill at ease.

She confided to her audience that she had a sore throat and was running a fever. What she didn't say was that less than two hours before the program went on the air, she collapsed in the studio and had to be taken to Roosevelt Hospital for medication.

Mr. Rudd and Miss Quinn intend to give their show a folksy, informal flavor by indulging in ad-lib comments on the news and feature items presented. Yesterday, it was demonstrated that they'll have to be prudent about what they say.

For example, after a grim report on the plight of migrant farmers and the backbreaking work their children do in the fields, Miss Quinn commented, much too glibly, that she always considered child labor to be nothing more vexing than, as a kid, having to spend half an hour cleaning her room.

She fared much better with an afterthought on a zany video-taped routine by Marshall Efron, in which Mr. Efron made a salad using dollar bills in place of real lettuce, reasoning that the genuine article was too costly for salads nowadays.

Miss Quinn held up the dollar bills and explained that they had been cleaned after the videotaping. "Which proves," she said laconically, "that you can launder money without sending it to Mexico."

[That was the only line I hadn't written.]

What it has most going for it is a certain zippy smoothness and willingness to experiment.

It's producers seem to have their sights on a fresh approach, and want to avoid copying the National Broadcasting Company's "Today" Show, although Miss Quinn has been brought in as a counterbalance to "Today's" Barbara Walters.

A tape of yesterday's "Today" show left one viewer with the impression that, compared to the CBS show, its pacing was dolorous, if not downright torpid. . . .

Kay Gardella of the *Daily News* had written a nasty personal review which I didn't see until much later. Other reviewers from publications across the country were dribbling in too from the PR department, but I refused to read these. Things went on as though wipe-out reviews were an everyday occurrence. Hughes didn't mention the reviews. He was concerned about my health and how I was going to hold up that morning.

They must have been disturbed to say the least. But no one said a word to me. Perhaps they felt they had to protect me. Whatever the reasons, I never heard anything.

I felt horrible. I think I was more dejected than sick. I still had a temperature of about 102 and kept breaking out in a cold sweat, then freezing to death. I was dizzy, my throat was sore, and my whole body was racking as I doubled over coughing time and time again.

I lay in my tiny office in the pitch black. I had borrowed the *Morning News* pillow, a filthy, once-yellow Marimekko, and I brought a bright-yellow hand-crocheted throw to cover myself. The door was shut, but I could see the light through the crack and could hear the voices outside. They would get softer as they passed my door, then louder as they got farther away. They must be talking about me. I wanted to remain there in the darkness and never have to get up. I tried not to think about my job at *The Washington Post,* and how I never had gotten up before 10 A.M. I tried not to think about a lot of things. The only thing I could think of that didn't upset me was decorating. I started trying to remember specific rooms in decorating magazines and I would think of a room in a friend's house and decorate it. It took hours to pick out the right materials, curtains, rugs and the perfect little objects. It was the beginning of a whole new escape.

I had just chosen persimmon for my mother's study when the door opened, letting in a horrible shaft of light and the real world. It was Edith.

"Good morning, my darling," she said in her soothing voice. "I hate to do this to you but it's time for your hair."

She turned on a light and plugged in the electric rollers. I crawled up from the black plastic sofa and into my desk chair.

"Everybody on *Edge* just adores you," said Edith convincingly. "After the show yesterday they all thought you were terrific. And so brave. They couldn't believe how brave you were to go on the air so sick and all. And with all the publicity buildup and everything. And the *New York Times* review was wonderful. That man is so nice. And listen, darling. Don't worry one bit about that nasty review in the *Daily News*. That Kay Gardella woman is kooky, you know. I mean, everyone knows that and nobody ever pays attention to her. But you're my sweet little girl and nobody's going to hurt you. Because people with class know how good you are."

Edith was beaming at me beatifically with genuine pride. She seemed to me then almost like an Edith Bunker only smarter. There was a quality of enormous optimism and genuine kindness that I had rarely ever seen before. I loved her. Rickey came in to do my makeup. She was brisk and terribly friendly, always a bit late so she never had time for her own makeup, unlike Edith, who was always perfectly coiffed, made up and color coordinated. Rickey was also supportive, but a little more realistic than Edith. She helped me back down to reality with affection. Between them, they kept me from ending up as a total emotional and physical loss.

When makeup and hair were done, Jackie Hadley, the six-foot script person, brought my script, smiled at me, and said she hoped I could read it. It was about a quarter to seven. I wasn't nervous. Why wasn't I nervous? I knew I would be after the first stumble. Yesterday I had tried to say Phnom Penh three times and could not because of the throat spray. My upper lip had stuck to my lower one. What if Phnom Penh were in my script today? I started to look, then decided it would make me too nervous if it were. If it came, it came. My God, philosophical in only one day.

Hughes peered in, already made up.

"How are you?"

"Fine," I said calmly.

"We better get in there," he said, unconvinced.

I think it was that I didn't care. There was no way I could be worse than yesterday. The debut was over, a lot of people would have decided I was terrible and would no longer be watching out of curiosity. And besides, I felt too crummy to get worked up.

Hughes and I went into the studio, got into our seats and plugged in our earplugs.

The monitor was on us and we happened to look at ourselves. I quickly turned away, but Hughes yelled out, "Christ!"

I jumped. "What's the matter?"

"You look like an Amazon," he said. "And I look like a midget. We've got to do something immediately."

I looked at the monitor and I seemed enormous compared to Hughes.

"We can't go on like this," Hughes bellowed. "What are we going to do?"

We moved around a bit, jostling in our seats, experimenting with cushions, and it turned out that Hughes is very short-waisted and I am very long-waisted. With three extra pillows, Hughes, who is four inches taller than I am, looks the same height.

Betty, the secretary we both shared, came into the studio several minutes before we went on the air and brought Hughes's coffee and my tea, poured them into brown pottery mugs to give us the authentic early-morning atmosphere, and disappeared. Jackie rushed in with a few last-minute additions to the script, and we got the two-minute signal. I wasn't nervous. Maybe it was the drugs.

The stage manager held up his fingers in some strange hand gesture (it is not dirty, that's all I know) and then pointed at me.

"Good morning," I said into one of the cameras. It was

the one in front of me and I hoped it was the right one. "I'm Sally Quinn." So far so good.

HUGHES: And I'm Hughes Rudd. And while we all slept another Administration figure seems to be close to being touched by scandal. Vice President Agnew—this time. He's being investigated for allegations of bribery, extortion and tax fraud. The Vice President says he is innocent of any wrongdoing. The *Wall Street Journal* is reporting that these charges against Agnew stem from the award of state contracts while he was Governor of Maryland, and from Federal contracts since he became Vice President in 1968. We'll have more on that later. Sally?
SALLY: There is some other news. There's a report this morning of another incidental U.S. bombing in Cambodia. United Press International says four people were killed and the toll from yesterday's attack may be up higher than the three hundred killed or wounded reported earlier.

(I didn't have to say Phnom Penh)

Have you ever tried not to buy anything at all for one whole day? You'll get a chance to test your restraint. A California group has set today as Boycott Day.
HUGHES: Wheat is four bucks a bushel, which means that groceries are going to go up. An expert assesses Nixon's chances of hanging onto those tapes. And a summer bachelor worries about red tide in the bathtub.
ANNOUNCER: From our newsroom in New York, this is *The CBS Morning News* with Hughes Rudd and Sally Quinn.
SALLY: The big story today is Vice President Agnew's potential involvement in a scandal. Barry Serafin in Washington has the story.

Barry came on with the story. Then Hughes and I asked him some questions about the story.

A film piece followed about how a guy was offering a pair of Viking season tickets for a hindquarter of beef.

Then we were told to ad-lib. I don't know anything about beef. I don't like it. I know less about football.

SALLY: They sort of go together, football and beef. I mean. . . .
HUGHES: Yeah, yeah.
SALLY: You always think of great big strapping men going after a big football game to eat, to the . . .
HUGHES: Which is more alarming here, the fact that people are that beef nutty or the fact that people are that football nutty? I couldn't make up my mind. . . .
SALLY: I think probably both. I loved the story about the man who was going to trade his wife for a football ticket.
HUGHES: Yeah, season, well, it was a season ticket.
SALLY: Oh, season—oh, season ticket. Well, that's not so bad then.
HUGHES: At least for one game there is a limit. We'll be back in a moment, talking with an expert on the United States Constitution.
ANNOUNCER: It's fourteen minutes past the hour.

It wasn't great, but it wasn't a disaster.

We ad-libbed about the missing in action, a subject much too sensitive to ad-lib about—but we weathered it. There was a near mishap when I asked out loud, "I wonder how much it costs to bomb each day in Cambodia?"

There was another ad lib after a film piece on country music, about which I know nothing, though I had picked up a little from Hughes, who is a country music freak. We had a rather nice talk about it, though it was too long—long enough for me to make a profound statement, "Well, the point is, they're dealing with real problems . . ." and, "It's, you can't, you can't be realistic . . . I mean idealistic, today, anyway, and listen to music."

Hughes brightened things up with a funny essay about summer bachelors and how they ended up with mildewed towels and worse, in the bathtub. It was a plea for his wife,

Ann, to come back from France. And Hughes wasn't kidding. He hadn't had a maid all summer. He said it was too much trouble. I never saw his apartment. I refused to set foot in it after his description.

Hughes ended his essay with, "The summer bachelor is, in short, a prisoner of bacteria and booze, and freedom's just another word for nothing left to lose. In other words— Annie, come on home!"

QUINN: That's a good argument for women's liberation, because it's men's liberation. And that's all the time we have today.
ANNOUNCER: This has been *The CBS Morning News* with Hughes Rudd and Sally Quinn.

The next day, Lee Townsend told me he had complaints from some of the women at CBS, anonymous, about my use of "women's liberation." That expression, said Lee, for reasons he did not understand, was "out." I didn't understand why "women's liberation" was out, either. I meant women's liberation, the liberation of women. I told him to go back and tell them, whoever they were, what they could do. That really showed them.

As we left the studio that morning, I felt a little better than the day before. Everybody said again, Great show; terrific, wonderful.

When I got back to my office Townsend asked me to come into his office. He closed the door.

"I don't know how to tell you this," he said, "but we just got a call saying that Hughes's mother died during the night. He'll probably want to go out to Kansas right away. Do you think you could do the show yourself?"

I stared at him.

"Oh, my God, it's just not happening. Lee, I don't know what I'm doing out there. Hughes is the show. Do *you* think I could do it myself? Of course not."

"Well, we've got to do something. Maybe we could get Nelson Benton or Barry Serafin up here to do it with you. But we've got a real problem on our hands, and there may be no choice but for you to do it yourself. We'll talk to Gordon."

I thought about it for a long time. I was sitting on the sofa staring at a large map that covered Townsend's wall, thinking, "There's no way I could write a worse scenario." Then I began to think about what would happen if I did do the show alone. Maybe then there would be a backlash of sympathy, maybe they would say, "Isn't she a great little trooper," maybe they would give me credit for being able to handle a whole hour live news show alone with exactly two days of TV experience. I could do it, by God. I would do it.

"Of course," I said to Lee, who had been staring at the wall. "Of course I'll do it if I have to. You can count on me."

Hughes came back from the studio a few minutes later and Lee took him in and told him about his mother. He wasn't too shocked because she had been quite sick. He would, of course, go out to Kansas, but he would ask them to postpone the funeral until Saturday so that he could finish the week's shows. I thought then that Hughes was terribly brave. I also had the thought that it was too bad that I wouldn't get my big chance to star alone, to show the world I could do it. It made me feel ashamed.

Hughes talked quietly to people. He didn't want to go home alone. I had to get home because I felt so crummy. I went back into my office to gather my things.

There was a pile of reviews on my desk. No note or clue as to who had left them there. Some were clips, others were wire stories. I put them all in a manila envelope without looking at them. Warren had promised me that he would tell me about the good ones, or at least the good parts, and I would just never know about the bad ones. If I were going to get any better I simply couldn't read terrible things about myself. And at this point there were too many terrible things. I would wait a month or two.

After I left television, I sat down one rainy Saturday in February when I was alone and forced myself to read them all. I sat on my bed and sobbed as I read each review over and over and remembered the pain. I wanted to explain things to the critics, who had so much to criticize legitimately about CBS and about my ineptitude and lack of experience, but who instead contented themselves with cutting personal attacks. Now with some time in between and less subjectivity, I still don't think I have ever seen anyone in a performing situation come under such personal attack. And I still can't explain it.

Here are a few excerpts from the reviews I read that dreary February Saturday:

A headline in *Newsday*, "A Sex Symbol Off to a Dull Start," led a review by critic Marvin Kitman.

Sally Quinn, the great blonde hope at CBS, was a major disappointment in her premiere as a female sex symbol. With her political contacts in Washington, it was expected that she would bring some important news from the bathroom or bedroom. But the only intimate details she presented the first day were about herself: Her parents expected her to clean up her room as a child, and she was making her debut as a TV newscaster with a cold and a fever. This last was in the tradition of the show having to go on. But it left you wondering why that is so. . . . That *New York* Magazine article about her private life, I expected, would make it impossible for anybody to watch her without thinking of her private life. But after watching her yesterday morning I didn't care what her sex life was—she came across on camera as a very dull person, even if she is a good reporter.

Commentator Nicholas von Hoffman warned us that Sally wasn't a glamor girl but a good reporter. Everybody tells us she's a good reporter—even the CBS publicity department, trying frantically to disavow all that sexpot publicity, an effort that is very Nixonian in saying one thing and meaning another. The network hired her because she was a sexpot, but they don't want anyone to say she's a sexpot. An auxiliary to this kind of double-speak is: We don't want any publicity, but, thank God she got the cover of *New York* Magazine. . . .

Sally Quinn is bound to improve as a good sex symbol. Eventually, she may even replace Barbara Walters in the fantasies of early risers. . . .

Kay Gardella from the New York *Daily News*:

A blonde sex bomb? A city-room Tokyo Rose? A deadly, scrumptious threat to Barbara Walters? The new co-host of the *CBS Morning News* was dubbed all these things and more in a giddy salvo of magazine stories and newspaper features.

The result, at least in Sally Quinn's 7 A.M. premiere yesterday, was less than had been promised. . . . Somewhere along the line CBS News apparently had uneasy thoughts about Sally's buildup. So, on the first show, a *Washington Post* colleague of Miss Quinn's, Nicholas von Hoffman, was tapped to say a corrective word or two about Sally. He assured viewers that in Miss Quinn they were not getting a sexy personality who had titillated half of Washington, but rather a competent newsgal.

The *Village Voice* review was by someone I never heard of before, called Roslyn Locks.

Touted variously as sex-bomb, brilliant newswoman (four years of society reporting on *The Washington Post*), glamor girl, and "star material" in the publicity lavished on her beforehand, CBS TV's new "Morning News" anchorwoman is something of a let-down in Monday morning's debut. . . . Nicholas von Hoffman comes on in Sally's behalf. . . . Deploring some of the sappy stories that have gotten out (*New York* Magazine's cock count?)

von Hoffman assures us that "You're not getting a glamorous sex bomb in Sally." We're already—yawn—privy to THAT much.

Tom Donnelly in *The Washington Post*:

CBS, with more than a little help from *New York* Magazine, the wire services and the news media in general, has been promoting Sally Quinn in a manner worthy of yesterday's Hollywood, when there was always a brand new blonde bombshell to be sold by Metro or Fox, usually with none too subtle hints that a veteran blonde bombshell at Paramount or Warners was headed for oblivion: "The Yuuuumph Girl" vs "The Pinggg! Girl." . . . On the basis of a four day sampling, I'd say the new CBS Morning News is exactly the kind of program you'd get if a lot of people with no new ideas for a morning news show got together and put on a morning news show.

And he goes on to report the dismal quotes, ad libs, lack of preparation, etc., that we have already heard about. But there were two things about Donnelly's review that made me furious and frustrated because I thought they were so unfair. One was this: "At this stage, Sally Quinn doesn't do a lot for the show. She is not a smooth, assured, experienced newscaster like Leslie Stahl, who popped up a couple of times to show us how it's done."

That drove me crazy. Leslie is a friend and I respect her professionalism. But she had done several one-minute standuppers, written beforehand, on the *Morning News*. That is a different thing from one solid hour, live.

The other thing he wrote that annoyed me was this about Barbara Walters: "She had a lot of trouble saying the word 'exhibit' yesterday, she gave a humorous grimace, repeated it a couple of times, smiled in triumph at her success. It was a nice little fumble and recovery: we don't want machines on our morning shows, do we?"

I had done the same thing with Phnom Penh and Donnelly hadn't celebrated my nice little fumble and recovery.

Frank Getlein in the *Washington Star* reported:

She has not been happy in her comments . . . and her persona, so far, is that of a bright adolescent in over her depth and trying to sneak through by saying little. . . . Together they come on a bit like Edward Everett Horton without the nervousness and Bonita Granville playing his niece, just out of school and ready for the great wide world. Ms. Quinn has yet to appear as anything like as attractive as she is in still photographs or as sharp as she is in print.

Time Magazine:

Overall, the first impression was a letdown after the advance publicity that suggested Quinn would threaten Today show hostess Barbara Walters' ten-year feminine hegemony on early-bird TV.

Newsweek:

The . . . CBS high command is anything but cavalier about the new Morning News. With Sally Quinn as its great blonde hope, the network is bidding for a slice of its early morning ratings action, which has been resolutely dominated for the past 21 years by NBC's Today Show. . . . "They were looking for a starlet," scoffed one member of the CBS News team, "instead of a good television journalist." But judging from Miss Quinn's gaffe-plagued first week, CBS may have gotten neither.

It wasn't all horrible. There were two reviews which made the others bearable.

Ron Powers, a Pulitzer Prize winner from the *Chicago Sun-Times* began his review:

A little kindness is needed here. Sally Quinn is a bright, dedicated and certifiably superior print journalist who has distinguished herself at the *Washington Post*. Hughes Rudd is a veteran broadcaster of unexampled humanity, depth and perception.

The fact that the two of them are lamentably unsuited as a co-anchor team for the "reorganized" or "readjusted" or whatever the flacks are calling it . . . let's say the "new"—CBS Morning News should not be the occasion for personal ridicule directed at either of them. There was more than enough of that in advance on Monday's premier, most of it an eastern neosexist canard directed at Miss Quinn's image as a Washington glamour queen.

And all of it ignored the essential point that CBS, its big black eye greedily ogling the artist and ratings superiority of NBC's Today Show, was using the Quinn and Rudd personalities as ingredients in a synthetic "package" to attract the curious. This "package" owes its mentality to evening prime time entertainment, not news; it is designed specifically to get results (massive herds of viewers) right now. Not next October. . . . given this unreal context in which to announce and discuss news, Quinn and Rudd did their trouperish best to live up to CBS' ambitious vision. . . . on the whole the premier came off as an inept use of two talented people and a cheap shot at the image of the Today Show, television's most completely realized program.

One review I had read at the time was Cyclops' (a nom de plume of John Leonard) in *The New York Times*. I was not happy that Cyclops felt it necessary to put down Barbara Walters to build me up. Couldn't both of us have both good and bad features without Barbara being accused of an abrasive harsh approach, or Sally a snotty, Eastern debutante manner? Still, since I had so few favorable reviews, I was somewhat bolstered by Leonard's piece.

. . . the question is whether you prefer waking up in the morning with Barbara Walters or Sally Quinn.

Quinn has my vote—because of her high cheekbones, and because she never said Richard Nixon is sexy, and because she doesn't mumble or fidget, and flounder around as though the English language were a maddened duck attacking her. Nor is she obliged to sit in a studio that looks like a command module for a Mars landing, with Frank Blair [newscaster Lew Wood's predecessor] as the computer print-out. However, since most of the people who watch early morning TV are said to be women, Quinn's handsomeness and self-possession may be to her disadvantage. With Walters, it is possible to pretend that anybody can get a job on television. The attitude of her admirers toward her is both avuncular and slightly condescending. . . . With Quinn, television seems to be a nice place to visit for an upperclass rich girl who got bored on the Côte d'Azur. The terrible truth of the matter is that Quinn seems somewhat stuck-up.

I believe that this stuckuppityness is a mask or manner to paper over camera qualms. She is an amateur, of considerable intelligence and charm, but still an amateur, with no real notion of who might be out there in the armpit of America, grunting at what she says.

Hughes Rudd is intelligent, has a fine gravelly voice, knows how to be angry, consorts with wit and can write. Hughes Rudd in one week has become the best anchorperson on TV, Cronkite's larynx notwithstanding.

But earlier, when I was still on the program, I had talked to Barbara Walters about how to cope emotionally with bad reviews. She had told me it still upset her so she simply did not read them. And she warned me about a reviewer on the West Coast who had once written a vicious review of her, which had nearly killed her. Apparently, he had written an equally vicious one about me, and I should not read it. I took her advice until a few months ago, when I asked a friend of mine to send it to me. Barbara was right. The reviewer for the *San Francisco Chronicle* was Terence O'Flaherty. He wrote: "I could only conclude that someone at CBS either hates women as newscasters in general or likes one woman too much."

Barbara brought up the Cyclops review. She had been away and when she came back she found it in her typewriter so she had read it. "Still, I can't help myself. I just get terribly upset by personal attacks. But it gets better and you get more and more able to handle it. Just take heart in that."

Berry sent me an original drawing for his cartoon "Berry's World." A man is sitting at the breakfast table drinking coffee and watching TV. A haggy old wife in rollers and a wrapper is screeching at him, "I don't like the way you're looking at Sally Quinn." I know he meant it to be flattering, but it depressed me more than anything else.

Townsend came into my office after the broadcast Wednesday morning to tell me that I could watch the show rebroadcast at 10:00 A.M., as it was every morning, over closed circuit. This is so that the executives who drive in from Long Island or Connecticut can see it.

I said no, that I couldn't bear to watch myself on TV. That, in fact, I couldn't stand to look at pictures of myself. The few times I had seen myself on TV I had been horrified at my voice, my gestures, my appearance, everything. In fact I couldn't even stand to listen to a tape recording of my voice. Besides, I was too sick. I went home, crawled into bed, unplugged the telephone, and stared at the ceiling most of the day, listening to the sound of the buses roaring by on Riverside Drive and the children playing outside. Occasionally I would plug in the phone and call my mother or Warren and they would tell me how wonderful I was. I couldn't sleep even with the medicine. For one thing, I was coughing too much. I lay there all day and finally around 9:30 I went to sleep. I didn't hear.

The alarm went off at 1:17. I got up, threw on my clothes, and ran down to the limousine in exactly thirteen minutes. I hadn't done anything with my hair or face. I didn't care. It was terribly hot and couples along the street were coming home from their evenings out, holding hands and walking arm in arm, stopping to kiss on the street as the limousine purred its way down Broadway to Hughes's apartment.

I'll never be able to do that again, I thought, rather dramatically.

Hughes crawled into the back of the limousine.

"Did you get any sleep?"

"No, did you?"

"Oh, shit, no." He lit up a cigarette. We rode the rest of the way in silence.

Every day the first thing one of us asked the other was if he had gotten enough sleep. Sleep was everything. It was our major preoccupation. If I wasn't sleeping I was trying to sleep or worrying about whether or not I would be able to sleep. I know now that there's not enough money in the world to make it worthwhile to go without enough sleep.

When I got to the office I went to my cubbyhole and found a stack of mail. I was to get into the habit of reading some of it before I did anything else.

For the first month or so a lot of it centered around my personal life. They didn't like it. This Thursday morning there was a postcard for Salant: "Dr. Mr. Salant—I shall *not* watch Sally Quinn until she marries the character she's living with. What's going on with you people anyway? Include me out! Sincerely J. Joyce."

It was from the Bronx. I wondered whether it was a literary put on. One thing, J. Joyce was watching. On the top of the postcard Salant had scribbled, "For Chrissake—we need every viewer. Will you *please* discuss this with Warren?—DS."

If I ever see him again, I thought.

I did my lead-in's and tried to put together something on grocery prices from the wires. After a while I went back to my office and lay down. When Edith came in around six, I just groaned and asked her not to turn on the lights until the rollers had heated up.

"How are you, lovee?" she crooned and I felt better. I wasn't nervous and today was a big day. After the show, we were to tape an interview with a woman stockbroker. I knew nothing about Wall Street. I'd never owned a stock and had never balanced my bank book. Also, I had never done a TV interview.

"*Tiens*," I said out loud. We used to say that a lot at Smith when we were nervous but wanted to seem cool. Maybe it was that kind of comment Cyclops meant when he said I seemed snotty and didn't appeal to the armpit of America.

Our big interview that morning was with Samuel Dash, the chief attorney for the Democratic majority on the Senate Watergate Committee. As Hughes and I were settling into our chairs and Betty was pouring our coffee and tea, we put on our Telexes and heard a ruckus.

Then Townsend rushed in to tell us that Dash had canceled.

"What are we going to do to fill up that fourteen-minute gap?" I asked Townsend.

"Ad-lib," he said without a smile.

Everything seemed so unbelievable that I was beginning to accept the worst atrocities as normal.

We used some film pieces and filled in with more news for the Dash gap. It started out all right—and spiraled downward. I read a report on the decrease in crime statistics. We had over a minute to ad-lib, I heard through the Telex.

QUINN: I don't see the news of this decrease as anything to rejoice over. It doesn't sound very—for instance, yesterday I learned that a man on my block had been stabbed to death. And I was just sort of told that as a matter of fact—"Oh, by the way"

—and it happened at 11 o'clock in the evening on the way home from the theater.

HUGHES: Well, I think that around the country, outside of, oh, Chicago, Los Angeles, Kansas City, New York, in smaller towns and cities surely it isn't this bad. I can't believe that it is.

QUINN: Well, it's not—I mean, there are some places, obviously, but way out in the woods, where people do still boast about being able to go out and leave their doors unlocked. But then you have cases like the Clutter family. [The murdered family Truman Capote wrote about in *In Cold Blood*.]

HUGHES: Yeah. . . .

At the end of the program there was an ad lib about French bread and plastic eggs with ketchup on them and there were some good film pieces and news reports, but that was not what the critics were watching for, nor is it what I remember.

The woman who was to be interviewed was waiting in my office. Rickey had made her up and she was a nervous wreck. She could hardly speak, and she confessed to me in a frightened whisper that she had never done a television interview in her life.

I thought I would try to cheer her up. "Neither have I," I said brightly.

I don't think I have ever seen such a look of terror. Oddly, I find that other people's fear makes me feel calmer and more confident. And I am always surprised at how scared people get when they go on television. Even if the interview is taped. That cold, unfeeling eye stares at you.

The interview was a bomb. The woman's mouth was so dry you could hear her tongue scratching, and she sat rigidly and answered our questions as though she were a computer. I asked questions: "If you were I, what would you do with your money?" She froze.

It was after the interview that I panicked. Is this what all my interviews would be like?

Townsend said it was great. It never ran.

I went home immediately after the show, stayed in bed all day, and only fell asleep late that night. When the limousine picked me up I was dazed from exhaustion. I couldn't seem to get better, even with all the rest and the medicine, because I couldn't sleep. Nor did I know that I would start out this day with another foray into snobbism which would be pounced upon as one more example of how I could never appeal to the masses.

I was to open the show with a tellstory. I found a little wire story about horse meat and wrote it up. Then someone asked why didn't I do one of those great little Washington essays that I had done on the pilot. Well, I pointed out, I hadn't been in Washington in about six weeks and I didn't really know what was going on.

I was told to try anyway.

I remembered a conversation I had had with Nick von Hoffman earlier in the week, in which he told me he had run into Henry Kissinger and Kissinger had offered him a ride home in his limousine. Nick said that with Watergate and everything, they had to fumble around for a safe conversation and finally, after several moments of silence, Kissinger had asked Nick what he thought of Rockefeller's chances to run for President. We had both thought that was terribly funny, so I decided to write a short essay about it.

Thursday is Chinese day. That means that we order carry-out Chinese food for "lunch," which is usually about 3 A.M. Everyone looks forward to Thursday because you don't have to go downstairs to the Bay of Pigs, which is presided over by someone of misty ethnic origins named Oscar. He is very good-natured, too good-natured for that hour of the morning, and much too good-natured considering the slop he had to ladle out to the unfortunates who work the lobster shift.

I think I ordered beef with snow pea pods. When it came, everybody sat around the Bullpen pushing copy and eating this aromatic Chinese food (Jackie Hadley always had shrimp egg foo yong, which has a rather strong odor if you're not feeling too well). It was a macabre sight.

I left without finishing my pea pods and went to lie down until Edith and Rickey came. We were to tape an interview with Gay Talese, who was writing a book about sex in America. "Great," I told Hughes. "You'll just have to conduct the whole interview because there is no way I'm going to talk about sex the first week on television after all the publicity and reviews."

Hughes laughed and told me not to worry, that he would ask all the dirty questions.

Hughes opened the show with headlines, then passed it to me, for my tellstory.

QUINN: Well, before we start talking about food prices, there are still some more beef stories around. If your butcher seems to have a large supply of beef on hand it might be worth your while to check the source of his supply. What you're eating at home with a nice bottle of Beaujolais and some béarnaise just might be horse meat. In some places, of course, horse meat can be sold legally and openly. But the owner of a Cicero, Illinois, meat shop was just fined $510 for selling horse meat cut to look like regular steak. Officials say Nicholas Cardamone had been getting the horse meat in Wisconsin, where it's used to make dog food. Well, it's not that we may not be reduced to eating dog food before long, but it would be nice to know it. That way at least you wouldn't buy quite such a good bottle of wine.

But that wasn't the end. No, there was still my little Washington story.

QUINN: Summer is always a pretty dead time for those who have to stay in the city, but it's especially dead for Washingtonians. Congress is usually adjourned; political, embassy and White

House functions slow down to a halt; and so does conversation, which normally centers around the political scene. Part of this summer was saved, socially at least, by the Watergate hearings, which did keep conversation going and minimal political social activity worthwhile. It still remains to be seen whether the latest news about Agnew will keep things lively or not. A vice presidential scandal is never quite as riveting as a Presidential scandal. What any prominent host or hostess in Washington does not need is a drawn-out discussion of the wheat deal, unless, of course, it involves scandal. Not only that, but people are wary these days of being bugged, and who knows what recording machines lie under what Belgian-lace tablecloths? This, of course, puts a terrible strain on members of the Administration, who really have few topics which are comfortable to discuss. Henry Kissinger has been trying valiantly to draw attention away from Watergate by talking about the Administration's foreign policy achievements. But you can only talk about that so long before you get dropped from the invitation lists. Uncontroversial issues are hard to come up with, but Kissinger made a big effort recently when he ran into an acquaintance who was not of his political bent. After greeting each other and exchanging a few pleasantries, there was a short pause as Kissinger cleared his throat, then turned to his friend and asked, "What do you think of Rockefeller's chances?"

It didn't make it. I knew it when I wrote it. I knew it when I read it. It was forced and contrived and stupid. Why did I do it? Why did they let me? I began to question myself. It was the beginning of a rapid decline in my confidence as a writer (I began to forget what that meant), which deteriorated so badly that I began to think I would never write anything again.

After the show we had the Talese interview. It was a perfectly adequate interview, with Hughes asking all the provocative questions and me, most uncharacteristically, asking how his other books had sold and other boring questions. But mostly I just nodded and said, "Uh huh," trying to create a sympathetic atmosphere.

Afterward everybody said it was terrific. It never ran. Later I found out why. It wasn't terrific. Apparently you couldn't hear any of Talese's answers because all the mike picked up was my "uh huh's." Nobody ever told me this, and I often wondered in my paranoid state why it hadn't run. If I had known, it would have been a relatively easy thing to correct.

I went home and to bed and stayed there all day. My cough was still terrible and I was weak, but I was beginning to feel better. Besides, tomorrow would be Friday.

When Hughes got in the limousine that morning he said, "Hunter's coming today."

"Have you prepared your questions for the interview?" I asked Hughes.

"It wouldn't make any difference if I had," said Hughes. "He wouldn't answer them anyway."

Hunter Thompson was at the studio when we arrived. He wasn't supposed to arrive until after the show.

Hunter Thompson is the "political correspondent" for *Rolling Stone*. He is a brilliant writer and what you might call a "new journalist." Allegedly Hunter once defended his brand of journalism by saying, "Well, I would say that over forty-five per cent of everything I write is true."

Hunter once ran for sheriff of Aspen, Colorado, on the Freak ticket and he is thought by some to be crazy. Hughes thinks Hunter is the sanest person he knows. I'm not sure I don't too. But, nevertheless, he wasn't supposed to be there at 1 A.M. He had brought a friend, to whom I was never formally introduced, and several six-packs "to last them through the night." Hunter was wearing his usual short-sleeved Hawaiian-print shirt, heavy-duty Keds, and his head was closely shaved, as usual.

I have an image of Hunter flapping around, but I can't really remember much else about what he did except that at one point Hughes gently reminded him that he was here as our guest and that we just assumed he understood he was not to write about this experience.

"Shit," said Hunter, looking bewildered. "I've got to. I've already sold this story to a magazine for several thousand dollars."

"Hunter," said Hughes, "you're not going to write about it. You're supposed to be here for an interview at 8 A.M. Unless you promise us, we'll have to throw you out."

"Hunter," I said, *The New York Times* wanted to send a reporter and a photographer down here to spend the night with us and we refused. We can't tell some people no and then let others in."

"Okay," said Hunter. "I promise."

I don't know why, but I believed him. So did Hughes. So far he hasn't written anything.

When Edith arrived I went in to have my hair rolled up. Hunter came in, leaned up against the door, and watched. Hunter has a way of zeroing in on the problem.

"You're sick," he said to me.

"You said it," I said back to him.

"No, not that kind of sick," he said. "I mean mentally ill. Anyone who would do this job has got to be really crazy. So maybe you get a lot of money. But there's not enough money in the world that can pay you to live this kind of insane life. You're like the people who rob banks and stash the money away and spend seven years in jail so they'll be rich when they get out. But they still have to spend all that time in jail. What kind of life is that? You're a writer. So is Hughes. This isn't writing. This isn't journalism. This is bullshit."

Edith was fuming. "You need a bath," she told Hunter.

Hunter looked at Edith in disbelief.

Edith took Hunter by the arm and led him away. As they were going down the hall I heard Edith say. "I'm taking you upstairs to the ladies' room of the *Edge of Night* studio. They have showers up there. I'll stand outside and guard the door."

The interview with Hunter was a total loss. Neither Hughes nor I knew what to ask him, and we never did understand his answers. It was somewhat free-form.

Nobody said it was terrific.

The first week was over. Suddenly I didn't feel so sick. I decided I would go shopping to try to find some clothes with my great big fat clothes allowance. Everything I owned was blue and I had been wearing, for the past week, the few things I did have that were other colors. One was a heavy red winter sweater, another was a black winter sweater and I had nearly died in the studio under those hot lights. The yellow safari jacket I wore the first day brought out the yellow in my teeth and made me look like I had jaundice.

So I wandered around Madison Avenue, but I couldn't find anything that didn't have blue in it that looked pretty on me that was summery. I finally ended up with one black-and-red-and-white pullover, and I was about to faint from heat prostration and weakness. I had left on my stage makeup and it had begun to cake into my pores; my hair was dirty because I hadn't wanted to wash it while I was sick. My outfit was wrinkled because I'd been lying down in it.

For some reason I decided to take a bus home to Riverside Drive. A holdover from my frugal days. Plus, I think there was an element of—"I want to keep on being one of the people even though I'm a rich and famous star." That meant walking across 57th Street from Fifth Avenue, standing in line in the 90-degree heat, and standing on a hot, crowded Number 5 bus. I grabbed hold of a strap, clutched my package, and jiggled along with the rest.

Suddenly, a young woman sitting below me, pointed her finger at me and yelled, "Hey, I know you. You're Sally Quinn, the new TV star. I saw you on the *Morning News*."

Everybody turned and stared.

I could hear mumbles and whispers of, "That's really Sally Quinn," and, "A celebrity, right here on the Number 5 bus."

People started pushing and shoving to get a better look at me; women were holding the newspaper in my face to autograph (with no hands?); the woman who had identified me kept asking me what it felt like.

I kept apologizing about how I hadn't expected to be recognized, because my hair was dirty, and my makeup, and "It's so embarrassing, I'm not used to this. . . ." Mercifully, the ride came to an end and I collapsed in my bed for the rest of the evening.

Somehow that was not the way I had pictured "celebrity." It was my first taste of it and I didn't like it.

Warren and I had planned to go visit Ann and Walter Pincus on Martha's Vineyard for the weekend. We were to catch the 7:15 A.M. flight out of Kennedy airport on Saturday morning. We got up very early, which was fine with me. I had been awake since 3. We drove out to Kennedy, parked the car, took a bus from the lot to the airport, and arrived just in time to see our plane pulling out on the runway. The airline official had put the wrong time on the flight. The plane left at 7:05. We took the bus back to the car, drove back to New York and spent the rest of the weekend doing nothing.

I knew it was an omen.

During the first week, I had not seen or heard from Gordon. I debated whether or not to call him or leave a message, but then I figured if he wanted to see me he would have come back or sent a note. I will never understand why, after the first show, he didn't come screaming back to the *Morning News* and fire everybody, or put Hughes on with straight news, tell the world I had terminal pneumonia, and send me away to some hideaway studio in Connecticut with his trustiest producers and cameramen to work me over.

As far as I knew, nobody had seen or heard from Gordon. I waited each day for him to ask me into his office and explain gently that I needed some kind of training; that they were going to change the format, get a new set and a jazzy producer, set me up with taped interviews, get me out of reading the news, get me voice lessons, make me put on contact lenses, and demand that I grow my hair longer and cut out the ad libs.

Nothing.

The broadcast Monday was uneventful, including my first live television interview. It was—I still have a hard time believing this was the best person CBS could think of for my TV interview debut—the designer Emilio Pucci. I discovered that he was branching out from lingerie into sheets and men's wear.

Hughes did not participate. He wasn't all that anxious to, didn't particularly like to do interviews, and I'm sure he didn't have all that much to talk to Pucci about anyway, except the fact that they were both World War II pilots.

I called Gordon and left a message after the show. I was told he was out. Gordon soon became for me a Major Major Major figure from *Catch-22*. Hard to reach.

I felt better this week so I had a few lunches with Hughes and one with the producers, Lee Townsend, Helen Moed, Harry Griggs, and Hughes. I liked Helen and Harry and admired them both, but I felt from the beginning that they were both hard-news oriented and I also felt that the broadcast should have at least one hard-news type and one showbiz, razzmatazz person if we were going to compete with anybody. Hughes and I felt that the format didn't have enough spark or imagination. We felt there should be more humor, whimsy and certainly a lot more offbeat stuff. We wanted midgets and mean cab drivers, as well as the standard timely "Tell me, Senator, do you think the Vice President will resign" kind of thing.

The staff lunches we had were usually held in a little

French restaurant called the Mont St. Michel, on 57th Street, which is next to a good French restaurant. It was dark, dreary, depressing, had terrible food and worse service.

Hughes loved it there because he could *bavarder avec le patron*. After a preliminary discussion of what to do about the broadcast, during which nobody agreed, the SOP was for Hughes and me to concentrate very hard on getting drunk. He had discovered the previous week, as I was beginning to find out, that the only way to sleep in the afternoon was to get drunk enough to pass out. One day we each drank two full bottles of wine for lunch. I reeled out of the restaurant, got into a cab, staggered to my apartment, and took a shower, and fell several times. In bed everything swirled around so that I was nauseated. I put one hand and one foot on the floor and stayed that way with my eyes open until I did pass out, around 9 P.M. When I got up at 1 A.M. I was still drunk, and I didn't sober up until around 4. Then I had such a terrible hangover I had to lie down until it was time to go on the air.

So, each day by lunch time I had to make a decision. Should I get drunk and pass out, assured that I would sleep but also that I would feel awful the next morning, or should I have, maybe, one glass and go home to stare at the ceiling and then feel horrible because I hadn't had any sleep?

It was six of one. Usually I chose to get drunk.

During that second week I came out of my apartment one night and ran into a big burly man snapping my picture.

I screamed, threw my hands in front of my face, and ran back inside, yelling to the doorman to make him go away. The *paparazzi*, I thought. They're going to plague me the way they do Jackie. Maybe it's Ron Galella. I'll never have any privacy again. My mind raced to what I would wear in the courtroom when I sued Ron Galella to stay at least fifty yards away from me.

"Relax, sweetheart," I heard a gruff New York voice. "I'm

the photographer from CBS. Didn't they tell you I was coming along on the ride this morning?"

I was disappointed.

As usual, I hadn't done my hair or put on any makeup and I looked awful. He kept saying how great the before and after would be. When we picked up Hughes he acted as though a gnat were flying around in front of his eyes. But he seemed to remember someone saying something about an article for *Columbine,* the CBS house organ. Later that day someone called me for an interview. I was so suspicious by this time that I said I would call back, just to make sure it was *Columbine.*

The interview was the only really positive one written about me, but I had to laugh at one part.

"On the initial program an attack of the flu so bugged correspondent Quinn that she went to the hospital for emergency temporary relief. Still she let fly typical arrows of wit. After a Marshall Efron sketch that used money as a food substitute, Sally Quinn held up the cleansed props. She explained that no currency had been destroyed in violation of the law, 'which proves you don't have to send your money to Mexico to have it laundered.' "

It was, of course, the part I hadn't written myself.

Tuesday we ran an interview with Doris Kearns, a Harvard historian, which we had taped earlier. First as a White House Fellow, then on the Presidential staff, she had developed a friendship with Lyndon Johnson and was writing a much-discussed book about him. I thought the interview had gone well and so did everyone else. I was horrified when I saw it on Tuesday morning. I had done the same thing I was later to learn I had done with Talese, only not quite as bad.

After watching it on the monitor, in the middle of the broadcast, I was so embarrassed I could barely continue. It was the first time I had seen myself perform on television.

Doris was interesting and amusing, but most of what could be heard was my saying "uh huh."

The rest of the week was uneventful as to gaffes. On Tuesday we had had a report on striking cab drivers and I had allowed as how "they've got to live too." We had a piece about an old mill and I said I'd rather be there than "whirling around in outer space with the astronauts." On Thursday I got back to death and destruction. "I heard about a man who literally shot another—on a porch, at a deer that was on the man's porch." On canning: "If you don't get the right amount of air inside or outside, you can get diseases like botulism."

Friday was my big day. For the first time I made no terrible faux pas, didn't trip over any words reading the TelePrompTer, did a good essay, and conducted my second live interview fairly professionally.

My essay was prompted by a wire story we had seen that night about Mae West.

"When a famous beauty reaches forty, it's really big news. You might remember, Elizabeth Taylor had her picture on the cover of *Life* Magazine with headlines: 'Elizabeth Taylor Turns Forty.' As though it were an obituary. This country seems to be obsessed with youth, both for men and women. Old age just doesn't make it. Even men are beginning to dye their hair and lie about their ages. But for women it just gets worse. A woman past the first blush of youth is condemned for the rest of her life to hear compliments like, 'Well, she doesn't have a bad figure for her age,' or, 'She certainly is well preserved.' Women over a certain age learn that they can't wear long hair, that certain clothes styles are too young, that they must grow old gracefully. Husbands can leave their wives for younger women with hardly an eyebrow raised; but if a woman runs off with a younger man she's thought to be ridiculous. People feel sorry for her. 'Poor thing.' 'What a fool.' 'He'll never stay with her.' I asked a man recently who was married to a woman twenty years younger how he would feel if his wife were twenty years older than he was. And he looked at me in astonishment and replied, 'But it just doesn't work that way.' Well, sometimes it does. More and more women are deciding that being saddled with age is what's really ridiculous. And there's one woman who has refused for the last fifty years to get into her rocking chair and do her granny number. And that woman is Mae West, who turns eighty-one years old today. Mae West still wears plunging necklines, body-hugging clothes, false eyelashes and blonde wigs; she still works out on her bicycle machine each day, and she still lifts 15-pound weights. A lot of people laugh at Mae West. They say she's grotesque and absurd, that her way of dressing and acting is tasteless. But Mae West laughs back. 'They still come up and see me,' she said the other day. And they do. 'I still get diamonds from young men seventeen, eighteen, nineteen and twenty. They write letters. I send them pictures. And they come up and see me.' And she's still going at it too. She's just finished a book called *Sex Drive,* the stories of her battles with censorship in the 1930's. And who knows—she might even make another movie. One might think Mae West is some kind of weird anachronism, but she has had the courage to go against the prevailing social attitudes about women and old age, and that's not easy. But it does have its rewards. As she pointed out to a visitor the other day, 'Those yellow roses on the table over there are from a young admirer.' So, for Mae West then, it does work that way."

The interview was with John Emmet Hughes, a former White House advisor to Eisenhower. He was nervous, perspiring, and his hands were shaking. It could have been the early morning DTs, but nevertheless his fears calmed me, and I managed to get through an interview about the Presidency without disaster. I was feeling good. I decided that I had redeemed myself with the women—because of my essay, and because I had clearly been prepared for my interview, proving to the world that I-had-a-mind-as-well-as-a-body.

Warren and I went to Barbara Howar's in Easthampton that weekend and I slept at all the wrong times—for instance, at the table in the middle of dinner. The rest of the time I sat there in a sort of zombielike state, not really entering the conversations, many of which were spent avoiding the topic of my budding television career. It was my first taste of what life was going to be like, and I hated it. Warren hated it, too. He had been as cooperative and considerate as any human being could have been with my fear, hysteria, illness, sleep schedule, depression and total loss of humor. But I could tell it was beginning to get to him. His patience with me was being strained and I couldn't blame him, only I just didn't know what to do. I despaired particularly at 3 or 4 in the morning, when I would automatically wake up and not be able to sleep again. I felt so alone and helpless as I lay there all those hours with the horror of my own thoughts. I tried to sleep in the car on the drive back to New York on Sunday, but when we arrived at 7:30 I hadn't slept a wink. Nor did I get to sleep for hours.

Monday morning I felt horrible, but I was learning that I would always feel horrible. At about 4:30 I got a call at the office from Warren Beatty. "Don't pay any attention to those reviews," he said. "I've been watching you, and you're going to be all right. It'll take some time, but you're going to be good. You just have gotten really screwed by CBS. I've never seen anything like it."

I felt better, but I still couldn't pick myself up. Each morning about 4 A.M. I had to lie down just in order to be able to make it on the air.

I still hadn't heard from Gordon. Finally in the middle of the third week I got a call from his secretary asking if we could have lunch the next day. That night I didn't sleep at all. When the alarm rang at 1:17 I dressed and dragged myself down into the limousine. I could barely write my copy and finally I lay down in my office. After the broadcast I called Dr. Miller and he said he would see me. I explained that I just couldn't keep myself together, that I couldn't sleep or eat, and that I was tired and nauseated all the time. He examined me, pronounced me over the flu, but said I did seem a bit run down.

"Let me give you a vitamin shot."

"What kind?" I asked.

"Just a vitamin B$_{12}$," he said. "It'll fix you right up."

"I know, but what about feeling crummy all the time?" I asked him. "I don't want to just be fixed up today."

"Well, I recommend that you come in two or three times a week for these vitamin shots. There are other vitamin shots you can take, too, and they really keep you going. I have a lot of patients who are on television and most of them take these shots regularly. They really do wonders for you."

I was upset. The whole thing smacked of the Dr. Feelgood syndrome, and the constant shots and vitamins that John Kennedy allegedly had taken. And all those jet-setters.

"Dr. Miller," I said, "I don't want to have to live that way. I don't want to have to live bolstered up by shots and medicines all the time. That's just no life at all."

"But, darling," he said, "that's the life you have chosen."

I checked around. Dr. Miller was right. Most of the on-camera people I talked to took vitamin shots. I never did. Finally he advised me to take Unicap Therapeutic vitamin pills. I did, but as far as I could tell, they never did any good.

I felt too bad to go to lunch. Gordon and I made a date for the next day, and when I got to his office he seemed nervous and a little on edge, but he was making jokes as fast as he could. We got in the cab and he mentioned to the driver a place I'd never heard of. It's close," he said. "Very informal. I hope you'll like it."

We went to a little pub not far from CBS. Where one is taken to lunch says a lot. If you want to take someone's temperature in the television world, you measure where they take you to lunch.

This was bad news. A few college kids for waiters, too much air-conditioning, the no-reservations-we'll-have-a-table-in-few-minutes kind of place, and a choice of London broil, eggs benedict or bleu-cheese burgers.

Though I still felt sick, I had been looking forward to lunch because I would just pour it all out to Uncle Gordon and he would make it all right. I still hadn't gotten the message. I was sure once he heard how bad things were, he would do something right away. I was sure he had just been waiting to see how things went, and was trying to formulate just what changes needed to be made. What kind of help, advice, guidance I was going to require.

But, I decided, I would let him bring it up. We ordered drinks. I had a glass of Almadén, their best wine.

I had another glass. We gossiped about friends. We ordered lunch. They brought Gordon the wrong dish. We waited while he reordered. I had another glass of Almadén. We gossiped some more. I was getting drunk. They brought Gordon's lunch. I had finished mine. I ordered another glass of wine. We went on gossiping. We'd been there nearly two hours before I realized that Gordon had no intention of discussing the broadcast.

Just then we heard someone yelling our names from around the corner. I looked up and saw Mike Wallace, the CBS correspondent for *Sixty Minutes*. He was with several men I didn't recognize, and he was smiling and waving to us to come join them. Gordon waved back that he would. He paid the check and we went over. I was introduced to Don

Hewitt, the producer of *Sixty Minutes,* and two other men who were also producers on that show. We sat down. They started making cracks about the *Morning News,* riding me just a little. Mike was snide, I thought, but I kept smiling because I wanted to seem good-natured and a sport. I felt rather sick at my stomach because their remarks, though veiled, were derisive. Mike kept asking me with a smirk how it was going. I was embarrassed because I didn't know what to say. Gordon sat there looking uncomfortable and made jokes. It was a long cup of coffee. Finally I told Gordon that it was my bedtime and I had to get going.

As we were leaving, Hewitt called us back to the table. "Hey," he said to me, grinning. "I've got to tell you a great line. The day your show went on the air I went into Gordon's office and I said, 'Gordon, what's going on? You promised us *Deep Throat* and all we got was sore throat!'" He doubled over with laughter, and so did the others.

Gordon looked embarrassed. We left the restaurant without saying a word and got separate taxis.

I didn't see Gordon for a while, but I did come in one day that week to find a note scribbled on an envelope on my desk, saying that Arthur Taylor had liked one of my essays on women. Signed GM. I had done several. Not a single woman in the building had mentioned it. Only the president of the network.

While I was having lunch with Gordon, somewhere across town one of the major CBS correspondents was having lunch with Jack Schneider. Schneider, I have been told, has always resented the news side of CBS because they have done their best to make him feel lacking. He had been a salesman from Philadelphia, had worked his way up to CBS executive vice president, then after two years had gone back to being president of CBS Broadcast Group, which, though a powerful position, gave some the impression that he was out of the running for Paley's job. Everyone in the news area treated Schneider with disdain. He was a terrific broadcast salesman, they agreed, but that, for news people, is considered sort of a slimy profession. And Schneider comes on rather slick. He isn't their type, and they resent his influence over Paley and the fact that he has any influence over the news division. Gordon was the most disdainful. Schneider knew it and couldn't stand Gordon. He had begun to pick up vibes several years earlier that Gordon didn't have a very sophisticated understanding of television, and he had noticed that Bill Leonard, Gordon's counterpart for special events, had quietly started to put some distance between himself and Gordon.

Schneider was waiting for Gordon to make a big mistake.

"How's the *Morning News* going?" the correspondent asked Schneider at lunch.

"It's a disaster," he said.

"Well," asked the correspondent, "what are you going to do about it?"

"Nothing," said Schneider. "Just wait."

That third week, Jim Ganser, the producer who had told me that nobody would ever give me advice because I was a big star, gave me some advice. He came to my office one morning after the broadcast and told me I needed help. I fell on him with gratitude.

Each morning after the show he would go over that day's script, underlining the important words, and then I would read it into a tape recorder. The most important thing I learned from Jim was that you have to *sell* the news. That means you have to *punch* certain words that seem important.

"If you listen to a good newscaster," Jim pointed out, "you'll notice how he will speak almost in a singing voice, going up and down, occasionally hitting certain words. It's totally different from conversation, where you might not emphasize a word. On television, even if the meaning is not necessarily there, you must maintain a sort of cadence." For instance: "There's a *report* this morning, of *another* accidental U.S. *bombing* in *Cambodia. United Press International* says *four people* were *killed,* and the *toll* from *yesterday's* attack may be *higher* than the *three hundred killed* or *wounded* reported earlier."

"You would never talk that way in person but you've got to on television or you sound bored or unenthusiastic."

"I am," I told Ganser.

"Don't ever say that to anybody but me."

I took the recorder home and practiced, and then I went over it for about a half hour each day with Ganser, but I still couldn't quite get it. It just didn't seem important. Reading the wires and the newspapers, then rewriting stories into thirty-second tellstories and reading them over a TelePrompTer wasn't what I wanted. I just didn't give a damn. It showed.

The problem with trying to sell the news is that you read it with a different meaning. I got so that I was just punching and not paying attention to what I was saying. I was playacting the news and not absorbing it. I think I have never been more ill-informed than I was as an anchorperson on the *Morning News.* It amazes me now, going over the transcripts, to read major news stories that I was not even aware of while they were happening.

The superficiality bothered me. Major and complicated stories are condensed into a few seconds. Even if one could spend longer on them—two minutes is usually the limit—it would lose the audience. Most of what goes on the air is the barest bones of wire or newspaper stories that broke the night before. Sometimes the stories on air seem more comprehensive, because they are compilations of the stories from three or four papers, plus the wires. I wonder what would happen to television news if the Washington and New York papers and the two wires went on strike.

I was in trouble with the TelePrompTer too, Ganser told me. I was so afraid I would lose my place that I didn't look down at my script. The trick is to pretend that you're reading the whole thing from your script, but to remember enough so that you can keep looking at the audience. So I had to learn to read two or three lines from the page, then two or three lines from the prompter, then back to the script. That way I wouldn't get the glazed, zombie look that comes when it seems you've memorized an hour's worth of news. With Jim's coaching I finally mastered it, but I didn't feel as if I had achieved anything. Then the interviews. Apparently I had a tendency to jump in on people because I was afraid they would run out of things to say. I should be more relaxed and let them have their say. I also wasn't very good at controlling those who rambled on. Our sessions didn't last too long because Jim was sent out of town on an assignment.

I decided I needed a coach. I had run into a friend, Trish Riley, in the hallway. She had come from *Newsweek* to work at a local station and had been heavily coached from the moment she arrived. She was shocked to hear that I had had no voice training or coaching. I asked Townsend. He said he didn't care, it was up to me, but he had heard that Salant was against coaching for the network correspondents. He felt that it took away from the naturalness of the reading and made it all seem too glib and show-bizzy. He suggested I talk to Sandy Socolow. Sandy said sure, he had no objections. If I wanted a coach, I could get a coach. I said I was thinking about it. But then nobody seemed to know where to go, who was good or bad, or whether or not I could take it off my expense account (I heard they were $50 an hour, and in the shape I was in I was going to need a lot of hours). There was no enthusiasm at all for the idea and I never did anything about it. I'm not sure whether or not I did the right thing. I guess I knew it was only a matter of time before the nightmare would be over. I couldn't have cared all that much.

That week John Reiser, my agent's assistant, came over to the office to get me to sign some documents and sort out my financial arrangements. I wanted to go to the bank so he said he'd walk over with me. On the way, I turned to him.

"John, how do I quit?"

"What?"

"You heard me. How do I get out of this job? I hate it. I'll always hate it. It's not for me. It's a disaster. You know it and I know it and everybody else knows it. How do I quit?"

"Now calm down," said John. "It's not all that bad. You're discouraged but things will get better. But I'll tell you confidentially, Richard and I have discussed this whole thing and we've decided that we've seen a lot of horrible things happen on television but we've never seen them do anything as bad to anyone as they've done to you. And that's the truth. I don't blame you for feeling the way you do. But don't start talking about quitting now. It just isn't the right time."

"John," I said, "think of a way. It's just a matter of time. I've got to do it as gracefully as possible, but there's no way I can stand this job or this life much longer."

"Gordon's going to flip out," he said.

"Fine."

That week I sank even deeper into my upper-class-snob routine. It couldn't be helped. There was something compulsive about it. I did a terrible put-down of Cold Duck, that ersatz bubbling rosé, and when Hughes was doing an essay about what to do with buffalo meat I mentioned jokingly that it might be delicious as "Buffalo Diane."

That week the ratings came out.
Ratings are everything. You can have the most horrible

show in the world, but if the ratings are good you're there forever. You can have the best show in the world, but without ratings you're dead. Those who fail in television like to point out that taste, class and intelligence have nothing to do with the ratings. But anybody who goes into television can never forget for a second that *nothing else matters.*

The important thing is that they are mysterious. There is really no formula for making a good TV show. If there were, there wouldn't be so many pilots and new scripts to try out each year, or so many shows dropped. Merle Miller, in *Only You, Dick Darling,* his book about writing a script for a TV series, points out the foolishness of trying to develop a winning formula. Why does Johnny Carson stay on top and Dick Cavett lose? Why, suddenly, do the Dean Martin and Dick Van Dyke shows get dropped? Why is Lawrence Welk everybody's favorite? What happened to Glen Campbell and *Laugh In?*

Nobody knows. Trying to figure out what will work and what won't is a game of Russian Roulette. "Ratings" is a euphemism for money. Money is what the station or network gets for advertising. Companies don't advertise on shows that have low ratings because then fewer people will see their ads and buy their products, and they will make less money.

People get hired on television and stay there if they make more right guesses than the others who are trying to get hired or stay there. Everybody is afraid because they never know when they're going to guess wrong. These are the managers. The correspondents are even more afraid. They don't even get to guess right or wrong. They have to have the right "appeal." It doesn't matter how good you are, once you arrive at a certain level. There are ten or twelve really good people on each network, but only one will be the next Chancellor or Cronkite.

Cronkite is on top now, but not by much. He has always been well in the lead until recently, when the ratings started closing in. Some time in November 1973, Chancellor's ratings surpassed Cronkite's for a week or so, and that's all people talked about for days. The first thing Hughes and I were told the morning it was discovered was, "Chancellor is ahead of Cronkite and heads are going to roll." Later I asked Gordon if heads were really going to roll, and he looked solemn and raised an eyebrow. For all he knew, it could be his head. In a case like that, firing Cronkite would be a last resort, so somebody's got to take the blame. Happily for CBS News and everyone concerned, Cronkite got back on top before too long. Cronkite, who is one of the most decent people I know, was asked why he thought the ratings had dropped. He said it was probably because Roger Mudd had been replacing him during his vacation and it had caught up with him.

The primary motivation in the world of television is fear. People are scared to death. Ambition and enthusiasm and interest and the desire to excel are secondary. Because fear is an enormous motivating force, many in the medium are afraid to make decisions, take chances, do anything innovative. Manning had gone out on a limb with Hughes and me. For some imagination, no matter how ill-conceived, he gets points for courage. Manning was not as afraid as most. The only person I met who has no fear at all is Hughes Rudd. Hughes is the most fearless person I ever met. His lack of fear and his independence kept me going.

Cronkite's friends say that every time his contract comes up for renewal, he goes into a slump for fear he won't get renewed, on account of his age. And Barbara Walters has critics who feel she is too old for television (women are too old in television long before men are too old), so that when her contract comes up and the pressure is on, she feels it.

All this is irrelevant to how one is doing or what one's ratings are at the moment. It has to do with the possibility that people won't like you tomorrow, and that it will all be over. Cronkite was thought to be such a loser during the 1960 conventions that he was taken off the air. That experience may stick in his mind. Yet, three years later, he went on the *Evening News* as anchorman and is still there.

Gordon had told us that they weren't even going to think about ratings for the first six months. It was a lie. The ratings that came in were for the first week. Even after all that stupid publicity, CBS had made very little dent. From the 7 to 8 A.M. period our ratings had been 1.4 million viewers and our share, 26 per cent. The share, which I had never heard of, is more important than the ratings. Even if the ratings go up, if the share stays the same or goes down you're in deep trouble.

The share indicates percentage of the total TV audience. Suppose there are 10 people watching, and we get 5 and the *Today* Show gets 5. Our ratings would be 5 and our share would be 50 per cent. Then suppose that there were suddenly 20 people watching, and 5 were still watching us and 15 were watching the *Today* Show. We would still have a 5 rating, but the share would have dropped to 25 per cent. The week we went on the air our rating was the same—1.4 million—but our share had dropped to 18 per cent. The *Today* Show had a 4.5 rating and a 40 per cent share.

That was not good. But I took heart. All the publicity had not gotten us a bigger share of the audience. And the low share couldn't have been my fault, because I hadn't done anything yet.

On Wednesday, August 29, we did a film piece about Helen Thomas, the AP White House bureau chief. Part of it was about her relationship, as a reporter, with Martha Mitchell, the estranged wife of the former Attorney General. Afterward, I commented in a lengthy ad lib about Martha and Helen and the whole Washington reportorial scene.

I got a rave note from Salant saying it was a terrific ad lib, and why couldn't I do more of that? It depressed me. How could I when I was never alive when other people were, when I never went out, and when I wasn't even a reporter any more, when I didn't know anything that was going on? I was isolated. Confined. After only a little more than three weeks, I felt out of it. The only conversation I had left (and I didn't need it much since I never saw anybody but Hughes, for lunch, and then I got so drunk I never knew what was going on anyway) was about things I had done as a reporter at the *Post.* I was becoming more useless each day.

I couldn't learn how to write for TV, which usually meant in thirty-second blurts. The night editor was a harmless little guy named Bob Siller who lacked self-confidence. It seemed to me that he had resented me from the beginning, probably because of the salary, my lack of experience, and because I was a woman, but he was afraid to express his hostility. All he did—and it destroyed what confidence I had—was simply to throw everything back at me, saying it wasn't any good.

I would write a three-line lead-in to a film piece and he would ask me to rewrite it. If it was long, then it needed to be shorter. If it was short, it needed to be longer. Hughes wasn't all that crazy about him either, but he didn't cut Hughes the way he did me. He didn't seem to have any sense of humor, and he was beginning to get me down. I couldn't tell whether I was hopeless or paranoid. I heard that he was putting out the word that I couldn't write my own copy, and that made me angry. Writing was all I had left. He never threw anything back at Hughes, so one night I asked Hughes to write a tellstory for me.

I put my name on it and put it on Siller's desk. He came back, shaking his head and clucking in an annoying way he had, meaning this was the greatest disaster he'd ever seen, and in a loud, obsequious whisper he said he was sorry, it was no good, that I'd have to do it over, that it was too wordy and not to the point. I was delighted. Hughes blew up. We went in to Townsend to complain, and from then on I never had to deal with Siller. Harry Griggs, the assistant producer and a former newspaperman, edited my copy and things went much better, though I never really got the hang of it.

Friday, August 31, was the tenth anniversary of *The CBS Evening News* with Walter Cronkite. He was our interview that morning. I was excited because I admire Cronkite as both a good print journalist and a good television journalist. And for someone who has achieved such near reverence, he is easy, natural, unaffected, smart, gentle and funny. Cronkite has a beguiling, self-deprecating sense of humor and an appetite for an occasional salty joke. He has loomed as the power at CBS News, mainly because basically he edits and produces the broadcast. Though others have the titles, Cronkite has the final say. Yet there is no sense of arrogance or manipulation about him. Cronkite is comfortable to be around. Talking to him, you get the feeling you're sitting around a press room chatting with an old UPI reporter, which in fact he is. Cronkite's friends say he does a mean and funny striptease and plays the best bass in the business.

He came in a bit early and Hughes and I joked around with him about the *Morning News*.

"I was on the *Morning News*," said Cronkite. "I lasted all of six months. Let's see how long you two last."

We all laughed.

Cronkite had been one in a series of people, including Mike Wallace and Jack Paar, who had tried and failed to defeat the *Today* Show. That always made me feel better when I was sorely put.

I was surprised at how comfortable I felt, even at the start of the interview, because I had been ill at ease at the thought of interviewing such a veteran. But Cronkite, though not nervous, seemed less comfortable at being interviewed than we were interviewing him.

Hughes asked him if he missed reporting, getting out there on a story rather than sitting in an anchor booth. "Sally and I are getting a little restless at being trapped here after only a month, that we don't get out on the actual story."

Cronkite does get out sometimes but, yes, he does miss it. I asked him if he could explain the disdain that some print journalists have for television.

"I think there's a little bit of justice to it," he said. "The job we're doing in electronic journalism isn't exactly the job they're doing. . . . But I don't see they have any right for disdain. We have other problems."

The interview went well and ended on a nice note. So did the week. But we were still ad-libbing. And it was the "spontaneous" ad-libbing that was killing us. It's incredibly difficult to be clever and witty on cue. Hughes and I were both unhappy about it. It wasn't working.

I was getting Hughes worked up about things that were going wrong on the program, and the fact that nobody was helping me out. He felt protective of me, and yet dragged down by me at the same time. I was more unhappy with the ad libs than he was, mainly because I was making an ass out of myself and he wasn't. So every day we'd have lunch, and we'd get boozed up and I'd start whining, and Hughes would get furious and call Gordon.

"Shit, Gordon, you've got to *do* something," I could hear him yell from the phone booth of whatever little French or Mexican restaurant we were in. I would feel almost hysterical at the thought of it all, and then Hughes would come back to the table in a rage because Gordon had hung up on him. I would be in tears of laughter and he'd get furious with me. Then we'd fight a bit, until we got too drunk, and take a taxi back to our apartments on the West Side. We agreed that it was a good thing his wife, Ann, was coming home from France that weekend.

That Monday, two seconds after the broadcast was over, Ann called to tell me how great she thought I was, and Hughes was, and the show was. "I can't believe those reviewers were writing about the same people," she said. I loved her.

That day the three of us had lunch. Ann is terrific. She's a feisty, gutsy, bright, funny dame who doesn't mince words. She's nearly fifty and looks marvelous, dresses in pants and French jerseys, and loves to have a good time, tell earthy jokes, laugh heartily, and eat good food. She and Hughes have been married for years and have one of the best marriages I've seen. And Ann knows how to handle Hughes Rudd.

Ann's return cut down our daily drinking bouts. We still drank, but Ann regulated us a bit, and she and Hughes often lunched at home. That meant I had more time on my own if I couldn't drum up lunches with friends. I had lunch with the Rudds at least once a week. They treated me like friends and parents. Ann would get angrier than Hughes at the way things were going, and we'd all end up yelling at each other or screaming with laughter. Her return brightened things up considerably.

One night as Warren was coming in from a dinner party and I was going out to work around 1:30, he mentioned that he had seen John Chancellor and that Chancellor had told him that he agonized watching me on the air, knowing I wasn't getting any help, and that he'd be glad to talk to me or give me some advice if I needed it. I called him, practically in tears from gratitude. He invited me to come to lunch at his apartment with his wife, Barbara, who is also a friend. I don't know a newsman in either print or TV who has more integrity than Jack Chancellor, and who is as nice. He was shocked when I told him how I'd been hired and how little preparation there had been for the broadcast. He kept shaking his head, "I don't believe it."

He said my voice needed the most work, that I wasn't reading the news as forcefully as I should, and that he strongly recommended a voice coach. He had gotten one and it had helped tremendously in finding his natural stride and voice level and style of presentation.

I stayed for several hours, drank quite a bit of wine, had a very pleasant lunch, and left depressed. I had the strong impression that Chancellor felt there was no hope for me, though he never said such a thing.

That Wednesday we had Mike Wallace on the broadcast. He had done an interview for which there had been no space on *Sixty Minutes,* so he donated it to the *Morning News.* We were delighted to have it, because Wallace is good and we knew it would liven up the show. In fact, I had suggested we take their cuttings as a regular feature, since it was clear we weren't going to do anything of that quality.

I was wary of Wallace. I had known him before, though not so well, and everybody said to watch out, if you crossed Wallace he'd get back at you. I had heard from several reliable sources that Wallace was badmouthing me, and I believed it was true, especially after the scene in the restaurant. Wallace was not only telling everybody how unattractive and unintelligent I was, but was mocking my performances. It was hard to understand why, since he is so big; he certainly had nothing to worry about from me. The other correspondents had been extraordinarily nice and helpful and had sympathized. I was perplexed rather than angry.

I was in my office having my hair done. I heard a loud voice from down the hall saying, "Watch out, I haven't defecated yet this morning and I'm mean."

It was Wallace. I heard Hughes roar with laughter. "You're mean as a Gila monster this morning, aren't you, Wallace?" he said. (He later explained to me that Gila monsters don't defecate and therefore are mean.)

Wallace had interviewed two people on tape, a young man named William Lemner, who had been a government witness against the Gainsville Eight, and Barbara Stocking, a forty-three-year-old antiwar Quaker. Their conversation grew more and more heated and finally Lemner said to her, "Are you mad at me for taking you to bed?"

She said, "But you couldn't."

He said, "But we did and you know it."

She replied, "No, no, you tried and couldn't, Bill, don't you remember?"

Even Hughes and I were stunned. But it made the show and we got a lot of comment. Several days later a friend called and said, "Sally, you poor thing, I heard what happened on the air the other day, and I feel so sorry for you. I'm just horrified. How are you?"

"What happened on the show the other day?" I asked.

"Well, I was at a dinner party and one of the guests said he had watched your show. And he said that in the middle of one of your interviews the man you were interviewing said he had gone to bed with you. Then you got in a big fight and you said he tried but he couldn't get it up."

Several people at the party had nodded and said they'd heard the same thing. She said they couldn't believe that I would get into that sort of thing so soon after all the terrible publicity.

That week I did several more essays on women's rights. I still had not heard a word from any of my sisters.

On Saturday, September 8, my seven-year relationship with Warren Hoge ended. It was a mutual decision. I moved out of his apartment on Riverside Drive and into the Alden Hotel, a residential hotel on 82nd and Central Park West. I got two furnished rooms overlooking the Beresford, and Central Park if you leaned halfway out the fourteenth-floor window. It had a bedroom, bath, living room and kitchenette, with a tiny icebox, sink and hot plate. It cost $450 a month. The Alden, once elegant, had become what you might call a bit seedy. Its faded curtains and slipcovers and turn-of-the-century furnishings reminded me of a room in one of the nicer, but not the best, hotels in Bordeaux.

I began seeing Ben Bradlee, the editor of *The Washington Post* and my former boss. He had left his wife, Tony, at the end of July.

These moves were not taken lightly. The situation was difficult for all of us, and particularly traumatic for me because of my already-painful professional situation, the hours and the subsequent publicity.

Monday was our first month's anniversary on the show. When we went in, and after we'd finished writing, we all met in Lee's office. He had gotten a long, long memo from Salant on his views of the first month—what was good, what was bad, what should stay, what should go. The ad libs, he had concluded, should go.

I was joyful. Hughes seemed pleased, too. I don't even remember what else was in the memo. I never got a copy, and efforts to retrieve one have been unsuccessful.

Salant felt we should do longer news summaries at the beginning rather than Hughes and me skipping back and forth with little headlines. Salant also wanted me to do more interviews. I hated writing the news summaries. We agreed that Hughes would write the summaries and I would do the interviews. What that meant was that, aside from my lead-ins to interviews and film pieces and an occasional essay (Hughes did more than I), I really didn't have much to write, and I wouldn't have to read all the news when I got in. I began coming in later and later. The limousine would start picking Hughes up around 2:00 and go back for me around 3:00. Even so, there isn't all that much difference between 1:00 and 3:00. It's still going to work in the middle of the night. There was another side effect. I got so I never read the papers at all.

It was decided we needed more critics. Apparently Bill Paley loves criticism, and so we began searching frantically for a "media" critic. Gordon wanted his old buddy, the late George Frazier of the Boston *Globe*. Nobody else did. We lost.

Tuesday, a woman I know not well, but whom I like, called. She runs with a very rich, social, artsy New York crowd, a group I had seen on weekends when I lived in Washington. She wanted to get together for lunch and to tell me that she had been watching the broadcast and thought it was coming along. She waited for me to say I thought it hadn't been too hot before she went into a tirade about the critics. I was ready to agree.

Then she said, "You know, Sally, I have a very good psychiatrist you might want to go see to talk about the way you've been attacked and why, and the people who've attacked you."

"I don't need to go to a psychiatrist," I shrieked. "I'm perfectly fine. It's the people who've attacked me who are sick."

"As long as you keep on thinking that way," she said, "you're okay."

Wednesday, Hughes and I had a little relapse. Betty Furness, whom I know personally and who is married to CBS producer Les Midgely, was a guest along with Dr.

Dunlop, whom I had never heard of. At one point in the interview I called her Betty, and at another I called him Dr. Dunlop.

I heard about that from my sisters, anonymously. It was sexist. I explained to Townsend, so he could pass the word, that had Dr. Dunlop been the one I knew, I would have called him by his first name and Furness by her last. He later told me that was not an acceptable excuse.

Hughes was in worse trouble. He had come out of an essay on canning tomatoes and into Betty's intro: "And now," he said, "we have a couple of real home-grown tomatoes over there with a lot of common sense."

The sisters chewed his ass.

(On another broadcast I had started to talk about Europe. "When I was abroad—" "You're still a broad," said Hughes. We broke fast for a commercial.)

We had been taping interviews after the broadcast, though most of them never ran. They were, on the whole, boring interviews with boring people, and most of the time we didn't even know who the subject was to be until we arrived in the morning. The burden was generally on me, since I did most of the interviews alone.

We were constantly making suggestions and never hearing about them again. I was pushing for midgets. There was a big midget convention coming up in the Midwest, and I wanted to get some members of the local New York chapter to come on and talk about what it's like to be in that world. Hughes wanted to get outgoing Mayor Lindsay on with a mean cab driver and have them shout it out. We thought we had some interesting and offbeat ideas. Instead we got nutritionists and such, big yawns.

Hughes and I wanted to go out and tape some interviews, but Gordon was opposed to it: live interviews have more zip. There was no way we could change his mind, and maybe he's right that they have more zip, in principle; but a lot of individuals don't, at seven in the morning.

Including us.

In addition, we were getting a bad reputation. Several friends from publishing told me that they wouldn't chance putting on their authors because we had a bad reputation for killing interviews.

One of the things that appalled me and the rest of the staff was that we never had staff meetings. I discovered that they had them regularly on the old *Morning News*, but Townsend said he didn't believe in staff meetings.

I screamed and shouted and begged and cajoled so much, we finally had one, which Hughes and I both felt was productive. We never had one again.

The last weekend in September, Ben came up to New York. We were walking down the street on the East Side after lunch on Saturday afternoon when we ran into Mike Wallace.

"Well, well," he said. "I was just talking to Beverly Grunwald [wife of *Time* Magazine's managing editor, Henry Grunwald] and she said they're running a story this week that you two are getting married."

Ben and I laughed, thinking it was a joke. We chatted on about a few things, then parted.

The following Monday in *Time* Magazine's "People" section, this item appeared:

When a blonde ex-Junior Leaguer named Sally Quinn admitted during a job interview at *The Washington Post* that she had never actually written anything, the executive editor joked, "Well, nobody's perfect." Nevertheless, Ben Bradlee hired her and carefully molded her into a *Post* feature writer. Eight weeks ago he had to relinquish her to the great power base of the *CBS Morning News* opposite Barbara Walters. Sally moved to Manhattan, and the apartment of her long-time friend Warren Hoge, city editor of the New York *Post*. But soon she moved out again (Hoge had also been seeing socialite Amanda Burden). Now it seems Bradlee, 52, has decided to look after his Galatea, 32. Parted from Tony, his wife of 17 years and the mother of his two children, he plans to marry Sally as soon as he gets his divorce.

From then on out we were harassed with similar items and by people trying to do interviews and stories, including the *National Inquirer*, which threatened to "door-step" us if we wouldn't cooperate. And they did.

Around the third week in September, Lee had casually asked whether I would like to go to England in November to cover Princess Anne's wedding.

"Sure," I said.

"Well, you ought to get a little experience with film," he said. "I'll get Harry Griggs to get you to work on a film piece."

I was crazy to get out of the studio and back onto the streets, and I had visions of fabulous films on marvelous events where I could get a chance to do something decent.

On September 25th I was assigned to go to an A & P supermarket in Westchester County, a suburban community, with producer Norm Glubock to do a consumer piece on the difference in price between house-brand and name-brand products.

We did a stand-upper. That means I say to the camera, "We have here in this basket a group of name-brand products (such as Clorox). . . ." I do an interview with the manager and ask several housewives which make they prefer. It took most of the day, and I was tired, bored and furious. And I had learned nothing. I pulled my only prima-donna scene when I got back to the office. But I still had to go up to

Westchester twice more to finish it, and though the piece turned out well, considering what it was, it was not the kind of thing that was going to make me a big "TV star."

Two days later I had lunch with Charlotte Curtis of *The Times* at Sardi's.

Charlotte asked me how I liked television.

"I hate it."

"Good girl," she said, laughing. "I like to think of you as a reporter and a writer. I would have hated it if you had suddenly gotten carried away by the glamour of television."

Earl Blackwell, editor of the *Celebrity Register,* came oozing up to the table.

"Oh, God, here comes another autograph hunter," I thought. But of course he was looking for Charlotte.

"Darling," he gushed, "how divine to see you. Did you see Sylvia Miles over there? Isn't she wonderful? I'm just getting out this year's edition and I'm a wreck."

Charlotte, who is in the *Register,* introduced me to Blackwell, whom I had already met.

"Oh," he said, looking me over carefully, "you're the new one on television. Well, darling, it's too late for this year, but maybe we can get you in next year's *Register,* hmmmmmmmmmmm?"

As we left the restaurant Charlotte said quietly, "Let me know when you're ready to quit."

"It won't be long."

My health all along had not been good. I still felt dizzy and nauseated in the early mornings, and I was constantly exhausted though there wasn't anything wrong with me as far as anyone could see.

There was, however, a major cosmetic problem.

For the first time since I was seventeen years old, I was developing acne. And it was getting bad. Rickey switched to an allergenic makeup, but it didn't help. The makeup and the bright lights must be doing it, I decided. I should have my face cleaned.

I remembered that a classmate of mine from Smith had a mother who ran an Institute of Cosmetology on East 62nd Street, which I occasionally read about in *Vogue* or *Harper's Bazaar*. Her name was Vera Falvy, and she was a Hungarian with the most beautiful complexion I had ever seen.

Mme. Falvy examined my face carefully and asked about my eating habits, health and life style. She knew I was on TV but had no idea of the hours or the pressure. She felt the breakout was caused by emotional tension. I would need regular treatment. We made another appointment and she gave me a special lotion which I was to use under, or preferably instead of, makeup.

Altogether I visited Madame six times, and the bills ran close to $300. She did her best, but the tensions kept building and my face got worse. My complexion has never been the same. I have scars on my face to show for those horrible months.

The final week in September Lillian Hellman, who had just published *Pentimento* to rave reviews, was scheduled to be interviewed live. She has always been one of my great heroines, and I was terrified. To make matters worse, several interviews had appeared in the papers that week and none had really managed to draw her out, so I imagined she was a resistant subject. Her agent called to say that she wanted to have lunch with me before we did the interview, but the luncheon was canceled and so we had to do it cold turkey. Her agent also relayed the message that Ms. Hellman never got out of bed until noon, and wouldn't be herself at 7 A.M.

I never met Hellman before she came into the studio. We nodded as I adjusted my mike. She had her cigarettes, which she puffed incessantly while she kept clearing her throat. After a few perfunctory questions I turned to her life, which she had written about with great intimacy. I asked a question. She paused for centuries. Out of panic, I jumped in before she had a chance to answer—I was afraid she wasn't going to. The interview lasted more than twelve minutes, and I was dripping with perspiration as I thanked her for being on the show; but before I could get the words out, she had gotten up from her chair and was walking out of the studio, dragging the mike behind her and me as well. We were attached to the same hook-up.

The cameras panned quickly away as I raced back to the anchor booth.

I had no idea how it had gone.

The next day I got a scribbled note from Gordon; he thought it was terrible. Harry Griggs thought it was good but reminded me that I should let people finish their sentences. Gordon said I should have jumped in and interrupted her more.

I got more fan mail on that interview than any I had ever done on television.

When I saw Hellman again, she didn't mention it. I wonder what she thought.

Although we had agreed to stop the ad libs, occasionally we were called to fill in, usually around a boring or a controversial film piece. It was almost bound to make us look stupid, and I was determined to put an end to it. The moment came at the end of that same broadcast. We were winding up a film piece from Spain by Bob Trout about the new dirty flicks that were being shown and how the Catholic Church was in an uproar. As we came out of it they shouted that we had about twenty seconds to ad-lib.

"You know," I said to Hughes, "Spain being a very Catholic country, it always amuses me when the statement comes out that the church strongly disapproves, because how does the church know about all those dirty movies unless a lot of the higher-ups in the church go and watch them?"

Hughes looked stunned. He shook his head slightly to warn me, but I pretended not to notice.

"Oh, no," he said, "I'm sure there's a censorship office where somebody gets special dispensation to go do that sort of thing."

"Well," I said, "I know—I bet they're clamoring for those jobs." And I burst out laughing, pleased with my own daring.

Everybody was furious. I caught hell. Even Blackrock got in the act.

Dick Cavett called me several days later. He said the story was going aorund ABC about Sally's "latest."

I didn't give a damn, and we didn't have too many ad libs after that.

After about a month, Hughes and I were told we were getting more than seven times the amount of mail that Cronkite was getting. I never found out if that was true or not, but I did have the impression that the quantity of mail, not the quality, was what counted at Blackrock. At first I read all of mine. It ran about half hate and half good mail, which is about average, I was told. One of our favorites was from someone who wrote, "Dear Sally, you are just what the doctor ordered—a pill. And as for Hughes Rudd, somebody should do something about his throat. Preferably with a machete."

A fair proportion was ugly and vicious, attacking my looks, style, speech, dress, manners, everything. I found it debilitating, and I finally stopped reading it on the advice of Barbara Walters. One of the disadvantages was that I didn't see some of the helpful and honest criticisms. So I told

my secretary to give me mail that she thought I might bene-
fit from reading. Also, you had no idea what people were
saying to the management, since most of the hate mail goes
directly there. If people like you they write you; if they
don't, they write your boss.

The most heartening part of the good mail was that most
people were outraged at the critics. They had read all these
things about me and had turned on the television out of
curiosity to see what kind of monster CBS had wrought.

Many of the notes were requests for autographs, auto-
graphed pictures, articles of clothing or objects. Some of
these were for celebrity sales at schools and bazaars. There
were requests for recipes, for interviews and thousands of
requests to speak. I turned down all the interview and speaking engagement requests. I figured I was in enough trouble
already; why push it? And I had decided never to give an
interview again. I felt like a fraud. I wasn't a big TV star, I
was an impostor.

At first I tried to answer the mail personally. Occasionally
there was a note that touched me and I wrote back, but
mostly I sent it to the correspondence unit, where a form
letter is drafted that the "talent" approves. I liked to think
of the kook mail being answered automatically with those
letters.

Obscene letters—letters calling me, for one, a "penis lover"
—threats on my life and marriage proposals . . . all got the
standard form letter. Just keep those cards and letters coming, folks.

The last Friday in September the office called me at home
to say that Dick Cavett's office had called to ask if he could
be on the broadcast Monday morning. I was taken aback.
For some reason I jumped to the conclusion that Dick
watched me religiously, had decided I was the hottest thing
on television, and wanted to try me out as a possible co-star

on *The Dick Cavett Show*. I don't think I really thought that, but on the other hand, I think maybe I did.

Then on Sunday night I got a call from the office saying that the reason Cavett wanted to come on was that he had just taped a ninety-minute special with Katharine Hepburn and wanted to plug it. That deflated my ego a little bit, but still, he was coming, and he had asked, and it did add a little to my almost nonexistent cachet around the office. I started talking about him a lot, "Dick and I" this, and "Dick and I" that, so everyone would understand that I had important friends.

I interviewed him for nearly fifteen minutes, the longest interview I had ever done. I thought it went well. He was funny and amusing, and I was relaxed. I felt good when we came off the air. But before I could say a word, it was pointed out to me that I had insulted Cavett. He had made a remark about Walt Frazier, the basketball star, barely being able to fit in our tiny studio when I interviewed him, and I had replied, "Well, at least you didn't have any trouble" (implying that Cavett was small). I was reminded that I had insulted Cavett by several higher-ups, and I finally got so paranoid that I wrote him an apology. I didn't hear back. Later Cavett told me he had never gotten it. He didn't think I had been rude.

The first week in October Charles Collingwood was in town. Collingwood, CBS's correspondent in England, had been there so long they called him the Duke of Collingwood. He's more English than American, with the slightly British way of talking that Americans who have lived there for a while affect. He has his silk shirts made to order, belongs to the right clubs, wears a bowler, and is terribly pompous.

Gordon asked me if I wanted to have lunch with Collingwood, whom I'd never met, to discuss the coverage of Princess Anne's wedding. He and I were to co-anchor the five-hour live broadcast from London.

Collingwood had other plans, so we had to settle for a

special meeting the next day with Russ Bensley, head of the Special Projects division (weddings, conventions, space shots, assassinations, etc.).

I went upstairs to Bensley's office the next day, and we all sat around a big table with coffee and pads and pencils. I did not utter a word. Collingwood talked a lot. He said he knew a wonderful woman from the *London Sunday Times* whom we could get as commentator on the fashion and social side of it, and he would do the historical and political side of it, and I could do everything else.

It did not occur to me until after the meeting to inquire what everything else was.

The day after the meeting, *Ms.* Magazine gave a luncheon in honor of Helen Gahagan Douglas, the former Congress-woman from California whom Richard Nixon defeated in 1950, who was on their cover that month. I had been invited. I had debated whether or not to go. I knew and liked Gloria Steinem, Suzanne Levine, Mary Peacock and many of the women who worked there. But I was afraid. I hadn't appeared in public since I'd been on the air. I knew that there would be a lot of press, and further, I didn't have any idea how people would react to me. I was afraid of scorn or ridicule, or of just being ignored.

But I had decided to accept, because we were scheduled to do a filmed interview with Douglas after our broadcast the same morning.

After the broadcast I went back to the *Sixty Minutes* area, where we were going to film. What I did not understand was that there was a difference between filming and taping. And, naturally, nobody told me.

Filming is done on a camera that can be moved, like a movie camera. It has poorer quality in terms of the print. Taping, done on a TV camera, is much clearer and better, but is vastly more expensive. That's why, when we did an interview with tape, it generally lasted about twelve minutes and ran (if it did) the way it was done. With film you could run hours if you liked, and cut and edit to your heart's content.

The Douglas interview was a failure. I couldn't get her to stay on the subject, and I lost control of the interview. I was so hot under the lights that I kept looking down and rolling my eyes, which the camera caught, and I got so sidetracked by her digressions that I couldn't think of questions to ask, and there were awkward pauses.

I liked her very much, but all I could think was, "Thank God this isn't on live." The interview lasted an hour as we baked in the hot lights. Jim Ganser showed me the five minutes he had edited out, which he thought were salvageable, and we both agreed it wasn't worth putting on the air.

I was a failure. This had been my one big chance to really get my teeth in an interview.

When I arrived at the *Ms.* luncheon I stood at the door for several minutes and then went to the bar. The few people I recognized didn't pay any attention to me. I considered making for the door. Finally someone I didn't know asked if I was Sally Quinn, and when I said yes and she didn't say anything hostile, I was grateful to her.

Soon lunch was announced. I hadn't gone over to Gloria. Feeling like America's No. 1 woman failure, I didn't want to have to face her. I sat at a table with a group of people I didn't know, except for Suzanne Levine, managing editor of *Ms.,* who is a friend. The black man next to me had never heard of me. Which was good. Nobody wanted to talk about TV at lunch, except Suzanne, who was very sympathetic. She told me that a lot of the women were very pleased with my women's essays on the air. For a few moments I felt not like the No. 1 failure—but still pretty close.

After lunch, Gloria introduced Ms. Douglas, who spoke for a while; then it was over. In the ladies' room I ran into several friends.

"How *are* you?" they asked, with pity in their eyes. (I know it was pity.) I finished in the john and ran out of the ladies' room, and out of Jimmy's restaurant, and all the way down the street to Seventh Avenue. I fell down twice. Finally I got a cab and went home to bed.

That was my last social engagement until November.

That week I got a call from Barbara Howar. We chatted for a bit and Barbara, who had had her own TV shows, gave me a few pointers. She told me that I was coming along really well and shouldn't worry. Then she said, "Why don't you look at the right camera when the show is closing each day? Half the time the camera zooms out to the newsroom while you're looking straight ahead into the camera in the studio, and whenever the camera is in the studio you're looking across at the newsroom. You've got to keep your eye on the red light."

"Red light?"

"For God's sake," she screamed, "hasn't anyone told you about the red light?"

"No," I said. "What about it?"

"There's a light on the side of the camera," she said, "and when it goes on red it means that camera is on you and that's where you're supposed to look."

"Oh, no," I moaned. "No wonder. I saw that light flash on and off but I didn't know what it meant."

That week I had three very successful interviews, one with Pearl Bailey, one with an admitted homosexual, and another with Rosie Grier, the football star. Grier demonstrated how to do needlepoint, and pushed his needlepoint book. Afterward he wandered into my office. He stayed and "shot the bull" until finally I had to leave. I had nothing to do. I just didn't want to talk. I was becoming antisocial.

The next day I had a letter from Anthony Mazzola, the editor of *Harper's Bazaar*, asking me to lunch. I had never met him, and I was getting concerned about my fear of social contact. I accepted.

The morning I was to meet him, somebody from *Vogue* called to say they were doing a piece about my hair. They wanted to know who did it. I told them Edith. There seemed to be some surprise on the other end. Then she said they had consulted several top New York hairdressers and they all agreed my hair was wrong. One of them was André of Cinandre, then the most statusy salon. For some reason, I was infuriated. I inquired as to whether they had any idea of the pressures I was under, and especially the amount of time (usually fifteen minutes) we had to do my hair in the morning. She was sure they understood that.

I never heard from her again.

I was to meet Mazzola at La Caravelle, one of New York's most exclusive and expensive restaurants, at 12:15. And I was in a state. The call from *Vogue* had upset me. I was alarmed about my appearance. My face was so broken out that I had left my stage makeup on even though I knew that only exaggerated it.

And I was still sick. I had never really stopped being sick. I was more and more nauseated and my stomach hurt all the time. No matter how much sleep I got (and I was just beginning to get somewhat adjusted to the hours), I still had to lie down for an hour or two before I went on the air.

I wasn't up to being charming, and I certainly didn't look charming. Mazzola had said that they were thinking of some kind of spring layout on me, a picture layout, which I liked. I've never really cared about other kinds of publicity, but I have always secretly longed to be in *Vogue* or *Harper's Bazaar* in a beauty layout. I've also yearned to have my apartment in *House & Garden* or *House Beautiful*.

We had a lovely lunch, though I was nervous and tense.

I felt so sick I could barely eat, and each time I took a sip of wine, I felt nauseated. I waited in vain for Mazzola to mention the spring layout.

As I reeled down the street after lunch, searching for a taxi, I faced the truth.

It was the acne.

I threw up all night and barely made it through the broadcast the next morning. The Yom Kippur war had started, and we had three-way interviews live from Israel and Egypt. I was being carefully and quietly left out, and I felt so horrible I didn't care. All I managed was to read some of the news.

The coverage was brilliant. Dave Horowitz, the assistant producer who was in charge of the control room, had organized those broadcasts and he was considered one of the brightest young producers at CBS.

After the show I called Dr. Miller. He said to come right over. I told him I hadn't come for vitamin shots, that I thought there was something really wrong with me. He examined me and said he thought I had an ulcer and sent me down the street to his friend, Dr. Marshak.

I was ushered to the back room and told to strip and put on a gown. When I came out of the dressing room, I found Bess Myerson in an identical gown. The irony got me, two supposedly successful women coming in to check for ulcers.

We had never met, but we recognized each other. We each ignored the other. I went to the X-ray room and was told to drink what seemed like ten gallons of barium. Then I had to kill two hours before the X rays.

I got dressed, walked up and down Madison Avenue, and dropped into Encore, the secondhand store where Jacqueline Onassis is supposed to take her leftovers. I tried on everything in the store and finally bought a gray tweed winter coat for $50.

As I was leaving, my box under my arm, a woman stopped me. "Aren't you Sally Quinn?" she asked. I said I was. "What on earth are you doing shopping in here when you make all that money? Aren't you afraid you'll be seen. A big star like you?"

"I hadn't thought of it," I mumbled. I knew I could never go back. Would Barbara Walters be caught dead in Encore?

Back at Dr. Marshak's, I had X rays, drank more barium, then had more X rays.

The doctor called me into his office. He was a nice, friendly, chatty man.

"Gee," he said, "this is my big day!"

"How do you mean?"

"Well, first Bess Myerson, then you. I've never had two big celebrities like this in one day. Wait till I tell people."

"Do I have an ulcer or not?" I asked, a bit impatiently.

Actually, I was much more interested to know whether Bess Myerson had an ulcer, but I didn't dare ask.

He thought there was a potential one, but it was in the beginning stages and, with a proper diet, could be curbed. He sent me back to Dr. Miller for a list of things I couldn't eat or drink.

I only noticed one thing. No alcoholic beverages.

If I had been doing a third-rate movie I would have played funeral music during this scene.

This was out of the question. How could I sleep without getting bombed every day? I was desperate. I pleaded with him.

"I can't stop you from drinking," he said matter-of-factly. "But you'll have a bleeding ulcer before you know it if you keep it up." He advised me to take a laxative before I went home to bed. "Barium is constipating," he said.

I walked out of his office in a daze and went home, con-

vinced that I would never sleep again. I fell into bed at
5 P.M. and passed out.

The next morning when I woke up I was doubled over
with cramps. I realized immediately what it was. I was con-
stipated. I had forgotten to take a laxative.

I got in the limousine and we drove to pick up Hughes.
"Hughes," I said, "I've got to get a laxative. Do you know of
an all-night drugstore?"

He didn't, but the driver did, and we cruised down
Broadway to 50th Street, where the driver stopped at a
grubby all-night drugstore with one bright light overhead
and a few old-fashioned counters.

I looked like a gun moll going in for bandages for a
wounded Mafia boyfriend as I dashed out of the limousine.
Hughes crouched inside the depths of the car.

"Quick," I said to the druggist, clutching my stomach,
"give me your fastest-acting laxative."

"Right here, little lady," he said. "This'll fix you right up."

He gave me a bottle of carbonated citrus drink, which he
said really acted. I drank it there.

"It'll just be a few minutes," he said with a friendly wink
as I paid him.

I raced back to the limousine and told the driver to go as
fast as he could. I explained to Hughes that the druggist had
only given me a few minutes.

"Oh, Christ," said Hughes, howling with laughter. "I hope
we make it." We made it. We got to the office and I waited
around for a while, but nothing happened. So I went into
the Bullpen and started to write. At about 3:30 Hughes
looked at me quizzically and I shook my head.

Four thirty. Nothing. Five thirty. Nothing. Hughes started
to check every five minutes. He was getting nervous. As 6:30
came around and nothing, he was beginning to perspire. At

two minutes to air time, Hughes looked at me ominously. "Well, this will be the test to see whether you are a professional or not."

"What do you mean?"

"If Cronkite can do it so can you."

"Cronkite?"

"He once took a laxative and it worked right in the middle of the broadcast," he said with a straight face, even if it probably isn't true.

"What did he do?"

"He didn't miss a beat. Most professional thing I ever saw."

"Five seconds," shouted the floor manager.

Jesus, I thought, am I really going to have to say "Get me off this horse immediately" and mean it? "Good morning, I'm Sally Quinn."

I made it. So much for citrus carbonate.

The next week I did an interview with Barry Goldwater, who came on because he is a family friend. It worked better than most, and I felt confident and smooth.

The next day, an item appeared in "The Gossip Column" by Robin Adams Sloan in the *Daily News*. Robin Adams Sloan is Liz Smith, the writer who reviews movies for *Cosmopolitan*, and who does Igor Cassini as well. She was a friend.

Question: Now that CBS's Sally Quinn is going to marry a Washington newspaperman, how will she reconcile that with her early morning news show in New York? Answer: Her pals expect Sally to eventually give up her CBS job, return to Washington to live, and probably to work on the paper run by her husband-to-be, editor Ben Bradlee. (You can have your old job back when you are the wife of the boss.) Sally is already talking about her TV job in the past tense. The experience hasn't been a total disaster, however; she'll get an acid book out of it.

It is true that I hated the job, but I had told only a handful of close friends, and I had not told any of them I was thinking about quitting. I had no idea of going back to work at the *Post*. I was not engaged, and I had no plans to write a book.

Everybody joked about it, perhaps a bit uneasily. Hughes, a camera buff, pulled out his camera and began snapping pictures of me. He asked if he could illustrate the book. I told him certainly.

Ray Gandorff, a strong, silent, Hemingway type who had barely exchanged three words with me the entire time I had been there, said, not looking up from his typewriter, "If you do write a book, will you say I was a good lay?"

The next day after the broadcast, a handwritten note on thick ecru note paper was delivered to my desk.

It said, "Dear Ms. Quinn: May I apologize for the thoughtless remark reported in today's *Variety*. You continue to have my support and hope for the future. Sincerely, Arthur Taylor."

I ran for a *Variety*. Taylor had been in Washington the night before, speaking at a dinner meeting of the local chapter of Sigma Delta Chi, the honorary journalism fraternity. The article dealt with the primary aspect of his speech, then went on to say:

Sally Quinn was a highly visible reporter for the *Washington Post* before she took over the CBS Morning News slot, so several of the questions after Taylor's speech naturally asked if the blonde is having more fun.

"How is Sally Quinn doing?" queried a journalist. "I'm not dating Sally Quinn," Taylor replied, "and I don't know how she's doing." The allusion to Quinn's much publicized personal life, which has seen her most recently romantically linked to *Washington Post* exec editor Benjamin Bradlee, brought down the house.

Recovering from his own sense of humor, Taylor promptly expressed optimism for the beleaguered morning program, saying that "things are coming along" and "there is need to be a little bit patient."

I didn't have anyone to have lunch with that day, so I did what I usually did when I didn't have a lunch date, which was about half the time. I walked up to 57th Street to Henri Bendel and roamed through all the floors. Then I went next door to I. Miller's Capriotti shop and checked that out. Then I walked down Fifth Avenue to 50th Street, over to Madison Avenue and up through the East Sixties, then back down Fifth to 57th Street and over to Sixth Avenue. I bought a copy of the *New York Post* and went to Wolff's Delicatessen across the street about 4 P.M. to have dinner. Usually corned beef and cabbage, and sometimes I'd sneak a beer.

I also sneaked another look at the article and at the note from Arthur Taylor.

Around 5:30 I went home to bed.

The next day I had an appointment with Mme. Falvy. My face was worse. When she finished working it was red and splotchy. I put a scarf over my head and ducked along the sidewalks, trying to find a cab. Someone yelled, "Hey, aren't you Sally Quinn?" I looked up to find about ten people staring at me.

"No," I mumbled quietly. "But everybody tells me I look like her."

Several days later I decided I needed a haircut. I called up Cinandre and made an appointment. I had my hair washed, and went upstairs to the stark, modern second floor to wait for a cut and blow-dry. I had requested André, that season's in haircutter. For $25 a shot he will shape your hair and, as everyone knows who's read *Vogue*, the cut is everything. It was André who had told *Vogue* how terrible I looked and what he would do with my hair if he had a chance. I waited with wet hair dripping down the back of my neck, reading an old *New York Times* for more than two hours before the master could see me. By that time I was nearly deaf and blind from the screeching rock music that blared from speakers all across the room.

Once I was in the chair I waited for André to smile and say, "Ah, Miss Quinn, the moment I've been waiting for," but he asked blandly how I wanted it cut. He hadn't a clue who I was. So all his great advice must have been based on some picture of me he had seen.

"Oh, just do with it what you think best," I said.

He trimmed it, leaving it basically the same. "I think," he declared then with Gallic pomposity, "that you should have long hair. It softens the face."

I noted with satisfaction that the following month's *Vogue* said that Cinandre recommended "[cutting] Sally's hair to diminish the effect of her full face." The picture they used to illustrate this bit of wisdom showed me in an old pair of glasses I hadn't worn since I had gone on the air.

The week of October 22 the special events unit called a meeting to discuss the wedding coverage. I was to leave for London on November 9th, and we had a lot of planning to do. We met in Russ Bensley's office around 11:00, a nice sunny room on one of the top floors. It was hot and Russ had displayed endless charts and diagrams he was describing to the assembled staff. Hughes had come along, since he was to be the New York anchor. We both began to nod when Bensley started his newspeak—"We're going to brainstorm it." Bensley is a decent, soft-spoken man whom everyone had told us was terribly effective. He seemed undynamic to me, very competent and thorough, but with not much imagination. He had a slight paunch and an ill-fitting toupee.

Hughes and I slept through his spiel and learned nothing. Later, one of the secretaries told me she would begin gathering material about the wedding. Nobody seemed worried. That worried me.

Later that week I got a phone call from a man who said he was one of the head ad salesmen at Blackrock. Unfortunately I can't remember his name. I have doubtless blocked it out. I asked Hughes, and he said he thought he had heard of him.

He wanted to talk to me but he didn't want anyone in the news division to know about it.

"They get very uptight when we deal directly with the talent," he informed me.

He suggested lunch, I suggested coffee, he suggested a drink. We met at the Oak Bar in the Plaza Hotel at 11 A.M., my cocktail hour. I was not drinking because of the ulcer, so I had a Virgin Mary and he had a double martini.

He explained that he handled a certain account; he also explained that his wife didn't understand him. They lived out in the suburbs and the commuting was really getting to him. He was getting an ulcer and the doctor had told him to cut out the martinis. But how are you going to make it through the day?

"My account is looking for an attractive girl to advertise their products," he said. "That girl could be you. There's big money in it."

"But I'm an anchorwoman"—I stressed woman—"on a news show. We don't do commercials," I told him.

"Oh, I know they hand you that crap," he said. "But you could really be doing great things. This company, for instance, could sponsor you in your own special and you could advertise the products. You'd be great."

He ordered another drink.

"Yes, but ..."

"A girl like you? Just think of the money you could make. You don't want to spend your life on that news show that nobody watches, getting up at one in the morning, do you?"

You bet I don't, buddy, I thought, and smiled.

"Listen, do you like cameras? Huh?"

"Well, I'm not much of a camera buff, but Hughes ..."

"Hughes, huh. Great. Terrific. I've got a camera for him. Listen, I've got a great little camera for you. It's a movie camera where you can take the pictures and develop your own film right there and show the movie. It's dynamite and something you could work. How'd you like it?"

"Well, it sounds nice. . . ."

"Great, I'll have one sent to you and I've got a terrific one I'll send Hughes. Okay? But listen, mum's the word. It wouldn't look too good if I were giving cameras away to the talent. And for God's sake, don't tell anyone we had a drink."

I excused myself shortly, saying I had a lunch date. It occurred to me later that he had wanted to get laid.

We never got the cameras. I never heard from the company.

Thursday, October 25, Don Hewitt, the producer of *Sixty Minutes*, stuck his head around the door of my office. He was grinning and he seemed excited.

"Hi," he said in a very friendly manner, which threw me. I hadn't forgotten the day I'd had lunch with Gordon and Hewitt had made the remark about *Deep Throat* and sore throat.

"Guess what? I've asked to go to London with you to be your director for the wedding."

I couldn't believe it. Hewitt was the hottest director and producer in the business. He wouldn't touch anything he didn't think was a big winner and, it seemed, everything that he touched turned to gold. He was legendary. He was a winner. He didn't get involved with anything that smelled like a loser; he didn't have to. *Sixty Minutes* was off the air during the fall because of football; he had time to kill, I told myself. But still, Don Hewitt, asking to be my director. This was it, the beginning. I was going to make it. I was headed toward success. I was going to be a star. I would stun everybody by how I improved during the wedding coverage. Because Don Hewitt could help me. And he would.

Hewitt is a fairly short man in his early fifties with a Hollywood look. His wife lived in Washington and he lived a rather freewheeling life in Manhattan. He wears flared pants, tapered suede jackets, turtleneck sweaters and boots. His graying hair is carefully styled and he always manages to have a tan, which complements his shiny white teeth. He's a touch overly casual. He deals with women in a very familiar, easy, patronizing, careless way. The "sweethearts," "darlings" and "angels" come easily to him.

"Now, the first thing we're going to do is get rid of those terrible glasses," he said. "Then we're going to find you something to wear for the wedding. I think maybe a green-corduroy Levi pant suit, maybe with a scarf, something casual and sexy. Then we've got to do something about your voice—it doesn't have punch—the makeup has got to be darker, and the hair maybe a little longer and looser."

I nodded my assent. Everything seemed to make sense. I did have a slight impression of a Hollywood makeover. I wouldn't have been surprised if he had suggested plastic surgery. However, Hewitt was really the first person to pay any serious attention to me, and I was determined to go along with everything he advised. I must have seemed passive and unsophisticated to him, in contrast to all the publicity.

We made an appointment for the next day to pick out a new pair of glasses. "We're going to make you a star," said Hewitt as he left my office.

The next day I met Hewitt at my glasses shop near Bloomingdale's on 59th Street. We tried every pair in the store, finally found a good-looking pair of horn-rims, and ordered them. The woman behind the counter said we couldn't have them for a week or so. But I needed them for the tryout so Hewitt could see how they looked. Hewitt began to put the charm on the woman, and I could see her turning into putty. Before long "Darling" was promising the glasses in a few days.

Hewitt had a shit-eating grin on his face as we walked out of the store and over to Bloomingdale's to find the green suit. That venture was unsuccessful and Hewitt had to leave, but he advised me to keep looking, gave me a quick peck on the cheek, told me I was terrific, and dashed off.

I felt like Cinderella. Finally somebody cared, and the somebody was the hottest producer in the business. I felt golden again as I had the day I first talked to Gordon about the job.

That week I tried especially hard to be as good as I could, and everyone said I had improved. We had Teddy Kennedy on, and the interview went smoothly. There was more on the Middle East, and I was included in the three-way interviews more often. All in all, it seemed that I was becoming more professional, and my spirits were high.

Hewitt worked with my voice all one morning and even that seemed to improve. The glasses arrived. I got Rickey to put darker makeup on me and it looked better. I asked Edith to take the hot rollers out sooner and my hair was looser and softer.

Hewitt had a talk with me about my attitude in London. I shouldn't be the snotty bitch I had a reputation for being, and I shouldn't put down the wedding. There were a lot of sweet little old ladies out there watching who just loved weddings, and they would switch me off if I got too arch. I admitted my weakness, and he told me just to watch it.

Several days after Hewitt had started hanging around my office, and I his, someone from the *Morning News* warned me to watch out for him when we got to London, that he had quite a reputation as a ladies' man. I brushed it off. It was absurd. He knew Ben and knew I was involved with him. And I knew his wife. There was no way he'd make a pass at me.

On Wednesday, October 31, a week before I was to go to London, Gordon took me to lunch. We went to a tiny French hole-in-the-wall I'd never heard of, though I thought it was a step up from the pub.

We got on the subject of London quickly. Gordon asked me if I'd had a chance to talk to Hewitt about it. He said Hewitt had requested that he be sent over on a special assignment just to be my director.

"Gordon," I asked, "is Hewitt going over there to make me a star or is he going over there to make me?"

"The latter," said Gordon matter-of-factly. "But don't worry, you can handle it."

I felt the blood rush to my face.

"Listen," said Gordon. "Hewitt is the best. Just do what he says and he'll make you look good. I've seen him operate for ten years, and he's a genius."

I changed the subject. For several weeks I had been trying to think of a way to get out of the job and I had decided to ask Gordon to send me to Washington. About halfway through the lunch I got up the courage to ask if there was any possibility I could be taken off the anchor job and sent to Washington as a reporter doing the same kind of thing for CBS that I had done for the Style section of the *Post*. The kind of thing that Bill Small had been trying for several years to hire me to do.

He said no. I asked if I could get off the anchor job a

couple of days a week to do film pieces, or maybe even go to Washington for two weeks for a trial period.

He said no.

Saturday, November 3, friends of mine, James Goodale, the senior vice president of *The New York Times*, and his wife, Toni, gave a party in my honor. Among the guests were Barbara Walters; Abe Rosenthal, managing editor of *The New York Times;* Charlotte Curtis; Barbara Howar and the writer Willie Morris; Oz Elliott, editor of *Newsweek;* and Morley Safer, *Sixty Minutes* correspondent.

Hughes and Ann didn't come because he didn't change his sleeping schedule around. Gordon and his wife refused at the last minute.

I was a nervous wreck as I dressed. I hadn't been to a party since I had gone to work at CBS. My face was so broken out I could hardly bear to look at myself in the mirror. I spent hours dressing in new black matte jersey pajamas, doing my hair, and caking my face with makeup. The only reason I was going was because Ben had come up from Washington and he wouldn't have let me back out. When we got to the party I realized that I didn't know how to make conversation any more and I kept hanging around the periphery of the group, listening. I couldn't maintain a one-to-one conversation with anybody. If a group was about to break up I would move to another so as not to get stuck with one person. At dinner I got my buffet plate and clung to Ben.

It was only after dinner as we were getting coffee that I ran into Morley Safer. We began talking about CBS and I found myself opening up and beginning to talk to someone.

Morley told me he thought CBS had fucked over me. He was the first person at CBS to say it. I don't remember anything else about the conversation. That was enough. I felt grateful.

The special events office was sending me clips and books on the wedding and royal family. A young man named Mark Harrington, who seemed awfully kind and helpful, had come down to chat with me and explained he would be my liaison with Central Control during the wedding. I hadn't read any of the material, and it was piling up. I would study it on the plane going over.

The Monday before I was to leave, Hewitt called from the airport at 9 to say he had just seen the show and that I looked sensational. He would pick me up at the airport in London on Wednesday. I was flattered but I insisted that he not go to that trouble. Heathrow is miles from London.

On Tuesday I made a horrible faux pas on the broadcast. Hughes led into a tellstory as though it were to be one of his funny essays. I hadn't heard it before, and was waiting for the punch line when all of a sudden I heard him say "and the nightmare of many travelers came true for a man from Beaumont, Texas. He was aboard a National Airlines DC-10 jetliner on a flight from Houston to Las Vegas Saturday night when, at 39,000 feet, one of the jet engines flew apart, tearing holes in the aircraft cabin. That caused violent decompression and as pressurized air inside the cabin rushed out, it took G. F. Gardiner with it through a smashed window. The airliner made a safe landing at Albuquerque a few minutes later. Sally?"

I burst out laughing. Hughes moaned. I tried to recoup. "But you never said what happened to him . . . you didn't . . ." Hughes just glared at me.

"Coming up," I fumbled into the camera, still trying not to laugh, "we have interviews with . . ."

Later, a number of people told me that they had known that was the beginning of the end.

I went to Kenneth's. Kenneth is the classic hairdresser in New York. He does *everybody's* hair. I had never been before, although I had interviewed Kenneth once and had thought he was a nice man. I am intimidated in expensive hairdressers' and boutiques. It stems from the days when I was an Army brat with no money. Even if I had money, I was always afraid they'd add something on the bill and I wouldn't have enough. But I thought Kenneth's would be the proper send-off. I needed to have my hair streaked, and I figured they must have the best.

The place looks like some kind of Oriental palace, with elevators and hundreds of floors, and thrones to sit in instead of chairs. I wondered how many decorators and how much time it took to get it to look that way.

I resisted intimidation. I kept reminding myself that I was a famous TV star (though nobody recognized me) and that they were just hairdressers' assistants. I was washed and streaked and sent off to another floor to be set. I got lost and ended up in an elegant-looking little salon with a hushed, temple-like atmosphere, when someone came rushing over and asked what I was doing there. "I'm trying to find out where to go to have my hair set," I explained. "You can't come in here," he said. "This is where Kenneth works."

I was tempted to get down on my knees and salaam.

I finally got my hair set and dried. I paid downstairs (you leave tips in envelopes at the desk). The bill was over $80.00.

I went home to rest up and pack, staying up much later than usual, and I got hungry around seven that evening. The Alden Hotel has what passes for a dining room off the lobby, a large room with columns and a linoleum circle in the center where years ago the *grandes dames* of New York swirled to waltz music as champagne flowed under the crystal chandeliers.

Now it looks like a geriatrics ward. Most of the residents of the Alden are either very old or very young, because the rents are so cheap. About six tables were occupied, as they usually were, by single elderly types. Only one light was on and it was drab and depressing. The waiters looked, for the most part, to be young gays moonlighting. (The dining room closes at eight.)

There was a choice of chicken, steak, or fish. I had the steak and read an interview with Barbra Streisand in *Cosmopolitan* Magazine. I always read *Cosmo* when I'm eating or flying. It relieves the boredom or terror. Barbra Streisand was talking about fame and success. It struck me that she was uttering some of the most profound thoughts I had ever heard.

"Somebody once said that fame is the aggregate of all the misunderstandings that collect around a new name. . . .

"There's a line in Joan of Arc about she who tells the truth shall surely be caught. It's absolutely true. There is no place for truth today.

"Part of our society kills what it loves, despises what it's created. It really hates success. It's for the underdog . . . you've got to be destroyed, buried, pushed right back down again."

I felt at one with Streisand. My eyes welled over with tears. I took another sip of my Almadén rosé (the Alden house wine), wiped my eyes, and looked around the room. People watched me on television and thought, What a glamorous life, and here I was, way past my bedtime, sitting in a seedy hotel dining room alone, reading *Cosmo* and feeling sorry for myself.

I took my suitcases to the office. That morning I interviewed Eugene McCarthy and Hughes announced that I was going to London.

Salant was coming to work as I was leaving, and he offered his limousine to take me to the airport. He kissed me goodbye and wished me luck. At the airport I found writer and film critic Rex Reed, who was taking the same plane, so we gossiped as we waited for the flight and agreed to meet after the meal because he wanted to sleep and I had to study.

By this time I had such a pile of background I didn't see how I could absorb it, but I began weeding through it anyway. I was already sick of Princess Anne, and the story seemed irrelevant at best. I couldn't imagine what amount of drivel we would have to come up with for five hours, but I knew one thing. It would be drivel. And I knew it was the kind of story I could write much better. I was already getting depressed.

Toward the end of the flight Rex came up and sat with me. Neither of us was flying first class. We chatted for a while, and then the attendants handed us our little cards to fill out with passport numbers and all, and I realized that I had forgotten my passport. I panicked. I knew they were going to put me on the return flight for New York. It was all right in the end. The man had me fill out a little form; but what he didn't tell me was that I couldn't get back home unless I got a new passport. That was the law. Nobody told me until two days before I was to leave, and I heard it over dinner. It took my last two days to get one.

When I arrived at the airport in London, Don Hewitt was there. He gave me a kiss and a hug, and as we went to get my luggage he told me that Barbara Walters had just landed. Don was talking about all the plans, and I began to feel a sense of anticipation.

We got into the CBS car and started toward London. We were about five minutes on our way when Don said, "God we're going to have fun. London is such a great place to have an affair."

Gordon had said it would happen but that I could handle it. But how? As they say a drowning person sees his past, I saw my future pass before me. If I didn't go to bed with Hewitt he'd probably ignore me and certainly not give me any help. That would mean that I would spend five hours live on the air looking like an ass. If I did go to bed with him he'd spend every minute with me, be attentive, massage my ego, advise me, help me, coach me, in effect make sure I looked fabulous on the air. Hewitt decided who was positioned where and who the camera was on. Simple as that.

"Oh, Don," I chuckled indulgently, "I couldn't think of anything nicer if I weren't already in love with someone else."

"Yeah, but he's there and I'm here."

"Yes, but he's here with me in spirit," I said, laughing lightly.

"Oh, don't give me that shit," Hewitt laughed. "You're not that naive. Listen, are you hungry? I know a great little place I go to all the time with Tony Armstrong-Jones. It has marvelous pasta. We could go there."

I decided that it would be best to go for the dinner and have a heart-to-heart talk about how we weren't going to have an affair, and how I really needed his help. I would appeal to Hewitt's sense of chivalry. San Lorenzo, the in spot in London at that moment, is dark with, I think, gravel on the floor and little round tables in the corners. We got one in the darkest corner. I kept trying to talk about what we were going to do for the broadcast. Hewitt wanted to talk about personal matters. I told him my fears and explained why it was important that I remain emotionally calm and happy on this trip if I were to do a good job. He thought that I would be much more relaxed and do a better job if I were "getting it."

I said it was late and I was tired.

Hewitt took me to my hotel, a horrible modern hotel near Harrod's that looks like the Intourist in Moscow. He was very aggressive.

After Hewitt finally left I called Ben in Washington to

tell him what was happening. I was in tears. When I hung up the phone, it rang. It was Hewitt.

He said, "I've been trying to get you but your line's been busy. I bet you were calling your boyfriend to tell him."

"Yes," I said, "as a matter of fact, I was."

Hewitt, undaunted, went on about the affair we were going to have in London. The whole thing was almost obscene. Finally, when he was through arguing and ready to hang up, Hewitt said, "Well, if you won't sleep with me, I'll sleep with Barbara Walters."

Gordon had had more faith in me than I had. I was going to have to do some fancy maneuvering to bring this one off.

The next day, I went to the office. Hewitt arrived fresh and smiling. I didn't see him again that day. That morning, I was set up to do a film piece, a travelogue of London. You have to memorize an open and a close, usually about a minute's worth, and recite them in front of the camera on location, which in this case was a barge on the Thames. After that you go to a park where the outdoor sounds are quiet and consistent and read the rest into a recorder to be used for the voice-over. Jim Ganser had written the script. Unfortunately, he had never been to London, so it read more or less like an excerpt from the *Encyclopaedia Britannica*.

I was disappointed with it, but the others were pleased and sent my part off to be aired the next day. In the meantime, everywhere we went, there was Barbara with her camera crew.

I knew she was doing fabulously. That afternoon there was a press conference about the wedding. Barbara was there. I asked her if Hewitt had called her. She said he'd left a message but she hadn't talked to him. I told her what had happened. She laughed and thanked me for warning her. We agreed to talk the next day.

Later I went back to the office, where I met Mark Harrington and another young man on the staff, Barry Jagoda, with whom I would be dealing directly. Both were funny, sympathetic and extremely helpful and supportive. They said they had felt all along that I had gotten a rough deal, and they wanted to help me look good as much as they could. They were staying at the Connaught, London's most exclusive hotel. They asked me if I'd like to move, and when I said yes they managed to come up with a room within minutes.

We had a lot of conferences. Barry would be in the control booth, and Mark would sit in a small hole and pass messages or information to me on cue cards the day of the broadcast.

They were happy to have me do much of my own reporting, if Russ Bensley would let it on the air. I had gathered some juicy background (things like how the royal household was getting fed up, what the best man really thought of Princess Anne, and which royals hadn't been invited or had refused to come) which they both liked and thought would liven up the program. It was trivia, but much more interesting and bitchier than what we did on the air.

We had one big problem. Collingwood. The second night I was there he invited me and Russ Bensley for drinks to meet Ernestine Carter, an American married to an Englishman, and the former women's editor of *The Sunday Times*. Charles wanted her to do the social tidbits while he did the political side.

I liked Ernestine. She was funny and clever and knew London very well. But I also knew that if she were there I would be aced out completely. Hewitt hadn't been too hot on Ernestine at the beginning, but under the circumstances he wasn't going to interfere.

We sat for an hour or so while Collingwood pontificated about his role, major of course, in the entire ceremony. He finished up his soliloquy with, "So, in effect, I'll be doing the skeleton and most of the meat of the subject, and when I'm not talking you two girls can natter on about whatever you like."

Bensley scratched his toupee, said, "That sounds fine," and we all stood up to leave.

I raced back to the Connaught and got Mark and Barry together for a strategy meeting. Did Bensley really mean "fine," I wanted to know, or was he just humoring Collingwood? If he meant it, I didn't see what I was doing there, not to mention the outrageous sexism of the whole conversation.

They assured me that Bensley was humoring Collingwood. I went back to my room and studied some more. I had read mountains of material. When I wasn't out doing film pieces, all I did was study and order room service. I had made notes on papers and had filled yellow pads with quotes, dates, facts and other items I had picked up by calling everyone I knew in London. I was unhappy because I wasn't writing a story. I had gathered a marvelous notebook full of good stuff that I would never get on the air.

I wasn't experienced enough at television to know what would be all right and what wouldn't. I soon found out that most of it wouldn't be. What people want on television is plain straight facts. Too much inside information is confusing and could be interpreted as snide or sarcastic. They want to know who is who.

I was getting more frightened, frustrated and depressed as the time drew near. Hewitt hadn't spoken to me. Barbara and I had had a long chat. I didn't know what to do about the Collingwood situation. The only person I could really talk to was Barbara. She was supposedly my competition, and she was the only one giving me advice. She didn't tell me how to do my job, just ways of handling specific producers who were hurting me. She tried to get me to assert myself more, but she didn't understand how little I really knew.

"They still deal differently with me than they would with Frank McGee," she said. "And I imagine they always will. If a man were in your shoes, the situation would be entirely different."

Finally I arranged dinner with Jagoda, Harrington, Hewitt, Bensley and his wife, whom he had brought along as an assistant director. I managed to sit next to Hewitt. We were going to talk about things. We didn't invite Collingwood.

We ate at the Connaught, which is supposed to be the best restaurant in London. The food was awful. The service was worse, and the table was too big for conversation.

Hewitt never mentioned the broadcast, and every time I brought it up Bensley looked nervous and changed the subject.

I began to get panicky. For one thing, I was terribly confused. Bensley had never once sat down with me to discuss what I was supposed to be doing, but I concluded that was because he had been told that Hewitt was there for that purpose, and since there was already some friction there, he had decided it would be easier for everyone if he just stayed out of it.

I felt the same way I had the week before we first went on the air. I knew I didn't know anything, but I didn't even know enough to know what I didn't know.

I didn't know, for instance, what exactly I expected Hewitt to do for me. Vaguely I had the idea that he was going to continue to work with me on my voice as he had begun to do in New York, help me choose my outfit, see to it that I had the proper makeup and hairdresser, rehearse me over and over on the chronology of the event and the parts I should concentrate on, let me spend time in front of a camera learning proper angles on the actual set, rehearse me on commercial cues, encourage me, keep Collingwood under control and, most of all, once I was on the air, give me some direction. And perhaps help me in areas I didn't even know existed.

Maybe it was unrealistic of me to expect all these things, though he had given me reason to in New York. But the absence of *any* help or advice at all I could not explain away by anything except the fact that I had refused him.

Monday I was to do an interview with Mr. and Mrs. Mark Phillips, the parents of the groom.

Barbara Walters had driven three hours up into the country to interview them at their home, but Bensley thought we should interview them in the London studio. I disagreed, but I was overruled.

I arrived at the hotel in London to pick them up. They were terribly nervous. We drove, nearly in silence, except for my hollow voice trying to make conversation, to the studio. They had never been in a studio before, and they were petrified by the time they got seated. I went upstairs to find the hairdresser and makeup woman. There was nobody. Finally somebody found a makeup woman who put a little powder on my face and I combed my hair. My complexion was worse than ever. I looked as awful as I had ever looked, I thought.

I was to read an intro live to Hughes, and immediately afterward tape an interview that they would use at the end of the New York broadcast.

Hughes asked me, "Well, are you settling in pretty well, Sally?"

I couldn't think of an answer. I said, "What a mean question. I think I have the London Stomach, but other than that it's really fun."

What a dumb thing to say, I thought. Who wants to know that?

The interview was a disaster. The Phillipses wouldn't talk. To everything I asked them, they answered, "I think this is an area we quite frankly don't want to get into . . . in terms of discussing it."

That was it.

I raised hell afterward about no hairdresser or makeup woman. I got a makeup woman for the broadcast. That morning the best hairdresser in London went first to Ernestine Carter's house to do her hair, then to Claridge's to do Barbara Walter's hair. I did my own.

Tuesday, the day before the broadcast, I did a round-table discussion about the wedding with Collingwood and Bob Trout, our French correspondent. I anchored the discussion live, from our set.

I haven't described our set. It was Hewitt's idea. It was on the roof of a building directly across from Westminster Abbey, so that the spires of the abbey were behind us, as well as Big Ben. It was beautiful, and freezing cold, though we did have heaters under the booth, and it was partially enclosed by glass. It had cost CBS $250,000, I was told. The *Today* Show was spending virtually nothing, and Barbara was broadcasting from the studio.

It seemed to me that if CBS was going to spend all that money, it might have been a good idea to have prepared the correspondents. No one had really even talked to Ernestine, not to mention my own predicament.

After the round table I asked Hewitt if we could have lunch. He took me to a chic little restaurant, all white, with flowers everywhere, modern, and with delicious pasta. I begged for some help or advice about the broadcast the next day. I told him I was scared to death and didn't know what to do or say.

"The best advice I can give you is to get laid tonight," he said, grinning. "That'll make you relaxed tomorrow."

That night I stayed up very late memorizing names, dates, facts. I woke up quite early and saw to my horror that my face was so broken out that it would be noticeable no matter how much makeup I put on. But at least I felt well prepared enough that I wouldn't look excessively stupid.

I wore a black pants suit, white satin blouse and pearl earrings. The perfect thing for a wedding. Simple but elegant. Especially when the American broadcast would begin at 5:30 in the morning EST.

We got to our anchor booth around 8:30 London time. It was freezing. We were made up and took our places. Ernestine was nervous, but her hair looked terrific. It didn't make any difference for very long. It was blowing so hard.

I was surprised at how quickly the broadcast went. It could have been that I was bored most of the time listening to Collingwood, who took over completely and droned on throughout in the most pompous manner.

Whatever hope I had left that Hewitt's direction would make me look good was not fulfilled, to say the least. Hewitt made sure the camera was rarely on me, and that I never got the commercial or takeout cues. Often, even when I was talking, Collingwood would interrupt abruptly and take us out to the commercial. It made me look as if I were too stupid to know what was going on, or as if what I was saying was so hopeless that I had to be cut off. All I did was ask Ernestine questions, when I knew the answers anyway, and most of the time we were interrupted by Collingwood, who babbled on about the glories of the monarchy.

Immediately after, Hewitt emerged from the control booth and rushed over to me at the anchor booth, a big grin on his face. He patted me on the head patronizingly and said, "A star is born!" I never saw him again.

That night Collingwood and I had to do a half-hour filmed recap of the wedding for those who had missed the morning show. It was to be aired at 10. It turned out to be an exact replica of the morning show, with Collingwood taking over. This time, however, our scripts were written by someone else and there was no ad-libbing, so I did get one or two lines in.

Afterward I was told I would have to stay the weekend because I hadn't done enough film pieces for the *Morning News*, and there was a possibility that I would get an eight-minute interview with Ingrid Bergman.

I had planned to leave for Washington first thing the next morning to spend the weekend, and I did not want an eight-minute interview with Ingrid Bergman. She has a reputation for being a terribly difficult interview. And I resented being told at the last minute that I hadn't done enough film pieces when I had spent the whole time waiting for instructions. I blew up. I announced that I had a private life as well as a professional life and that I was fed up and that I was leaving and I didn't care what they said.

People were taken aback. It was the first time I had really shown a temper since I had been at CBS. But now I refused to be everyone's up-front scapegoat for everything that went wrong. I left.

Hughes and Ann took me to lunch the first Monday I was back in New York. Hughes was furious with me. What was all this crap about my walking off the set, refusing to do film pieces, acting like a prima donna, announcing that my private life was more important than my job, throwing tantrums and refusing to work at all?

If I hadn't been so furious I would have laughed at the account of the "big TV star throwing her tantrum."

In an hour or so I explained everything to Hughes, including Hewitt, and how I had just had it.

He was terribly upset.

Later *New Times* Magazine printed an untrue story about how Barbara Walters had thrown a tantrum and threatened to walk off the set. I knew it wasn't true because we had talked every day and she had said she was having it pretty easy. But it stunned me to see how the stories were so similar.

I knew too that we wouldn't ever have seen those stories, or heard them, if Hughes and Frank had been there instead.

About a week later, I was about to go out to do a film piece on Frederick's of Hollywood when I got a call from Don Hewitt. He was livid.

Apparently, the night before in Washington, Joe Kraft, the columnist, and his wife, Polly, who are close friends of mine, had had a dinner party. Among the guests were Barbara Howar and Mike Wallace. In the course of dinner Wallace made some disparaging remarks about me, and Barbara, furious, said, "Well, don't talk about Sally when your producer took her over to London to make her a star and all he wanted to do was get laid."

(Obviously, I had told Barbara the story.)

Wallace couldn't wait to get back to Hewitt. I should have foreseen it. Once when a story had gotten back to Gordon, he traced it through Wallace to Hughes. Gordon had reprimanded Hughes in front of me for talking about anything private to Wallace, even at a dinner party. Wallace, Gordon said, was the worst gossip in the business.

Hewitt was in a rage. He screamed and shouted and raved on the phone about how he was going to tell everyone that I said that I would love to have an affair with him if I weren't attached to anyone else.

I explained to him that that was what you always said to someone who propositioned you if you didn't want to insult him or hurt his feelings. He could tell anyone he liked. I said I knew he had a reputation for that sort of thing. He wanted to know who had told me that. I wouldn't say. He was screaming at me and I was feeling sick at my stomach.

"I'm going to get to the bottom of this, I promise you," he said, and slammed down the phone.

After he called, I later learned, Hewitt marched into the *Morning News* section, called everyone together, and demanded to know who had told me that he had a reputation for screwing around. Everybody was terribly embarrassed and nobody came forth.

"I'm going to get to the bottom of this," Hewitt screamed, and marched out.

Nobody wanted to tangle with Hewitt.

A woman producer took me aside the next day. "Sally," she said, "everybody knows that Hewitt makes passes at women with aspirations in TV. But nobody talks about it. If you're smart you'll keep your mouth shut."

"The reason he does it," I said, "is because nobody talks about it. If people talked about it he'd stop doing it. It's the old Hollywood casting-couch syndrome. There's no excuse for it to exist today. It's outrageous."

I talked about it with Gordon. He was embarrassed too, but told me to keep my mouth shut. It was done with.

Hewitt called a week later. He wanted to apologize and could we be friends? He didn't want to read about what had happened in England in "any fucking book you might write."

I said we could be friends. That's all.

A week later Townsend informed us that we had creamed the *Today* Show in London. I was elated. Later I read an article about Barbara Walters in which she said the *Today* Show had run all over the *CBS Morning News* in ratings. I looked them up. She was right.

The same day Hewitt called, as if that weren't enough, I had lunch with my agent, Richard Leibner. One thing I have to say about Richard. He's straightforward. Since he was the only one who was, I generally appreciated it. We went to a tiny little French restaurant, out of the way, and were taken to a table in the corner, right next to someone I knew, though not well. It was definitely someone I did not want to overhear my conversation with Richard. I had barely ordered my Bloodless Mary (I still had ulcer problems) when Richard began.

"What's going on over there?" he said sternly. "I'm hearing terrible things about you."

"What things?"

"Like you threw a tantrum in London and stalked off the set, that you won't do any film pieces, that you don't write your own stuff, that you've gotten into a huge fight with Hewitt, that you make terrible gaffes on the air, that you haven't improved your voice, that you don't get along with any of the producers on the show, and that everyone is ready to quit because of you and that in general you are a prima donna and a snob and nobody likes you."

I stared at him. What could I say—"No, Richard, it's all lies"?

I thought about explaining, but then I decided the hell with it. If things had deteriorated that far, there was no point.

Then Richard dropped the big bomb. "You know that your fourteen weeks are up, don't you? That means that they can fire you any time they want to now."

I went weak. Certainly, I wanted out. But I wanted out my way. I wanted to be able to quit. And it hadn't occurred to me that I might be fired. It seemed too much in my present state.

"What should I do?" I asked. I was close to crying and I think Richard noticed and his tone softened a bit. He started to tell me what a rotten deal I had gotten and how they had really done a number on me, talking fast so that I wouldn't get a chance to weep.

"Listen, sweetheart, you may not have a choice. I don't know anything at this point, but I've been around this company long enough to see how these bastards work and I know what they're capable of. But let's try to think of something."

I told him that before I had left for London, I had suggested to Gordon that I go to Washington to do some film pieces. Richard loved the idea. I told him that I hated the anchor job and I had wanted out. I thought the Washington assignment might be one area where I might do okay.

We agreed that the Washington idea was a perfect way to get me out of the anchor job gracefully, and then if I hated it there I could quit and it wouldn't be such a big deal for everyone. We decided to go back to Richard's office and call Gordon. When we got there we talked the strategy over with John Reiser. We decided that I would listen while Richard spoke to Gordon.

It was a mistake. I felt like a woman who had decided at the last minute to undergo natural childbirth with neither anesthetic nor preparation. I sat as a witness to a painful operation.

Richard got Gordon on the line. "Gordon," he said, "I hear you're planning to fire Quinn. Her fourteen weeks are up and we all know how things are going. Let's not kid ourselves. But, Gordon, she's my client and we have a right to be able to know what's going to happen so we can prepare her. We would be very unhappy—I have to emphasize this to you, Gordon—very unhappy if she should get canned without any warning. I don't like to threaten you with recriminations, Gordon, but we'd like to know what's going on."

I felt sick. I didn't know what was being said from the other end. I watched Richard nod grimly. Gordon was trying to ease his way out of the conversation.

This went on for several minutes. Richard announced the Washington plan. He didn't ask, he told Gordon that that was a way out for everyone. Gordon apparently hedged. Richard got furious and started shouting. "I've known you for a long time, Gordon," he screamed.

"I can't stand by and watch this happen to one of my clients. We want an answer on this by the first thing next week."

Then I could hear Gordon scream back. "I was just leaving for a long weekend. You've succeeded in ruining my Thanksgiving eve." He slammed down the phone.

Richard smiled, "I think we've made headway," he said calmly.

He told me to be sure and call Gordon the first thing on Monday and sell him the Washington idea hard. At least force him to let me have a week's tryout in Washington.

I left, drained, and went home to bed. I cried myself to sleep. The misery seemed to escalate. I didn't know how much longer I could take it.

Thanksgiving was the next day, and we never had holidays off. It was the tenth anniversary of Kennedy's assassination. When I looked at the line-up that morning, I saw that the only scheduled interview was one I had done several weeks earlier with a woman who had written a diabetic cookbook.

I couldn't believe it. Hughes complained to no avail. That seemed like the final straw. On the tenth anniversary of a president's death we were to do a mediocre (at best) taped interview with a diabetic-cookbook writer. There was no hope for any of us, or that broadcast.

Without staff meetings, there was still no coordination. Things hadn't gotten better. Usually, we didn't know who the guest was to be until we came on the program, and half the time it was someone neither of us was interested in or wanted to interview. We wrote lists of suggestions and notes, but nothing ever came of them. It is not that the people on the staff were incompetent, but just that there was zero direction, that morale was low, and that there was no coordination.

We had a rule about not accepting guests if they'd already been on the *Today* Show, and they had the same rule about our show. What that meant was that we hardly ever got any of the good people because the *Today* Show had a much larger audience and no publisher would allow his author on our show unless he couldn't get him or her on the *Today Show.*

I thought that was dumb. I thought we should take people who'd been on the other show, then try to do a better, or a different kind of interview. We were in a no-win situation.

Another problem I kept hearing about third-hand from my friends was that some of them had talked their publishers into letting them go on our program because they were friends, and then for some odd reason they were rejected. This happened to Art Buchwald and Teddy White. There would be some vague explanation; but usually there were about three people involved in setting up the interviews, and often they weren't there when I was, so I couldn't find out. It was a mini-example of the total method of functioning at CBS. It was exasperating and, in the end, useless to try to do anything about anything.

The broadcast was beginning to take on a slight death smell. I had to get out.

The following Monday I went to see Gordon. Obviously he had been thinking over the weekend, and he had decided that the Washington deal might be a way out. He was pleasant and friendly, almost excited, the way he had been when he hired me.

He agreed that film pieces out of Washington might be something I could do.

Hughes gave his support. Hughes was aware that I could not stay on the anchor job, and I think he thought he could handle it more effectively alone anyway. Which he could and does. He also felt that I could be a valuable *Morning News* person in Washington (not replacing Barry Serafin, our *Morning News* Washington correspondent, but doing features). He seemed pleased for me. Hughes knew how miserable I felt, and the morale problems were getting to him as well. It was decided that I would spend two weeks in Washington and that I would begin there December 10. Things seemed to be looking up. We kept talking about the two-week time limit, but I was sure that once I got down there I would be able to talk them into letting me stay.

On December 3, an interview with Stuart Schulberg, the producer of the *Today* Show, appeared in *Broadcasting*, a trade magazine. He said, "The *CBS Morning News* people ought to quit and give the morning hour back to local stations unless they want the prestige of carrying the flag as our competitor." He never minded the competition. "It's a good idea for people to have a choice, and CBS's show is a good news show. It's not a failure as a program; it's only a failure as competition to *Today*—and if that's the only standard CBS is interested in, then the show's a failure."

He went on to point out that the tremendous amount of publicity that had been given to me had been "a strategic mistake by CBS. They were responsible for the oversell of Sally Quinn. No one, not even Ingrid Bergman, could have lived up to that buildup. The promotion had to make her an anticlimax. How could anyone possess the wisdom, the wit and all the sex appeal she was supposed to have?"

According to Schulberg I had "the kind of personality and sophisticated speech pattern that don't travel well across the Potomac and the Hudson."

Schulberg then commented on my remarks on the fourth newscast when I had said: "What you're eating at home with a nice bottle of Beaujolais and some béarnaise just might be horse meat. . . . Well, it's not that we may not be reduced to eating dog food before long, but it would be nice to know it. That way at least you wouldn't buy quite such a good bottle of wine."

Schulberg remarked that personality promotion is not pertinent to ratings success. "The *Today* Show is bigger than its personalities. I've always said if we do a *Today* Show in Ireland, and we all fly over in one little plane, and the plane goes down, there'd still be a *Today* Show the next morning. Edwin Newman or someone would sit in. The show has its own momentum to carry it through."

He pursued the point that personality is not CBS's only problem. "They might as well have stayed with Hart and Benton. Basically, their problem is that people do not want hard news early in the morning. They prefer the kind of morning entertainment we offer. CBS is like a newspaper. We're like a magazine, with a wide variety of things. . . .

I cut the article out, folded it, and put it in my wallet. About two or three times a day, I took it out. It helped.

My last week in New York I felt free. I spent a lot of time walking up and down the streets being recognized and signing autographs and accepting compliments. Like, for instance, "I saw you on television." That had gotten to be a compliment.

A number of people only watched me in motel rooms when they were traveling. At least every other person. It reminded me of the story about the woman with a cigarette holder who warded off jokesters who asked if her doctor had told her to keep away from cigarettes.

Shortly before I left New York, I heard that Frank McGee (who died in 1974) had left his wife of thirty-odd years, and his children, and had moved in with a young black woman, who was a script person. I was so accustomed to my personal life—and to Barbara's, for that matter—being reported in the papers that I expected to see it in the gossip columns the next day.

Not one word ever appeared in any newspaper or magazine. I asked several reporters why they hadn't used it in their columns, and they replied that it wouldn't be dignified, and besides, "That wasn't the kind of reporter McGee was."

It was the most blatant example of sexism in news reporting since the *New York* Magazine piece.

Barbara and I discussed it one day on the phone. She was reluctant to talk about it. But when I reminded her that everyone in journalism knew it, but that no one would print it, and that had it been either of us it would have been all over the place, she laughed resignedly.

"That's just the way things are," she said.

That first week in December, before I was to go back to Washington, I had lunch again with Charlotte Curtis in the *New York Times* executive dining room. I told her I didn't think I was going to last much longer but that I was going down to Washington to try film pieces.

"That might be fun," she said halfheartedly.

"I don't really think so, but I've got to get out of the anchor job and I might as well give it a try."

"Well," Charlotte said, "let me know when it doesn't work out."

"I imagine that will be soon," I said.

I packed my suitcase with a two-weeks' wardrobe, locked my door at the Alden Hotel with a special lock, and went to the office in the limousine, as usual.

I did the broadcast that morning, not thinking about the fact that it was the four-month anniversary of the day I had started on the air. Hughes and I left the anchor booth for the last time together.

I took the Metroliner to Washington. It was December 7, Pearl Harbor Day.

PART
THREE

THAT NIGHT Katharine Graham, the publisher of *The Washington Post,* had a dinner party. It was a large and formal dinner, a quintessential Washington party filled with the important politicians, members of the Administration, and journalists. The guests were seated at round tables in the dining room. I felt at ease, at home. I knew everyone fairly well, and they treated me, not with pity as people did in New York, but as though I had gone off on some kind of curious sabbatical but had, at last, come home. Not making it in New York's terms is not to get ratings and to be trounced by the critics. That's show biz, and you either make it or you don't. If you don't, they move along to something or someone else.

Washington is different. The world of television (New York television, anyway) is regarded with suspicion, not really respected by most newspaper journalists. Not to make it in New York is a confirmation of what everyone suspects in the first place—that TV can ruin a journalist. And if you make that mistake, you can come back.

It was a nice feeling.

I chatted with Teddy Kennedy for a while, reminding myself to call his office on Monday and ask for a filmed interview with his son, who had just undergone surgery for bone cancer a month or so earlier. That had been Gordon's idea. After dinner Henry Kissinger came in. He grinned and walked over.

"Sally, my dear," he said with his German accent, "how are you? I watch you every morning. In fact, I watch you forty-five minutes and Barbara only fifteen."

"Henry," I replied, "I know perfectly well that you tell Barbara the same thing, and now I know why you're such a good negotiator."

He laughed, enjoying his ploy but pleased that I had caught him up on it.

"I should take you with me the next time I have to do some negotiating," he said.

I would tell my producers Monday that we ought to do a film piece on Henry and that it might be nice to do something on one of his trips.

I was beginning to have visions of grandeur.

Monday morning I went into the small Washington CBS office on M Street just before five. The *Morning News* offices were on the third floor, along with *Face the Nation.* Barry Serafin and I interviewed former Senator Fred Harris. Paul Liebler, one of the associate producers, was in early, and I studied the prepared notes and clips on Harris and wrote the lead-in to the interview.

After the broadcast I met Bill Crawford, the *Morning News* Washington producer, who has a fine reputation. Somewhere along the line he and Gordon had fought and, as far as most people could figure, as long as Gordon was around, Crawford had had it.

I liked him immediately. He is wry and quiet, and has an ironical, resigned sense of humor and an understanding of television that most people either didn't have or didn't reveal.

I told him what I wanted to do and that if I worked out in the next two weeks, I would like to stay in Washington. Bill said he would like to have me on his staff, though it was obvious to him I had had no training at all. He said the rest of the staff was naturally suspicious of me, but that that was up to me to deal with. "And besides," he added with a straight face, "they've already got a blonde." It took me a second to realize he was kidding and a few weeks to realize they weren't.

I asked if he knew what was going on in New York, or at least at Blackrock.

"I think they want you off the air," he said bluntly. "The show hasn't made it. The ratings haven't gone up. They haven't gone down either, but the share has. That's not the point. This was supposed to be a big success and it bombed. You are a living testimony to their failure. As long as you're on the air they're constantly reminded of it." He felt my coming to Washington might give them an out.

Crawford told me I needed a lot of work, but that it wasn't impossible. He would help me out on my film pieces and he would talk to Bill Small, the CBS Washington bureau chief, about keeping me on the staff in Washington permanently if I worked out. There was no reason why I shouldn't. I knew the town. That was more than half of it right there.

Small called upstairs and asked me to have lunch with him. So far, things were going along fine. If he asked to have lunch the first day, it must mean that he wanted to talk about my staying in Washington. After all, he had been trying to hire me for a few years.

I met him at Le Provençal, a French restaurant which is CBS's hangout in Washington. There sat Bill Small and Eric Sevareid. Sevareid is a friend of mine and a man I admire tremendously. He is gentle and thoughtful and totally un-affected by his television popularity. At first I was pleased to see him and glad he was there, but as things went on and we did not talk about me or what I was going to do, I realized that Small had invited Sevareid so he wouldn't have to talk to me frankly.

It was a bad sign.

The week progressed with little excitement. The intro for the *Morning News* was "The *CBS Morning News* with Hughes Rudd and Sally Quinn on assignment in Washington." I came in around five and did meaningless eight-minute interviews with Barry Serafin, whom I like very much. Then we'd sit around the office and try to figure out film pieces for me to work on. I had suggested an interview–life style piece on the Iranian ambassador, Ardeshir Zahedi, whom I had met in Iran when I was covering the Shah's 2,500th anniversary bash several years earlier. Everyone thought that was a good idea, but it would take nearly two weeks to do it because we would have to cover the next several parties he was giving. The other two producers for the *Morning News,* Charlie Wolfson and Peter Kendall, were both bright, talented and decent. They were kind to me and as helpful as they could be.

The *Morning News* in Washington was a pleasant place to work. The only problem was that it was even more boring than the anchor job.

It wasn't that putting together a film piece and seeing the product was boring. Thinking of ideas that would work on film was difficult. People weren't cooperative. And then a film is cut with producers and editors and film cutters, and most of it ends up on the cutting-room floor. In the end it may not be anybody's product. Even so, I felt more pride and satisfaction from a very brief but solid film piece than I did after anchoring a whole show.

I had begun to brood about the difference between TV news and newspapers. I couldn't quite figure out what it was

I detested so about television, what I had instinctively felt about it even beforehand, or what it was that was so satisfying about writing.

I suppose I first became disturbed when I walked down the street and people followed, pointed at me, asked for my autograph and told me in worshipful tones that they had actually seen me on television. I knew it meant nothing. I also knew that they would have mobbed Charles Manson or Cinque or anybody else they had seen on television. There was no discrimination. How could I possibly feel flattered? It was irrelevant. I remembered with nostalgia the satisfaction when somebody said they liked an article or quoted from it. No one ever said, "I saw your byline in the paper," and then stared in fascination.

Some in the television business adore, thrive on and need this kind of personal recognition. I know them. Some have never known the other. Even some who, like myself, went into television from journalism are at first thrilled and flattered at the attention, but most soon realize how empty it is.

It's awful to have your privacy invaded. Not to be able to look like a slob if you want to. One wants to be known and admired among one's peers, but I have decided that the ideal kind of fame is to have everyone know and admire your name and no one recognize your face. A writer can have that kind of fame; a television personality cannot.

Then there is the entertainment factor. Everyone in the news side of TV is quick to defend it and desperate to make it seem unfrivolous and serious, and they always talk about "hard news." But it really isn't much more than show biz. In the end the ratings determine everything because the news has to have sponsors. And advertisers want their products to sell, and the products won't sell unless people watch the broadcast. If people like Chancellor better than Cronkite one week and reverse it the next, it's not because one's a better newsman.

Background, lighting, makeup and glasses, shirts, ties,

voice levels and smiles and laughs and mustaches and side-
burns and hairdos and jewelry are all *very* important in television. Television magnifies personalities and distorts them,
like photographs. Some people who look wonderful in person
look terrible on camera. Some people who are complicated
seem busy and overworked or fuzzy on camera.

Others who are simpletons may come across as warm,
honest, intelligent people on TV. Everyone has to act a little,
even the newscasters. You have to take voice lessons, or learn
how to "deliver." Even the best ones do it. If you do it well
you can manipulate your audience. And if you can do that
you can raise the ratings. And that is what matters.

Sometimes blandness is better. Or lack of commitment.
Very few people can offer opinions on television and survive.
David Brinkley and Eric Sevareid do. But they are both former newspapermen, and they had built up familiarity and
confidence for years before they did.

The ad lib is anathema to newscasters. Every ad lib is
dangerous. It is an occasion to slip up. I felt like a terrific
loser until I read that Barbara Walters had commented
about the prerequisites of the man who would replace the
late Frank McGee. The important thing, she said, was to find
someone who could deal with those ghastly thirty seconds of
ad lib at the end of the *Today* Show. Thirty seconds. As a
novice I had been thrown on the air live with five minutes of
unplanned ad lib a day.

I've often asked myself how CBS could have made so
many mistakes, how they could have let me go on the air
with no experience.

Part of my despair during that terrible time had stemmed
from trying to fathom where I had gone wrong. The thing
is, nobody really yet understands the medium. Television
isn't even fifty years old. Shows go on and off every month,
people are hired and fired ruthlessly, because nobody knows
what will work and what won't. They don't know what ter-

rible vibes a great-looking or -talking person may give out over the air or what good vibes a clod may transmit. So they don't want to make decisions—especially long-term ones. Therefore nobody does. It's what Sander Vanocur calls the "how-about?" school. Somebody said, "How-about-Sally-Quinn?" and there was a generalized mumble, and that was it. They hired me and nobody ever did anything about it again. Mainly because they didn't know what to do.

So much money is at stake—millions and millions of dollars in advertisements—that those who make mistakes cost their company a lot of money. If they do that too often they lose their jobs. On newspapers everything doesn't ride on one story or one series but on the long run. Everyone in television is basically motivated by fear.

And television news is run by the network. It is not really autonomous. Those in charge of entertainment have ultimate charge over the news programs. CBS News has a buffer between the management and the news division: Richard Salant. In fact, that is his primary function. He is a lawyer, not a newsman, and he is able to negotiate the vast differences of approach between the news side and Blackrock and to work out acceptable compromises.

I was also brooding about my own feelings, even aside from my more obvious failures. An old-time newspaper reporter once told me that the feeling of finishing a story on deadline was post-coital. And he was right. But I never felt any satisfaction after a broadcast. I just felt empty, as though I had poured myself out and had to be refilled. I soon found that if I knew too much I would do less well than if I knew too little. I stopped reading the books of authors before my interviews, which were usually seven minutes long, because it was less confusing and I could get more information across to the viewer if I didn't know so much. Most of the time after I'd finished the program I had forgotten what I had said or even done from one day to the next.

For a reporter there is another thing. If a journalist is too famous, too recognizable, he loses his effectiveness. He becomes one of the people reporters cover. There are places he cannot go and things he will never see. I saw this in California when Walter Cronkite tried to cover Hubert Humphrey at a speech during the Primary. Humphrey was abandoned by thousands at a shopping center when Cronkite appeared, and Cronkite had to leave so that Humphrey could get the crowd's attention.

Ironically, with all the fame and adoration and attention, television is really a producer's medium. Journalism is a writer's. You can go anywhere you like and you have it all there. A pad and pencil are all you need, and even without them you still have your eyes and ears. When the product is finished, it is yours and no one else's. I don't want to ignore television's extraordinary impact or to diminish the achievements of those people who have become successful and who do their work professionally and well. From my brief encounter with CBS, I know only too well just how hard they have worked, what obstacles they have had to overcome, how much they have had to learn, how much they have had to be afraid of. Those who have reached the top—and most of them are friends whom I admire and respect—are survivors in the truest and best sense of the word.

Thursday of the first week, Small asked me to come down to his office. Gordon was sitting there. I was surprised, to say the least. He hadn't told me he was coming down. He asked where I would be later in the day. He said he would call.

He called around 3:30 and asked if I could have a drink with him. I suggested he have a drink with Ben and me, since they were old friends.

He hedged. Then he said he could get a hotel room and stay over if I wanted him to. We could have dinner. I suggested we all have dinner. He hesitated. I couldn't figure out

what he wanted. "Well, Gordon," I said finally, "what do you want?"

He mumbled something about dinner for the two of us and how he could get a hotel room. I said I thought it would be more fun with the three of us. He blew up.

"Well, if you don't give a damn about your career, then the hell with it."

"Well, why didn't you say it was to talk?" I had thought if he wanted to have just a business meeting he would have said so. So I figured it was social. Now it was clear that he was embarrassed to have Ben involved in the discussion.

"Why don't we meet at my apartment at the Watergate and have Ben join us for dinner at the Terrace?" I suggested.

He agreed to be there at 7:00. I told Ben to come at 8:00.

During the hour-long conversation, I couldn't make out what Gordon was trying to say.

"Gordon, before you go any further," I finally interrupted, "I just want to tell you one thing. I have no intention of ever returning to the anchor job."

"What do you mean?" he asked.

"Exactly what I said. I'm not going back. Have you talked to Small about my staying down here?"

"Well," he said evasively, "there are some problems. They have a very tight little bureau here and, well, there are problems."

"What problems, Gordon?" I was getting angry. "Bill Crawford has said it was fine with him. I know the town. Small tried to hire me before. What are the problems?"

"How about doing film pieces in New York?" he asked hopefully.

"Forget it," I said. "How many feature film pieces a year get on network television from New York? None. I want to work in Washington."

He looked sheepish. "Well," he said hesitantly, "I could order it."

"Gordon, what's with Small? You're not being honest."

"Small doesn't think you've got it," he blurted.

"That's ridiculous and you know it," I replied. "You know how often he's tried to hire me. If he had hired me six months ago, I would have had a lot less experience than I've got now. I've had four months of one-hour-a-day live TV. Nobody gets that kind of experience right away. And Small wouldn't have wanted to hire me if he didn't think I would be good. But Small would have made sure I was good, because if he'd hired me it would have been his ass on the line. And I could have been okay, Gordon, and you know it. Small's problem is that I'm somebody else's mistake, like yours, for instance. And he doesn't want any part of it. I've got the kiss of death written all over me, and anyone who gets involved is going down with me. Right?"

By this time I was screaming at him. He was sweating nervously and gulping his drinks.

Ben arrived.

I told him what Gordon had said about Small.

"That's a lot of shit," Ben said to Gordon.

"Well," Gordon said defensively, "Blackrock doesn't think she's got it."

"That's a lot of shit, too," said Ben. "She's good and you know it. Her problem is she got a big buildup and no training and terrible reviews. Nobody could have overcome those handicaps. She's a victim of bad management. Look, Gordon"—Ben was getting mad too—"I'm in management. I know how it works. You make a mistake, somebody's got to pay. It's your ass or hers."

"Listen," I shouted. "Don't tell me I don't have it. If I don't have it, what about someone else? If you took Walter Cronkite out of the UPI bureau tomorrow and he'd never been on TV in his life, and you built him up as a great new star, and announced he was going to wipe out John Chancellor, and put him on the air four weeks later with no training, you know what would happen. You'd be laughed out of

the business. If I don't have it then why didn't you or Salant or Schneider or Bill Paley, for that matter, figure that out? You all approved me. You all thought I would be terrific. And you've all been in the business a long time. Don't try to tell me I don't have it and then tell me any single correspondent you have, or anybody else for that matter, would have done better under the circumstances. If I'd had half a chance and direction and any training and a format and a good producer, I could have made it. And I will not have you or Bill Small or Blackrock or anyone else tell me I don't have it."

I was shaking with rage. All the anger and bitterness and resentment I had stored up over the past four months came pouring out so fast I thought I was losing control.

Ben put his hand on my arm to calm me.

We all stared at the floor in silence. Gordon looked as if he were going to cry. Suddenly I felt sorry for him. He hadn't done anything mean to me. He had wanted it to work as much as I had. But he knew that a large part of the failure had been his fault. He knew what he had done to me. And he probably knew then that there would be consequences for him too.

"Gordon," I said quietly, "I'm going to quit CBS. I'll try to be out in about six weeks. But I've got to find a job first. Just get Small to let me stay in Washington until then. I can't—·won't go back to the anchor job. But I don't want to just quit and have it look like I was a total loss. I want to have a great job to go to. Will you do that much for me? Just hold them off for a while?"

He looked relieved. "I'll do it," he promised.

We walked in silence to the Watergate Terrace Restaurant and made polite conversation through dinner. Nobody ate anything. I ordered gazpacho but I couldn't swallow it. As we were leaving I asked Gordon what I had been longing to ask him since we went on the air.

"Gordon, why did you do it? Why did you hire me and

then throw me on the air like that with no training? Why
did you do it to me?"

"What if I had told you we wanted to make you the anchor on the *Morning News* but that you'd have to have about
three to six months' training on one of our local stations
first. Would you have done it?"

"Of course not."

"That's why."

The next few weeks before Christmas I did very little
work. An occasional early-morning interview, a few film
pieces. The Iranian film piece worked out well, and so did a
piece on *The Washington Post's* sixty-five-year-old social
writer, Dorothy McCardle.

Others I was less happy with, including a Washington
mood piece, a piece on corn-rowing hair, an interview with
Deborah Kerr, a White House Christmas decorations piece,
and a piece about toilet paper.

Except for the interview with Kerr, none were things I
would have bothered with as a *Post* reporter. It was increasingly difficult to persuade people to come on the *Morning
News* or even to be taped. The program had no clout. Almost
daily, someone we had tried and failed to line up would
appear on the *Today* Show, or in an interview in the *Post*.

Christmas week was miserable. My major preoccupation
was trying to find a job. As far as I could see, there were
three possibilities: *The New York Times; Newsday*, which
had the same wire service the *Post* did, so my pieces could
appear in the *Post;* or syndication.

Returning to the *Post* was out. Ben and I had had one brief
discussion about it and had agreed that it would present too
many problems. The Washington *Star-News* was out because
I didn't want to work for the competition. Syndication was
out because I didn't want to lock myself into having to pro-

duce a set number of pieces every week, even when I had nothing to write about. A lot of good writers have been hurt that way. That left *Newsday* or *The New York Times.* Both appealed equally. At *The Times* I would be competing with *The Washington Post,* but the advantage there was that it was a better and more prestigious newspaper than *Newsday.* If I left CBS for *The Times* it would look like a step up. *Newsday's* editor, Dave Laventhol, had been my first editor at the *Post,* however. And he is terrific. I liked the idea of working with him and of being fairly free in a small Washington bureau. Also, the *Post* could get my stories off the wire and run them.

I was scheduled to go to New York on January 4th to do a film piece. I had been invited several months earlier by Gael Greene, the food writer, to be one of twelve women of achievement at a dinner for women only, cooked by the famous French chef Paul Bocuse. It was to be held at the Four Seasons, and I had gotten permission to cover it as well.

I called Charlotte Curtis at *The Times* and set up an afternoon interview. She had just been made editor of *The Times'* Op Ed page, replacing Harrison Salisbury, and was terribly busy. We agreed to meet at 3. I telephoned Dave Laventhol and made a lunch date. I flew up to New York that morning intending to go to the Alden Hotel, leave my suitcase, then go to my interviews. I had been away for a month, and on this trip I was going to have to pack all my clothes and get them back to Washington. I had also arranged to leave some things with a friend so that I could give up my hotel room. I had had a special lock put on so that it would be burglarproof. I arrived at the hotel about 11:30. When I walked in, the manager gave me a big smile and said how glad he was that I was back. I got the doorman to come upstairs with me so he could unlock the special lock.

When he opened the door, I was stunned. The apartment was in shambles—drawers opened and dumped out, pieces of clothing strewn about, papers everywhere. I raced to the closet where I kept my fur coat. It was gone. I went into the bedroom and flung open the door where my clothes were kept. Empty. I ran over to the dresser drawer where I kept my jewelry. Nothing. A few pieces of clothing that had been tried on and discarded were lying about. I sat down on the edge of my bed and cried.

I called down to the manager in a rage. Did they know I had been robbed?

Well, actually they did know, because they had entered the room a week earlier to fix some pipes and discovered it then.

Why hadn't they contacted me in Washington? Had they called the police?

Well, no, they hadn't called the police. They were waiting for me to come back.

But they didn't know when I was coming back, I shouted. Were they never going to report it?

There was a lot of stammering on the other end.

Why hadn't they told me about it just now when I came in?

They didn't know why.

"You get on that phone and you call the police immediately," I yelled, choking with anger. "I'm leaving now for an appointment. I'll be back at 4:30. I want the police to be here when I arrive."

I grabbed my bag and ran out of the apartment to meet Laventhol. I drank a lot at lunch.

We talked about the possibilities on *Newsday*. He was excited about the idea. He would arrange for me to meet the publisher, Bill Atwood, and the bureau chief, Marty Schramm, in Washington early the following week.

I went to see Charlotte. I was so depressed about my robbery that I didn't seem to have much enthusiasm. Charlotte suggested I should write a piece about it for the Op Ed page. That would cheer me up. We talked about my coming to *The Times*. She said she was no longer in a position to hire me now that she was on the Op Ed page. But she would tell Clifton Daniel, the Washington bureau chief (and husband of Margaret Truman) that I was looking for a job, and see if he was interested.

At the hotel two detectives were waiting. They wandered into the room, glanced around, and asked me a few questions.

"Aren't you going to take fingerprints?" I asked.

"That's just a hoax that you see in the movies and on television," said Detective Friis-Skotte. "You can't find out anything with fingerprints. Sometimes we do it just to make the victim feel better, though."

"I think it's an inside job," I said with great authority, though I had only the following evidence. "For one thing, the manager didn't exactly kill himself to notify me or the police. And for another, who would know I was away except the people in the building?"

"Are you kidding?" he asked. "Every morning on television the announcer says, '*The CBS Morning News* with Hughes Rudd and Sally Quinn on assignment in Washington.' All you personalities are just sitting ducks for this kind of thing. That's what you get for being a star."

That evening I had nothing to wear except a black wool jump suit since all my evening clothes had been stolen. The party went well. Among the women were Pauline Trigere, Bess Myerson, Marya Mannes, Lillian Hellman, Charlotte Curtis, Louise Nevelson and Julia Child. I was pleased and flattered to be there but so miserable about the robbery and about my job status that I couldn't relax. It was the best meal I have ever eaten, ten courses, and the mood was hilarious. We got terrific film footage, and I had a good interview with Bocuse in French, which I later translated and used as commentary.

Then I went back to my empty hotel room to spend my last night there.

The next day I went down to the studio to work with Charlie Wolfson on the Bocuse dinner piece, which was to run on Monday morning. It was like going into a tomb. I wandered into my old office to look around. It was completely empty, as though I had never even been there. It gave me an eerie feeling. I felt like a non-person. Charlie worked on the film while I wrote the script; then we picked out the best parts. That was fun because we had a lot of good material to work with. I was pleased and so was Charlie. Around 1:30 Charlie said he didn't think he'd need me any more, but to call around 4:00.

I went to a friend's apartment, where I was staying, to have lunch; then I was going back to the Alden to move what was left of my things to the apartment.

Somehow, after a few glasses of wine, I started to cry and I couldn't stop. I cried hysterically for nearly three hours, until I was so weak I couldn't move.

My friend, though alarmed at the condition I was in, had to leave for the weekend, so I managed at last to pull myself together and get over to the Alden. I called Charlie at the *Morning News*, but there was no answer so I figured he had had no problems and had left for Washington.

I moved my things over to the apartment, got into my wrapper, and began to watch television. I started to cry again. I kept it up for a few hours. I couldn't stop until I finally went to sleep. The next morning I woke up and started to cry. I was getting worried. I began to think I was having a nervous breakdown. I still couldn't stop. The phone rang once and I picked it up, but I couldn't get myself together enough to speak. I cried most of the day, not eating, not even brushing my teeth. Just sitting in my nightgown on the bed, sobbing until my guts ached. I was trying to read Sylvia Plath's *The Bell Jar*. I was supposed to be in Washington for work the next morning and I knew that I should have left a number where I could be reached, but I couldn't function enough to do anything about it. I didn't want to upset anyone, either. My parents were in Jamaica and I didn't know how to reach them, and Ben was off somewhere in the woods at a *Post* conference and I didn't want to bother him.

That night I cried until I went to sleep. I didn't have any energy left, and I hadn't eaten since Friday night. Monday I woke up in the same state. But I knew I had to get out of there. I forced myself to take a bath and get dressed and brush my teeth. Somehow I got packed and got to the airport. About halfway to Washington a stewardess came over to tell me how much she enjoyed me on television. I got up and ran into the ladies' room and burst into tears.

I got home and cried the rest of the day.

Sometime that night I woke up in a fury. What in the hell was I doing sobbing and moaning and feeling sorry for myself? If I was going to be a pitiful creature, then that's what everyone would think of me. If I couldn't get myself together and get out there and get a decent job, then I deserved exactly what I had gotten already. I wasn't a quivering mass of insecurity, and if I wasn't strong enough to weather a few setbacks, then I wasn't much.

I was angry with myself for being so weak. I took an objective look at myself and I was revolted by what I saw. And I knew one thing. If I couldn't help myself, nobody was going to help me. If I couldn't hack it, nobody was going to do it for me. I was going to go out and get a great job and quit CBS with flair and style, and people were going to have to say, "By God, she did it."

Wednesday I met with Bill Atwood and Marty Schramm of *Newsday.* They were in favor of my coming to the paper. We had a drink and a pleasant exchange. I told them I was also talking to other people but that I would let Laventhol know the following week.

The next day Clifton Daniel called. He said he wanted to talk to me, but not where we could be seen and cause gossip. We agreed to meet at his house Sunday afternoon.

The meeting with Daniel went smoothly. He confirmed that as far as he was concerned we had a deal. If I were willing I could go to work for them, but he wanted to talk to the New York office first because it was an unusual situation. He would let me know in the middle of the week. I didn't want to bank on it, but it was beginning to seem like the better offer.

And no one could say that leaving the CBS anchor job to be a Washington correspondent in *The New York Times* bureau was a comedown. To me it was a step up, and to most of my colleagues.

It was a good exit. It had class.

The next day I had to go to New York to do a film piece on Halston, the designer. It was a snowy, slushy day and rather depressing. The interview went fine, for a TV interview, but I liked Halston and was frustrated not to be able to write it. I knew it would end as a pedestrian four- or five-minute question-and-answer piece.

That Wednesday night, Clifton Daniel called me at home. "Congratulations on being the newest member of *The New York Times* Washington bureau," he said jovially.

I was ecstatic. Everything had gone so badly until then, it didn't seem possible that something would finally work out. A few minutes later the phone rang again. I knew it was going to be Daniel, calling back to say he had changed his mind.

It was Abe Rosenthal, managing editor of *The Times*. He was calling to congratulate me. We had a pleasant chat and hung up. It was way past my bedtime. I had to get up at 4:30 A.M. to do an interview with Dr. John Knowles, president of the Rockefeller Foundation.

For the last time, I thought.

That morning I could barely wait to get through the boring interview to tell everybody. I went to breakfast with Bill Crawford, Barry Serafin and Bob Schiffer. We were hilarious, and Crawford asked finally why I was in such a good mood. I told him I would tell him when we got back to the office.

The first thing I did was to call Hughes. He was immensely pleased for me, and we had a few teary moments on the phone. There was nothing we could say to each other. It was hard to say anything except thank you.

Next I called Gordon.

"We love you," he said, a bit sadly. "I'm sorry for the experience we put you through. I'm sorry for all the scars there must be on your lovely soul."

I realized he meant it.

Next I called Richard.

"You signed a three-year contract, sweetheart," said Richard. "I'm not sure they're going to let you out of it."

"They'll let me out of it," I said. "Just talk to Gordon."

"There are an awful lot of people around here who are worried that you're going to write a book," said Richard. I'm sure they'd be much more lenient about letting you out of your contract if they could have some assurance that you weren't going to write anything."

"Richard," I said, "fuck 'em."

That night I got home, kicked off my shoes, fixed myself a Dubonnet and soda on the rocks, and plumped down on the sofa to watch the *Evening News*. I was half daydreaming, half watching, when I heard Walter Cronkite say my name.

"Sally Quinn," he said, "who, since August, has been a cor-respondent on the *CBS Morning News*, today resigned to become a reporter in the *New York Times* Washington bureau."

The morning after I quit, Hughes signed me off: "Sally Quinn is leaving CBS News for *The New York Times*—not necessarily sadder, but certainly wiser. And we hope she's happier there than she was here. For one thing, the help over there don't have to get up as early as they do here."

I thought it was touching and funny in Hughes' own gruff way.

Later that morning Richard called to say that Don Hamilton, Director of Business Affairs, wanted that day to be my last day. I pointed out that I had two film pieces to finish and that I intended to work two more weeks, that I had two further weeks of vacation coming to me, and that therefore they could count me on the payroll for another month. I wasn't to start at *The Times* until March 18.

Richard said Hamilton wouldn't buy that. I told Richard that I would call Salant or Bill Paley if I had to, and give interviews about what a cheap crumby outfit CBS was if I heard another word on the subject. Just get me the four weeks' pay. I didn't care how he did it.

Richard understood that I meant it. A half hour later he called back and said, "It's all set."

It still made me chuckle, though, that such a huge corporation would be so unbelievably cheap, especially under the circumstances. But I don't know why I was surprised, after what I had been through.

Saturday, I got a letter from Dick Salant.

Dear Sally,

In case you missed the AP story, I am attaching it. It quotes me absolutely correctly.

· I am terribly sorry that things did not work out as we all expected and hoped. The fault, I honestly believe, was ours—mine.

In any event, best wishes for every sort of satisfaction and happiness. And if you can bear it, do drop in so I can say goodbye and good luck.

All the best,

Dick Salant.

The AP story was enclosed. It said; "CBS News President Richard Salant said Thursday that CBS would not hold her to her contract. Asked if he considered Miss Quinn's move a slap at CBS, Salant said, 'No, not at all. She doesn't owe us a thing. We owe her a lot. And we damn near ruined her by making a mistake and pushing her too far too fast.' "

On February 7 Gordon Manning was fired from his job as news director. He was given a job as "vice president and assistant to the president of CBS News."

Gordon had been news director for nine years. His ten years were up in June and he was to receive a pension. That's why he was given that job, to hold him over so he could get his pension. He was fifty-seven in June, 1974. Somehow Gordon managed to redeem himself, partly by landing Solzhenitsyn for Walter Cronkite to interview. He stayed on after June and became a producer for the public affairs division of CBS News.

Bill Small was given Gordon's job, Sandy Socolow was given the Washington bureau. The day the change was announced Small was in Gordon's office.

Reached there, he said he was completely surprised by the promotion. "I've only been at this desk for six hours," he said.

"I'm just trying to find out where the men's room is and where they keep the key to the liquor cabinet."

On February 28 Lee Townsend was fired. They had no ready title for him to assume. He was later assigned to the investigative unit. The new *Morning News* producer was the Rome bureau manager, Joseph Dembo.

On February 12 I did a long freelance piece for *The Washington Post* on Alice Roosevelt Longworth. Mrs. Longworth had promised me a ninetieth-birthday interview a year earlier, when she became eighty-nine. I had offered the piece to the *Post* in December, when I knew I had to get out of the CBS job and start writing again.

Friday, February 8, just before I went off to see Mrs. Longworth for tea, I telephoned Clifton Daniel at *The Times* as a courtesy to tell him. We had agreed that I would probably do some freelancing before I started to work for *The Times*, and he posed no objections.

I had a terrific time with Mrs. Longworth and began writing the piece on Saturday. Saturday night I was at home, feeling better about myself than I had in six months, when the phone rang. It was Clifton Daniel. He was in a rage. He admonished me for having done the piece, told me I was disloyal to *The Times* and said I would always be under suspicion there. "We at *The Times*," he kept repeating, "are shocked," at what he called my lack of sensitivity for having accepted the assignment. Our relations, he told me, would never again be cordial.

I apologized profusely and declared my everlasting loyalty to *The Times*. I offered him the piece. He refused it. I offered to let him see it. He refused. I offered to kill it. He insisted that wasn't necessary. I asked what he would have me do. He slammed the phone in my ear.

Ten minutes later he called back. "You run that piece in the *Post*," he said in a voice tightly controlled but seething with fury. "But I want to warn you that this will never, never happen again." From now on, he told me, my loyalty to *The Times* would always be questioned and I had soured our relationship forever.

"Do you understand?" he finished.

"I do," I said.

He hung up.

It was clear to me then that I could not go to work for *The Times*.

Monday, however, I received a marvelously pleasant letter from Daniel with no mention at all of Saturday night's tirade, just the details of my starting time, salary, job description at *The Times*, and a little postscript about how they were all looking forward to having me in the bureau. I can only assume that his outburst on Saturday was the result of his having been bawled out by his editors in New York.

Tuesday morning the piece ran in *The Washington Post*.

Tuesday noon Howard Simons, the managing editor of the *Post*, called me in to say it was ridiculous for me to work for *The Times*. He offered me my job back at the *Post* and I accepted.

Tuesday afternoon I had a letter hand-delivered to Clifton Daniel, saying that under the circumstances I felt it would be uncomfortable for me to work at *The Times*. He wrote an extremely cordial and congratulatory note back, saying that he understood perfectly and wished me all the best.

Later I learned from friends that the consensus at *The Times* was that the Longworth story could never have run in that newspaper. It was too long and too sensational. Mrs. Longworth had talked at length about lesbianism and "dear old men's things, men's penises, my dear."

I had quoted her exactly, and she loved the story. But it would have been a bit much for *The Times*.

I was supposed to begin my new job with the *Post* on Monday, March 25. I woke up around quarter to seven that morning with a terrible sore throat and a fever of 101. . . . For a moment I felt terror. I began to break out in a cold sweat; fear engulfed me. Then I remembered. I smiled, propped myself up in bed, and switched on the TV set.

"Good morning," said the gruff, friendly voice.

ANNOUNCER: From the CBS Newsroom in New York, *The CBS Morning News* with Hughes Rudd. . . .